Codes, Designs, Cryptography and Optimization

Codes, Designs, Cryptography and Optimization

Editor

Raúl Manuel Falcón

MDPI • Basel • Beijing • Wuhan • Barcelona • Belgrade • Manchester • Tokyo • Cluj • Tianjin

Editor
Raúl Manuel Falcón
Departamento de Matematica
Aplicada I. Universidad
de Sevilla
Spain

Editorial Office
MDPI
St. Alban-Anlage 66
4052 Basel, Switzerland

This is a reprint of articles from the Special Issue published online in the open access journal *Mathematics* (ISSN 2227-7390) (available at: https://www.mdpi.com/journal/mathematics/special_issues/CDCO).

For citation purposes, cite each article independently as indicated on the article page online and as indicated below:

LastName, A.A.; LastName, B.B.; LastName, C.C. Article Title. *Journal Name* **Year**, *Volume Number*, Page Range.

ISBN 978-3-0365-4355-0 (Hbk)
ISBN 978-3-0365-4356-7 (PDF)

© 2022 by the authors. Articles in this book are Open Access and distributed under the Creative Commons Attribution (CC BY) license, which allows users to download, copy and build upon published articles, as long as the author and publisher are properly credited, which ensures maximum dissemination and a wider impact of our publications.

The book as a whole is distributed by MDPI under the terms and conditions of the Creative Commons license CC BY-NC-ND.

Contents

About the Editor vii

Preface to "Codes, Designs, Cryptography and Optimization" ix

José Andrés Armario
Boolean Functions and Permanents of Sylvester Hadamard Matrices
Reprinted from: *Mathematics* **2021**, *9*, 177, doi:10.3390/math9020177 1

Víctor Álvarez, José Andrés Armario, María Dolores Frau, Félix Gudiel, María Belén Güemes and Amparo Osuna
Hadamard Matrices with Cocyclic Core
Reprinted from: *Mathematics* **2021**, *9*, 857, doi:10.3390/math9080857 9

Víctor Álvarez, Raúl M. Falcón, María Dolores Frau, Félix Gudiel and María Belén Güemes
Pseudococyclic Partial Hadamard Matrices over Latin Rectangles
Reprinted from: *Mathematics* **2021**, *9*, 113, doi:10.3390/math9020113 23

Laura M. Johnson and Stephanie Perkins
A Discussion of a Cryptographical Scheme Based in $\mathfrak{F}$-Critical Sets of a Latin Square [†]
Reprinted from: *Mathematics* **2021**, *9*, 285, doi:10.3390/math9030285 43

Yansheng Wu and Yoonjin Lee
Self-Orthogonal Codes Constructed from Posets and Their Applications in Quantum Communication
Reprinted from: *Mathematics* **2020**, *8*, 1495, doi:10.3390/math8091495 57

Carlos Roncero-Clemente, Eugenio Roanes-Lozano and Fermín Barrero-González
A Multi-Criteria Computer Package-Based Energy Management System for a Grid-Connected AC Nanogrid
Reprinted from: *Mathematics* **2021**, *9*, 487, doi:10.3390/math9050487 71

Hyeokdong Kwon, YoungBeom Kim, Seog Chung Seo and Hwajeong Seo
High-Speed Implementation of PRESENT on AVR Microcontroller
Reprinted from: *Mathematics* **2021**, *9*, 374, doi:10.3390/math9040374 95

SangWoo An, Hyeokdong Kwon, YoungBeom Kim, Hwajeong Seo, Seog Chung SEO
Efficient Implementation of ARX-Based Block Ciphers on 8-Bit AVR Microcontrollers
Reprinted from: *Mathematics* **2020**, *8*, 1837, doi:10.3390/math8101837 111

Matea Ignatoski, Jonatan Lerga
Comparison of Entropy and Dictionary Based Text Compression in English, German, French, Italian, Czech, Hungarian, Finnish, and Croatian
Reprinted from: *Mathematics* **2020**, *8*, 1059, doi:10.3390/math8071059 133

About the Editor

Raúl M. Falcón

Dr. Raúl M. Falcón is an Associate Professor of Applied Mathematics at the University of Seville, from which he received his Ph.D. in Mathematics (2005). His research interest focuses on the study of Latin squares and related structures, on the classification of finite-dimensional algebras into isotopism classes and on graph coloring. He is the author of about 50 research papers on these topics in peer-reviewed journals.

Preface to "Codes, Designs, Cryptography and Optimization"

Novel synergies are continuously being developed among research areas in coding theory, cryptography, combinatorial design, and combinatorial optimization, giving rise to new applications in other fields and to the real world, including algebraic geometry, artificial intelligence, communication networks, computer science, hardware and software design, design of experiments, logistics, machine learning, and scheduling or transportation networks, among others. With researcher contributions from six different universities from five different countries, this book consists of a compilation of some relevant and recent investigations concerning this area. It covers a vast range of topics, such as: Ryser's formula over Sylvester Hadamard matrices by enumerating Boolean functions; the study of Hadamard matrices with cocyclic cores; the fundamentals of the pseudococyclic development of Hadamard matrices over quasigroups; the use of critical sets associated with autotopisms of Latin squares for describing secret sharing schemes; the study of binary linear codes through the use of order ideals in hierarchical posets with two levels; the use of computational algebra systems to control grid-connected nanogrids with hybrid energy storage systems composed of batteries and supercapacitors; a series of implementation techniques for lightweight cryptography, namely, PRESENT and its electronic code book (ECB) and counter (CTR) on low-end embedded processors; the optimized implementations of ARX-based Korean block ciphers (LEA and HIGHT) with a CTR mode of operation, and CTR_DRBG using them on low-end 8-bit AVR microcontrollers; the analysis of algorithms for text compression in different languages.

As the Guest Editor of this Special Issue, I would like to thank the authors of the articles for their fascinating contributions, the referees for their valuable reviews, Mr. Nikola Yuan and Mr. Claude Zhang from MDPI for their kind and valuable assistance during the entire process, and the journal Mathematics for inviting me and providing me the opportunity to publish this book.

Raúl Manuel Falcón
Editor

Article

Boolean Functions and Permanents of Sylvester Hadamard Matrices

José Andrés Armario

Departamento de Matemática Aplicada I, Universidad de Sevilla, Avda. Reina Mercedes s/n, 41012 Sevilla, Spain; armario@us.es

Abstract: One of the fastest known general techniques for computing permanents is Ryser's formula. On this note, we show that this formula over Sylvester Hadamard matrices of order 2^m, H_m, can be carried out by enumerating m-variable Boolean functions with an arbitrary Walsh spectrum. As a consequence, the quotient $per(H_m)/2^{2^m}$ might be a measure of the "density" of m-variable Boolean functions with high nonlinearity.

Keywords: permanent; Sylvester Hadamard matrices; Ryser's formula; Boolean functions; Walsh spectrum; high nonlinearity

MSC: 15A15; 05B20; 06E30; 65T50

Citation: Armario, J.A. Boolean Functions and Permanents of Sylvester Hadamard matrices. *Mathematics* **2021**, *9*, 177. https://doi.org/10.3390/math9020177

Received: 27 November 2020
Accepted: 15 January 2021
Published: 17 January 2021

Publisher's Note: MDPI stays neutral with regard to jurisdictional claims in published maps and institutional affiliations.

Copyright: © 2021 by the author. Licensee MDPI, Basel, Switzerland. This article is an open access article distributed under the terms and conditions of the Creative Commons Attribution (CC BY) license (https://creativecommons.org/licenses/by/4.0/).

1. Introduction

The theory of Boolean functions is a fascinating area of research in discrete mathematics with applications to cryptography and coding theory. Claude Shannon's properties of confusion and diffusion are fundamental concepts for achieving security in cryptosystems. The notion of diffusion is related to the degree to which the influence of a single input plaintext bit is spread throughout the resulting ciphertext, and the notion of confusion is related to the complexity of the relationship between the secret key and ciphertext. Boolean functions with high nonlinearity can be used to provide confusion in block encryption algorithms [1,2]. Nonlinearity is the minimum number of bits which must change in the truth table of a Boolean function to become an affine function. The Walsh transform is the most important mathematical tool for the analysis of cryptographic properties of Boolean functions. The understanding of the Walsh transform of a Boolean function uniquely determines the function; therefore, working fully with the Walsh transform is possible.

Here we study a connection between the Walsh spectrum of m-variable Boolean functions and Ryser's formula of the permanent for Sylvester Hadamard matrices of order 2^m.

In 1812, Cauchy and Binet independently introduced the notion of the permanent as a matrix function.

Definition 1. *Let N be the set $\{1, \ldots, n\}$, ($n \in \mathbf{Z}^+$). The symmetric group S_n is the group of all $n!$ permutations of N. The permanent of an $n \times n$ matrix $A = [a_{ij}]$ is defined by*

$$per(A) = \sum_{\sigma \in S_n} \prod_{i=1}^{n} a_{i,\sigma(i)}.$$

At first glance, it seems to be a straightforward version of the determinant, but this is a misleading impression. For instance, the determinant of an arbitrary matrix can be evaluated efficiently using Gaussian elimination; however, the computation of the permanent is much more complicated. Valiant [3] proved that it belongs to the class of ♯P-complete problems, which basically means that there is almost no possibility of finding a polynomial time deterministic algorithm for computing the permanent in general. Precisely, the central problem studied in arithmetic complexity theory is the permanent versus determinant problem, which is considered the arithmetic analogue of the NP vs. P problem (see [4]).

There are wide applications of the permanent of certain matrices, such as 0,1 and/or sparse matrices with special structures. Especially in combinatorial counting and graph theory [5]. For instance, if G is a balanced (the two parts have equal size) bipartite graph and M_G is its adjacency matrix, the per (M_G) counts perfect matchings in G. Nevertheless, as far as we know, there is not any clear combinatorial interpretation of the permanent of Hadamard matrices. Here we give some ideas towards an interpretation of the permanent of the Sylvester Hadamard matrices in terms of Boolean functions with high nonlinearity.

Notation. Throughout the article, we make use of $-$ for -1 and 1 for $+1$. We write H_m for a Sylvester Hadamard matrix of order 2^m. The cardinality of a set S is denoted $\sharp S$. We use I_n for the identity matrix of order n and M^T for the transpose of M. The Galois field with two elements is denoted by $GF(2)$ and the m-dimensional vector space over $GF(2)$, equipped with the canonical basis by $GF(2)^m$. $\langle g_i, g_j \rangle$ means the usual inner product for $g_i, g_j \in GF(2)^n$.

2. Preliminaries

Basic concepts and results on Hadamard matrices and Boolean functions will be reviewed. We refer the reader to [6] for more details about Hadamard matrices and see [7] and the references therein for some of the theories of Boolean functions.

2.1. Hadamard Matrices

A *Hadamard matrix* H of order n is an $n \times n$ matrix with entries ± 1 and $HH^T = nI$. If a Hadmard matrix has its first row and column all 1s are said to be normalized. A Hadamard matrix can always be normalized by multiplying rows and columns by -1. It is well-known that n can only be either 2 or a multiple of 4 and it is conjectured that Hadamard matrices exist for every $n \equiv 0 \mod 4$ (see [6]).

It was observed by Sylvester in 1867 that, if H is a Hadamard matrix of order n, then

$$\begin{bmatrix} H & H \\ H & -H \end{bmatrix}$$

is a Hadamard matrix of order $2n$. Matrices of this configuration are called *Sylvester Hadamard* and are defined for all powers of 2. The Sylvester Hadamard matrix of order 2 is given as

$$H_1 = \begin{bmatrix} 1 & 1 \\ 1 & - \end{bmatrix}.$$

Sylvester Hadamard matrices of order 2^k, denoted by H_k, can be formed by $\overset{k-copies}{H_1 \times \cdots \times H_1}$ the Kronecker product of k copies of H_1. These matrices have many interesting properties (see [8]), for instance $H_m = [(-1)^{\langle g_i, g_j \rangle}]_{g_i, g_j \in GF(2)^m}$.

Two Hadamard matrices H and H' are said to be *equivalent* when one can be acquired from the other by a series of row and/or column interchanges and row and/or column negations. The question of classifying Hadamard matrices of order $n \geq 36$ remains unanswered and only partial results are known.

We recollect that Hadamard proved that $n^{n/2}$ is an upper bound for the absolute value of the determinant of an $n \times n$ matrix with entries from the unic disc, and this bound is attainable by matrices with entries ± 1 if and only if they are Hadamard. However, the permanent of a Hadamard matrix has hardly been worked on, and it is considered a very difficult problem. From what we know, the permanents for all Hadamard matrices of orders smaller or equal to 28 were calculated in [9], but for orders greater than 28 the permanent remains unknown in general. The permanent of the Sylvester Hadamard matrix of order 32 is 6829323892021002240 ([10]).

2.2. Boolean Functions

A *Boolean function* is a mapping

$$f: GF(2)^m \to GF(2).$$

We denote by $\mathbf{B}_m$ the set of all m-variable Boolean functions. Since there are 2^m possible inputs of length m, $\sharp \mathbf{B}_m = 2^{2^m}$.

Example 1. $f(x) = \langle x, g \rangle + c$ where $g \in GF(2)^m$ and $c \in GF(2)$ represent a Boolean function, the so-called affine function. In particular, if $c = 0$ then $f(x)$ is called a linear function. We denoted by $\mathbf{A}_m$ the set of m-variable affine functions and $\sharp \mathbf{A}_m = 2^{m+1}$.

A Boolean function can be displayed in several ways. One prospect is to simply list all values in a fixed order. To this end we denote g_i as the binary representation of the integer $i-1$ with m bits. For instance, $g_1 = (0,0,\ldots,0)$ and $g_2 = (0,\ldots,0,1)$, hence this list $g_1, g_2, \ldots, g_{2^m}$ contains all the elements of $GF(2)^m$. The vector

$$[f(g_1), f(g_2), \ldots, f(g_{2^m})]$$

is called the *truth table* (TT) of a Boolean function f. The *support* of f is the set $S_f = \{g \in GF(2)^m : f(g) = 1\}$, and the *weight* of f, $wt(f)$, is the cardinality of the support, i.e., $wt(f) = \sharp S_f$.

The *Hamming distance* between two Boolean functions f and h on $GF(2^m)$ is defined as $wt(f+h)$. The *nonlinearity* of f and denoted by N_f is the minimum distance between f and the set of all affine functions. This concept has several applications in cryptography and coding theory. For instance, nonlinearity can be utilized as a measure of the strength of cryptosystems (see [11]). The Walsh-Hadamard transform is the main tool to study the nonlinearity of Boolean functions, which is defined for an m-variable Boolean function f, such as

$$W_f(g) = \sum_{x \in GF(2)^m} (-1)^{f(x) + \langle x, g \rangle}, \quad g \in GF(2)^m.$$

The vector $[W_f(g_1), W_f(g_2), \ldots, W_f(g_{2^n})]$ is called the *Walsh spectrum* (WS) of a Boolean function f. Each component $W_f(g)$ of WS is called a *Walsh coefficient*. Its magnitude is the correlation between f and the corresponding linear function $l_g(x) = \langle x, g \rangle$ for $g, x \in GF(2)^m$.

Now, we recall some results involving the Sylvester Hadamard matrix and the WS of a Boolean function.

Proposition 1. *Assuming that f is an m-variable Boolean function and $H_m = [h_{i,j}]$ is the Sylvester Hadamard matrix of order 2^m. The following identities hold,*

1. $[F(g_1), F(g_2), \ldots, F(g_{2^m})] H_m = [W_f(g_1), W_f(g_2), \ldots, W_f(g_{2^m})]$, where $F(g) = (-1)^{f(g)}$.
2. $\sum_{i \in S_f} h_{i,k} = 2^{m-1} \delta_{g_1}^{g_k} - \frac{1}{2} W_f(g_k), \quad k = 1, \ldots, 2^m$ where $\delta_{g_1}^{g_k}$ is Kronecker's symbol.

Proof. The first identity follows from the fact that $H_m = [(-1)^{\langle g_i, g_j \rangle}]_{g_i, g_j \in GF(2)}^m$. For the second, we have to take into account the following facts:

- $W_f(g_k) = \sum_{i \in S_f} h_{i,k} - \sum_{i \in \bar{S}_f} h_{i,k}$ where $\bar{S}_f = \{1, 2, \ldots, 2^m\} \setminus S_f$.

- $\sum_{i=1}^{2^m} h_{i,k} = \begin{cases} 2^m & k = 0 \\ 0 & 0 < k \leq 2^m \end{cases}$

□

3. Ryser's Formula for H_m and the Walsh Spectrum of Boolean Functions

H.J. Ryser found the following alternative method to evaluate the permanent of a matrix $A = [a_{ij}]$ of order n,

$$\text{per}(A) = (-1)^n \sum_{r=1}^{n} (-1)^r \sum_{\alpha \in Q_{r,n}} \prod_{j=1}^{n} \sum_{i \in \alpha} a_{i,j}, \quad (1)$$

where $Q_{r,n}$ denotes the set of all strictly increasing sequences of r integers taken from the set $\{1, 2, \ldots, n\}$. This is one of the fastest known general algorithms for computing a permanent. By counting multiplications it has an efficiency of $O(2^n n)$ (see pp. 31–11 [12]).

Proposition 2. *Assuming that $H_m = [h_{i,j}]$ is the Sylvester Hadamard matrix of order 2^m, f an arbitary m-variable Boolean function and $\Phi(f) = \prod_{j=2}^{2^m} \sum_{i \in S_f} h_{i,j}$. Then,*

1. $\Phi(f) = -2^{1-2^m} \prod_{j=2}^{2^m} W_f(g_j).$

2. $\text{per}(H_m) = \sum_{r=1}^{2^m} (-1)^r r \sum_{s_f \in Q_{r,2^m}} \Phi(f).$

Proof. The first identity follows from Proposition 1 and the second one is immediate. □

The following result studies some properties of the function Φ that we will use later.

Lemma 1.
1. Let f be an arbitrary $f \in \mathbf{B}_{m-1}$ and $h = [f|f]$ be the result of concatenating the TT of f to itself. Then $\Phi(h) = 0$.
2. Let $l \in \mathbf{A}_{m-1}$, $f \in \mathbf{B}_{m-1}$ and $h = [f|l]$. If $\Phi(f) = 0$ then $\Phi(h) = 0$. For instance, $\Phi(h) = 0$ when $wt(f) = 2$ or 4.
3. Let $l(x) = \langle x, g_j \rangle + c \in \mathbf{A}_m$, $f \in \mathbf{B}_m$ and $h = l + f$. Then $\Phi(h) = \dfrac{(2^m - 2wt(f))}{W_f(g_j)}(-1)^c \Phi(f).$

Proof. Identities 1 and 2 follow from

$$W_h(g_k) = \begin{cases} W_{f_1}(g_k) + W_{f_2}(g_k) & 1 \leq k \leq 2^{m-1} \\ W_{f_1}(g_k) - W_{f_2}(g_k) & 2^{m-1} + 1 \leq k \leq 2^m \end{cases}$$

for $h = [f_1|f_2]$ and $W_l(g_k)$ is null for some $k > 1$. For identity 3, we have to take into account that $W_h(g_k) = (-1)^c W_f(g_j + g_k)$. □

In the sequel, we will try to extract some consequences of the Proposition 2. Firstly, it may help in finding an interpretation of the permanent of H_m in terms of nonlinearity.

Since

$$W_f(g) = 2^m - 2wt(f + l_g),$$

the nonlinearity of f is computed from the Walsh sprectrum by

$$N_f = 2^{m-1} - \frac{1}{2} \max_{g \in GF(2)^m} |W_f(g)|.$$

If a maximum absolute value of W_f occurs at g_k, then either l_{g_k} is the best linear approximation of f (when $W_f(g_k) > 0$) or its complement, the affine function $1 + l_{g_k}$, is as good as, or better than, the best linear approximation (when $W_f(g_k) < 0$).

It is a simple corollary of Parseval's identity,

$$\sum_{i=1}^{2^m} W_f(g_i)^2 = 2^{2m},$$

that

$$\max_i |W_f(g_i)| \geq 2^{\frac{m}{2}}. \tag{2}$$

Therefore, for any Boolean function in m variables,

$$N_f \leq 2^{m-1} - 2^{\frac{m}{2}-1},$$

and this bound is achieved only when m is even and $|W_f(g_i)| = 2^{\frac{m}{2}}$, $\forall i$. Hence,

$$wt(f) = \frac{2^m - 2^{m/2}}{2} \text{ or } \frac{2^m + 2^{m/2}}{2}.$$

An m-variable Boolean function with m even and maximum nonlinearity is called *bent*. Furthermore, if f is bent then $|\Phi(f)| = 2^{m2^{m-2}}$. This is the maximum of $|\Phi|$ in $\mathbf{B}_m$ and $\Phi(f) < 0$.

The affine functions are the other extreme, with respect to the Walsh spectrum. There is only one non-null Walsh coefficient for an affine function, and its value is either 2^m, when it is linear, or -2^m otherwise. Therefore,

$$\Phi(l_{g_k} + c) = 0.$$

By Parseval's identity, if some of the Walsh coefficients are smaller than average in absolute value, especially if some are 0, then the others must be larger. Thus, if f is a Boolean function with a small N_f and $wt(f)$ even then it can be expected that $\Phi(f)$ will be null. For $wt(f)$ odd and after carrying out some computer searches up to $m = 5$, we found that Φ more often takes positive than negative values.

Although the formula for nonlinearity is sign free, the quotient $\frac{\text{per}(H_m)}{\sharp \mathbf{B}_m}$ could provide some information of the "global" nonlinearity of the whole set m-variable Boolean functions. Especially, when $\frac{\text{per}(H_m)}{\sharp \mathbf{B}_m} < \frac{\text{per}(H_{m'})}{\sharp \mathbf{B}_{m'}}$ could indicate a better density of Boolean functions with high nonlinearity in $\mathbf{B}_m$ than in $\mathbf{B}_{m'}$. For $m = 2$ and 4, this is confirmed with the behaviour of the quotient between the number of bent functions in m variables between the number of Boolean functions (see [2], Chapter 7). Attending to our observation we also claim the following.

Conjecture 1. If m is even, then

$$2^{(m-2)2^{m-4}} \leq \text{per}(H_m) \leq 2^{m2^{m-2}}$$

and if m is odd, then

$$2^{(m-1)2^{m-2}} \leq \text{per}(H_m) \leq 2^{(m+1)2^{m-2}}.$$

Secondly, we will try to take advantage of computing the permanent of a Sylvester Hadamard matrix from partitioning $\mathbf{B}_m$ in classes under the affine equivalence relationship.

Definition 2 ([2]). *Two m-variable Boolean functions f and h are said to be affine equivalent if there exists an invertible matrix A with entries in $GF(2)$ and a constant $b \in GF(2)^m$ such that for all $x \in GF(2)^m$ it holds that*

$$f(x) = h(A(x) + b).$$

The following Lemma studies the Walsh spectra of affine equivalent Boolean functions f and h. As immediate consequence, we have $N_f = N_h$.

Lemma 2 ([13]). *Let f and h be two affine equivalent m-variable Boolean functions, $f(x) = h(A(x) + b)$, then*

$$W_f(g) = (-1)^{\langle b, (A^{-1})^T(g) \rangle} W_h((A^{-1})^T(g)).$$

Another important consequence is,

Proposition 3. *If f and h are affine equivalent m-variable Boolean functions then*

$$\Phi(f) = \Phi(h).$$

Proof. This follows from Proposition 2 and Lemma 2. Since $(A^{-1})^T(g)$ runs over all the elements of $GF(2) \setminus \{0\}$ when g runs over all the elements of $GF(2) \setminus \{0\}$ and the number of times that $\langle b, (A^{-1})^T(g) \rangle = 1 \mod 2$ is even for any fixed $b \in GF(2)$ when when g runs over all the elements of $GF(2) \setminus \{0\}$. This last statement is due to the fact that the number of elements of $GF(2)^m$ with concrete values in certain positions divides 2^m. □

Now, the formula for the permanent of H_m can be rewritten in terms of classes under the affine equivalence relation for the set of m-variable Boolean functions.

Proposition 4.

$$per(H_m) = \sum_{r=1}^{2^{m-1}-1} (-1)^r (2r - 2^m) \sum_{i=1}^{\sharp \Omega_{r,m}} \sharp [X_i^r] \Phi(f_{X_i^r}). \quad (3)$$

where $\Omega_{r,m}$ is the set of classes under the affine equivalence for the m-variable Boolean functions of weight r, $f_{X_i^r}$ is a representative of the class $X_i^r \in \Omega_{r,m}$, $r = wt(f_{X_i^r})$.

Proof. It is immediate from Proposition 2, Proposition 3 and the fact that $\sum_{i \in \alpha} h_{i,j} = -\sum_{i \in \tilde{\alpha}} h_{i,j}, j \geq 2$; where $\alpha \cup \tilde{\alpha} = \{1, 2, \ldots, 2^m\}$. □

Example 2. *Now we are going to compute $per(H_3)$ using formula (3)*,

$$H_3 = \begin{bmatrix} 1 & 1 & 1 & 1 & 1 & 1 & 1 & 1 \\ 1 & - & 1 & - & 1 & - & 1 & - \\ 1 & 1 & - & - & 1 & 1 & - & - \\ 1 & - & - & 1 & 1 & - & - & 1 \\ 1 & 1 & 1 & 1 & - & - & - & - \\ 1 & - & 1 & - & - & 1 & - & 1 \\ 1 & 1 & - & - & - & - & 1 & 1 \\ 1 & - & - & 1 & - & 1 & 1 & - \end{bmatrix}.$$

Taking into account that $\Phi(f) = 0$ for any 3-variable Boolean function with $wt(f)$ even. Then,

$$per(H_3) = (-1)^1 (2 - 8) \sum_{i=1}^{\sharp \Omega_{1,3}} \sharp [X_i^1] \Phi(f_{X_i^1}) + (-1)^3 (6 - 8) \sum_{i=1}^{\sharp \Omega_{3,3}} \sharp [X_i^3] \Phi(f_{X_i^3})$$

(Using Table 1, we get)

$$= 6 \times (8 \times 1) + 2 \times (56 \times 3) = 384.$$

Therefore, the problem of computing the permanent of a Sylvester Hadamard matrix of order 2^m can be carried out by enumerating m-variable Boolean functions with an arbitrary Walsh spectrum. This enumeration problem, although of interest in cryptography [14], requires a huge amount of computational resources. For instance, the number of bent functions (those Boolean functions with flat spectrum) so far has only been known for dimensions up to and including 8 (see [15]). Thus, Formula (3) only has a theoretical interest.

Finally, we give another formula for the permanent of H_m as a straightforward consequence of some results from [16,17]. Let $Sym(E)$ be the group of permutations on the set E and $\varepsilon(\sigma)$ be the parity $+1$ or -1 of σ for each $\sigma \in Sym(E)$. Then, $\Gamma(f)$ is defined as the set $\{\sigma \in Sym(GF(2)^m) \colon \forall a \in GF(2)^m, f(a + \sigma(a)) = 1\}$.

Now, taking into account the following facts:

1. Theorem 1 of [16] proves that the Walsh spectrum of f coincides with the spectrum of G_f, the Cayley graph associated to f, where the vertex set of G_f is equal to $GF(2)^m$, while the edge set E_f is defined as follows:

$$E_f = \{(g_i, g_j) \mid f(g_i + g_j) = 1\}.$$

This connects the problem of analyzing the spectral coefficients of Boolean functions with the framework of spectral analysis of graphs. Let us denote by $w_f(g_i)$ the eigenvalues of the adjacency matrix of the Cayley graph associated to f.

2. Corollary 2 of [17] proves that the product $\Pi_{i=1}^{2^m} w_f(g_i) = \sum_{\sigma \in \Gamma(f)} \varepsilon(\sigma)$.

Therefore, the formula for the permanent of H_m given in Proposition 2 can be rewritten as

$$\text{per}(H_m) = \sum_{r=1}^{2^m} (-1)^{r+1} r \sum_{s_f \in Q_{r,2^m}} \frac{\sum_{\sigma \in \Gamma(f)} \varepsilon(\sigma)}{2^{2^m-1} w_f(g_1)}.$$

Table 1. Number of inequivalent m-variable Boolean functions of weight r under the affine equivalence for $m = 3$ and $r = 1, 3$.

r	# Inequivalent 3-Variable Boolean Functions	# Orbits
1	1	8
3	1	56

4. Conclusions

The paper demonstrates a connection between two different mathematical areas: Boolean functions and permanents. Firstly, Ryser's formula for computing the permanent of Sylvester Hadamard matrices has been rewritten in terms of the Walsh spectrum of m-variable functions. Although this formula does not represent a real shortcut for computing the permanent of H_m, it suggested the bounds given in Conjecture 1, since $|\Pi_{j=2}^{2^m} W_f(g_j)| = 2^{m2^{m-2}}$ when f is bent. Secondly, we show that the quotient $per(H_m)/2^{2^m}$ provides information about the density of m-variable Boolean functions with high nonlinearity (i.e., Boolean functions with linearity close to the minimum). We have checked until $m = 5$ that $per(H_m)/2^{2^m}$ is a strictly increasing function and the quotient between the number of bent functions in m variables and the number Boolean functions (2^{2^m}) is a strictly decreasing function (up to $m = 8$) which means that density Boolean functions with high nonlinearity are worse when m increase. Finally, let us point out the following asymptotic result about the linearity of random Boolean functions due to Olejár and Stanek.

Theorem 1 ([18]). *There is a constant c, such that if m is big enough, then for almost every Boolean function in m variables*

$$N_f \geq 2^{m-1} - c\sqrt{m}2^{m/2}.$$

Funding: This research received no external funding.

Institutional Review Board Statement: Not applicable.

Informed Consent Statement: Not applicable.

Data Availability Statement: Not applicable.

Acknowledgments: The author thanks Kristeen Cheng for reading the manuscript. This work is partially supported by the Research Projects FQM-016 from Junta de Andalucí a.

Conflicts of Interest: The author declare no conflict of interest.

References

1. Guesmi, R.; Farah, M.A.B.; Kachouri, A.; Samet, M. Chaos-based designing of a highly nonlinear S-box using Boolean functions. In Proceedings of the 12th International Multi-Conference on Systems, Signals and Devices, SSD, Tunisia, Mahdia, 16–19 March 2015; Volume 2015, p. 7348106.
2. Tokareva, N. *Bent Functions: Results and Applications to Cryptography*; Elsevier Science: London, UK, 2015.
3. Valiant, L.G. The complexity of computing the permanent. *Theoret. Comput. Sci.* **1979**, *8*, 189–201. [CrossRef]
4. Aaronson, S. $P\stackrel{?}{=}NP$ Chapter 3 in *Open Problems in Mathematics*; Nash, J.F., Rassias, M.T., Eds.; Springer: Berlin/Heidelberg, Germany, 2016.
5. Minc, H. Permanents. In *Encyclopedia of Mathematics and its Applications 6*; Addison-Wesley: Reading, MA, USA, 1978.
6. Horadam, K.J. *Hadamard Matrices and Their Applications*; Princeton University Press: Princeton, NJ, USA, 2007.
7. Carlet, C. Boolean functions for cryptography and error correcting codes. In *Boolean Models and Methods in Mathematics, Computer Science and Engineering*; Crama, Y., Hammer, P.L., Eds.; Cambrige University Press: Cambridge, UK, 2010; pp. 257–397.
8. Mitrouli, M. Sylvester Hadamard matrices revisited. *Spec. Matrices* **2014**, *2*, 120–124. [CrossRef]
9. Wanless, I.M. Permanents of matrices of signed ones. *Linear Multilinear Algebra* **2005**, *52*, 57–63. [CrossRef]
10. Szöllósi, F. (Department of Mathematical Science, Shimane University, Matsue, Japan). Personal communication, 2014.
11. Carlet, C. On cryptographic complexity of Boolean functions. In *Proceedings of the Sixth Conference on Finite Fields with Applications to Coding Theory, Cryptography, and Related Areas, Berlin, Germany*; Mullen, G.L., Stichtenoth, H., Tapia-Recillas, H., Eds.; Springer: Berlin, Germany, 2002; pp. 53–69.
12. Wanless, I.M. Permanents. In *Chapter 31 in Handbook of Linear Algebra*; Hogben, L., Ed.; Chapman & Hall/CRC: London, UK, 2007.
13. Preneel, B. Analysis and Design of Cryptographic Hash Functions. Ph.D. Thesis, Katholieke Universiteit Leuven, Leuven, Belgium, 1993.
14. Uyan, E.; Calik, C.; Doganaksoy, A. Counting Boolean functions with specified values in their Walsh spectrum. *J. Comput. Appl. Math.* **2014**, *259*, 522–528. [CrossRef]
15. Langevin, P.; Leander, G. Counting all bent functions in dimension eight 99270589265934337030578586124288. *Des. Codes Cryptogr.* **2011**, *59*, 193–205. [CrossRef]
16. Bernasconi, A.; Codenotti, B. Spectral analysis of Boolean functions as a graph eigenvalue problem *IEEE Trans. Comput.* **1999**, *48*, 345–351.
17. Mitton, M. On the Walsh-Fourier analysis of Boolean functions. *J. Discret. Math. Scien. Cryptogr.* **2006**, *9*, 429–439. [CrossRef]
18. Olejár, D.; Stanek, M. On cryptographic properties of fandom Boolean functions. *J. Univers. Comput. Sci.* **1998**, *4*, 705–717.

Article

Hadamard Matrices with Cocyclic Core

Víctor Álvarez [1,*], José Andrés Armario [1], María Dolores Frau [1], Félix Gudiel [1], María Belén Güemes [2] and Amparo Osuna [1]

[1] Department of Applied Mathematics I, University of Seville, 41004 Sevilla, Spain; armario@us.es (J.A.A.); mdfrau@us.es (M.D.F.); gudiel@us.es (F.G.); aosuna@us.es (A.O.)
[2] Department of Algebra, University of Seville, 41004 Sevilla, Spain; bguemes@us.es
* Correspondence: valvarez@us.es

Abstract: Since Horadam and de Launey introduced the cocyclic framework on combinatorial designs in the 1990s, it has revealed itself as a powerful technique for looking for (cocyclic) Hadamard matrices. Ten years later, the series of papers by Kotsireas, Koukouvinos and Seberry about Hadamard matrices with one or two circulant cores introduced a different structured approach to the Hadamard conjecture. This paper is built on both strengths, so that Hadamard matrices with cocyclic cores are introduced and studied. They are proved to strictly include usual Hadamard matrices with one and two circulant cores, and therefore provide a wiser uniform approach to a *structured* Hadamard conjecture.

Keywords: Hadamard matrix; circulant matrix; cocyclic matrix; difference set

MSC: 05B20; 05B10

Citation: Álvarez, V.; Armario, J.A.; Frau, M.D.; Gudiel, F.; Güemes, M.B.; Osuna, A. Hadamard Matrices with Cocyclic Core. *Mathematics* **2021**, *9*, 857. https://doi.org/10.3390/math9080857

Academic Editor: Abdelmejid Bayad

Received: 10 February 2021
Accepted: 9 April 2021
Published: 14 April 2021

Publisher's Note: MDPI stays neutral with regard to jurisdictional claims in published maps and institutional affiliations.

Copyright: © 2021 by the authors. Licensee MDPI, Basel, Switzerland. This article is an open access article distributed under the terms and conditions of the Creative Commons Attribution (CC BY) license (https:// creativecommons.org/licenses/by/ 4.0/).

1. Introduction

Hadamard matrices are square matrices of order n with entries from $\{-1,1\}$ such that their rows are pairwise orthogonal. They were identified as the extremal solutions of the maximal determinant problem for square matrices with entries from the unit disc [1].

It may be straightforwardly checked that, regardless of the elemental cases $n = 1$ and $n = 2$, as soon as three rows have to be mutually orthogonal, this implies that n is necessarily a multiple of 4. Unexpectedly, the converse assertion (that there exists a Hadamard matrix for every order $n = 4w$), remains one of the most famous open century-old problems in mathematics, the Hadamard Conjecture.

The techniques for constructing Hadamard matrices are usually organized into three types: multiplication theorems, "plug-in" methods and direct constructions [2,3]. Nevertheless, none of them has succeeded to provide a uniform method for constructing these matrices.

The cocyclic approach, as introduced in [4], tries to cast new light on this purpose. A cocyclic matrix (over a group G) consists of a matrix $(\psi(i,j))$ constructed from a binary (2-)cocycle over G, $\psi : G \times G \to \{-1, 1\}$, so that:

$$\psi(a,b)\, \psi(a,b \cdot c)\, \psi(a \cdot b, c)\, \psi(b,c) = 1, \qquad (1)$$

for all $a,b,c \in G$. It is called a 2-coboundary if a map $\phi : G \to G$ exists such that $\psi(a,b) = \phi(a)\phi(b)\phi(ab)$, for every $a,b \in G$.

Accordingly, checking whether a cocyclic matrix is Hadamard translates into checking if the summation of each row (but the first) is zero [5]. This is not the only advantage of this approach. It endows the matrix with an enriched structure, which is being successfully exploited to look for Hadamard matrices [2,6,7]. Nowadays, this framework is broadening its expected horizons, since more recently even quasigroups [8] and Latin rectangles [9] have come into play.

(Cocyclic) Hadamard matrices are intimately related to other combinatorial objects, such as designs, (almost) difference sets and (almost) perfect sequences. We next briefly recall these notions and relations, as they are introduced in [2,10], since they will be relevant in the exposition of the paper. For further information, the interested reader is referred to [2,10] and the references therein.

A (v, k, λ)-design is a pair $\mathcal{D} = (P, B)$ consisting of a v-set $P = \{p_1, \ldots, p_v\}$ of points and a v-set $B = \{B_1, \ldots, B_v\}$ of k-blocks, $1 < k < v$, such that each pair of distinct points is contained in exactly λ blocks.

If G is an automorphism group of $\mathcal{D}$ such that for each pair of points p_i, p_j there is a unique $g \in G$ such that $g(p_i) = p_j$, and similarly for blocks, the design $\mathcal{D}$ is called regular with respect to G, and G is called a regular group for $\mathcal{D}$.

Matricially, $\mathcal{D}$ is easily represented by its $v \times v$ incidence matrix $A_\mathcal{D} = (a_{ij})$, rows and columns in correspondence with blocks and points, respectively, such that $a_{ij} = 1$ if and only if $p_j \in B_i$, and 0 otherwise.

It may be straightforwardly checked that a $v \times v$ square matrix A with entries 0,1 is an incidence matrix of a (v, k, λ)-design if and only if $AA^T = (k - \lambda)I + \lambda J$ and $AJ = kJ$, for I the identity matrix and J the all 1s matrix.

In particular, there exists a Hadamard matrix H of order $4w$ if and only if there exists a square $(4w - 1, 2w - 1, w - 1)$-design $\mathcal{D}$. Actually, noting $A' = 2A_\mathcal{D} - J$, the matrix obtained from $A_\mathcal{D}$ by replacing 0s by -1s, then $H = \begin{pmatrix} 1 & \mathbf{1} \\ \mathbf{1}^T & A' \end{pmatrix}$, is a Hadamard matrix, and vice versa.

Other combinatorial structures intimately related to Hadamard matrices and designs are difference sets.

A (v, k, λ)-difference set in a group $(G, \cdot)$ of order v is a k-subset $D \subset G$ such that the $k(k-1)$-list of quotients $d_1 d_2^{-1}$ of distinct elements d_1, d_2 of D contains each non-identity element of G exactly λ times. The order of the difference set is $n = k - \lambda$. The difference set is called cyclic or abelian, if G has the respective property.

Remark 1. *Notice that if D is a (v, k, λ)-difference set, then $G \setminus D$ defines a $(v, v - k, v - 2k + \lambda)$-difference set, the so-called complementary difference set of D.*

Let G be a group of v elements, and $D \subset G$ a k-subset, $1 < k < v$. Then D is a (v, k, λ)-difference set in G if and only if $\mathcal{D} = (G, \{gD : g \in G\})$ is a (v, k, λ)-design with regular group G, and vice versa. Therefore, as soon as a $(4w - 1, 2w - 1, w - 1)$-difference set exists, there exists a Hadamard matrix of order $4w$ in turn.

Now we turn our interest to (almost) perfect sequences, as introduced in [10].

Consider a cyclic binary sequence (a_i) with entries from $\{-1, 1\}$ of period v, such that $a_{i+v} = a_i$, for $i \geq 0$. The autocorrelation of (a_i) for shift t is defined as the sum
$$c_t(a_i) = \sum_{i=0}^{v-1} a_i a_{i+t}.$$

A sequence (a_i) is called perfect when $c_t(a_i) = r$ is constant for $0 < t \leq v - 1$, and equals the smallest possible max $|c_t(a_i)| \in \{0, 1, 2\}$, since $c_t(a) \equiv v \mod 4$.

Remark 2. *Notice that a perfect periodic sequence with period v, k positive entries per period and autocorrelation $c_t(a_i) = r$, $0 < t \leq v - 1$, is equivalent to a cyclic (v, k, λ)-difference set: it suffices to take $D = \{i : a_i = 1, 0 \leq i \leq v - 1\}$, so that $|D \cap (D + t)| = \lambda$ and $r = v - 4(k - \lambda)$.*

Depending on the value $c_t(a_i) = r \in \{0, \pm 1, \pm 2\}$, the existence of perfect sequences (a_i) is summarized in [10]. In particular:

- The case $r = 0$ corresponds to circulant Hadamard matrices of order v, which are conjectured to exist just for $v = 4$.
- The case $r = 1$ corresponds to $(2u^2 + 2u + 1, u^2, \frac{u^2 - u}{2})$-cyclic difference sets, which are conjectured to exist just for $u = 1, 2$.

- There is no known example for the case $r = 2$, and experimental results suggest that none might exist.
- The case $r = -2$ gives just one difference set, the $(2, 1, 0)$-difference set.
- The case $r = -1$ gives the so-called Paley–Hadamard difference sets, with parameters $(v, \frac{v-1}{2}, \frac{v-3}{4})$, whose existence implies in turn the existence of Hadamard matrices of order $v + 1$. These include very well known families of difference sets [10].

Remark 3. *The case $r = -1$ is of particular interest in this paper, since it includes the so-called Hadamard matrices with one circulant core [11], of the form $\begin{pmatrix} 1 & 1 \\ 1 & A \end{pmatrix}$, for A being a circulant matrix whose first row consists of a perfect sequence (a_i) with $c_t(a_i) = -1$, $0 < t \leq 4w - 2$, and $\sum_{i=0}^{4w-2} a_i = -1$.*

When relaxing some conditions, the combinatorial structures described above may be generalized, in some sense.

For instance, given a k-subset D of a group $(G, \cdot)$ of order v, it might occur that the number of occurrences of each non identity element in G among the list of quotients $d_1 d_2^{-1}$ of distinct elements $d_1 \neq d_2 \in D$ is either λ or $\lambda + 1$, not just λ. Then D defines a (v, k, λ, s)-almost difference set, where s denotes the amount of elements of $G \setminus \{1\}$ that appears precisely λ times in the list $d_1 d_2^{-1}$, the remaining $v - s - 1$ elements of G appearing exactly $\lambda + 1$ times.

Almost difference sets are related to almost perfect sequences, in the following manner. A sequence (a_i) is called almost perfect when two possible values r_1, r_2 are allowed for $c_t(a_i)$, for $0 < t \leq v - 1$, with $|r_1| + |r_2| = 4$. As noted in [10], this is equivalent to $D = \{i : a_i = 1, 0 \leq i \leq v - 1\}$ being an $(v, k, k - \lfloor \frac{v}{4} \rfloor - 1, kv - k^2 - (k-1) \lfloor \frac{v}{4} \rfloor)$ almost difference set, for $k = |D|$.

As claimed in [10], computer experimentation seems to suggest that balanced (i.e., half of the entries are of opposite sign) almost perfect sequences might exist for every $v \equiv 1 \pmod 4$. As soon as two such balanced sequences (a_i) and (b_i) combine to give $c_t(a_i) + c_t(b_i) = -2$, for $0 < t \leq 2w - 2$, a Hadamard matrix of order $4w$ would exist in turn: this is one of the most prolific techniques for constructing Hadamard matrices of order $4w$, the so-called two circulant cores "plug-in" method [3,12,13].

Actually, the Hadamard matrix would consist in:

$$\begin{pmatrix} -1 & -1 & 1 & 1 \\ -1 & 1 & 1 & -1 \\ 1 & 1 & A & B \\ 1 & -1 & B^T & -A^T \end{pmatrix}, \quad (2)$$

for A and B being the circulant matrices based on (a_i) and (b_i), respectively.

As a matter of fact, among the most prominent "plug-in" methods for constructing Hadamard matrices, precisely the two circulant cores technique and the Goethals–Seidel arrays [14] were the only ones that remain out of the cocyclic framework, as indicated in [15]. Actually, Goethals–Seidel arrays have been recently characterized as (pseudo)cocyclic matrices over quasigroups in [16].

Finally, we now recall the characterization of cocyclic Hadamard matrices in terms of certain difference sets and designs, as introduced in Theorem 2.4 of [17], and which is used in [6] to provide an exhaustive classification of cocyclic Hadamard equivalent matrices of orders less than 40. For the sake of simplicity and readability, we will not detail the definition of these particular combinatorial structures, as they are not needed for the comprehension of the paper.

Theorem 1. *[17] The following statements are equivalent:*
1. *There is a cocyclic Hadamard matrix over G, $|G| = 4w$.*
2. *There is a (normal) relative $(4w, 2, 4w, 2w)$-difference set in a central extension of $\langle -1 \rangle$ by G, relative to $\langle -1 \rangle$.*
3. *There is a divisible $(4w, 2, 4w, 2w)$-design, class regular with respect to $\langle -1 \rangle$, and with central extension of $\langle -1 \rangle$ by G as a regular group of automorphisms.*

The aim of this paper is to settle a theoretical background for the study of Hadamard matrices consisting of cocyclic cores, instead of circulant cores. Actually, Hadamard matrices with a cocyclic core will be shown to be placed in some sense halfway from full cocyclic Hadamard matrices and usual Hadamard matrices, as $4w \times 4w$ Hadamard matrices with a cocyclic core will be proven to exist if and only if there exist $(4w - 1, 2w - 1, w - 1)$-difference sets (Theorem 2), which are already known to imply the existence of full Hadamard matrices, as commented before.

The paper is organized as follows. In Section 2, we characterize the existence of Hadamard matrices with a $(4w - 1) \times (4w - 1)$ cocyclic core, in terms of some perfect sequences and difference sets. Section 3 is devoted to the characterization of Hadamard matrices with a $(4w - 2) \times (4w - 2)$ cocyclic core, in terms of certain almost perfect sequences and almost difference sets.

2. Hadamard Matrices with a $(4w-1) \times (4w-1)$ Cocyclic Core

As introduced in Section 1, Hadamard matrices with one circulant core consist of matrices of the type $\begin{pmatrix} 1 & 1 \\ 1 & A \end{pmatrix}$, for A being a circulant matrix whose first row consists of a perfect binary sequence (a_i) with $c_t(a_i) = -1$, $0 < t \leq 4w - 2$, and $\sum_{i=0}^{4w-2} a_i = -1$. They were extensively studied in [11].

In this section we study the conditions under which a cocyclic (instead of a simply circulant) matrix M_ψ (for ψ as in (1)) may be plugged in a structure of the type:

$$\begin{pmatrix} ? & ? \\ \alpha & M_\psi \end{pmatrix}, \qquad (3)$$

in order to provide a Hadamard matrix as well, for $\alpha = (\alpha_{g_0}, \ldots, \alpha_{g_{4w-2}})$, given an ordering $\{g_0 = 1, \ldots, g_{4w-2}\}$ of G.

Notice that the first row of such a structure is not of interest, since every partial Hadamard matrix of size $(4w - z) \times 4w$, $1 \leq z \leq 7$, is known to be extendable to a full $4w \times 4w$ Hadamard matrix [18].

Theorem 2. *There exists a Hadamard matrix of order $4w$ with a $(4w - 1) \times (4w - 1)$ cocyclic core if and only if there exists a $(4w - 1, 2w, w)$-difference set (or, equivalently, a $(4w - 1, 2w - 1, w - 1)$-difference set).*

The following sequence of lemmas will help in the task of proving this result.

Lemma 1. *The first row (and column) of M_ψ consists of a common single value, either 1 or -1.*

Proof. This is a common fact of cocyclic matrices, and it may be straightforwardly derived from Equation (1): as soon as one fixes $a = b = 1 \in G$, it follows that $\psi(1, 1) \cdot \psi(1, g_k) = 1$, for every $g_k \in G$.

A similar argument applies to the first column, taking $b = c = 1$ in (1) instead. □

Remark 4. *Cocylic matrices M_ψ for which $\psi(1, j) = \psi(j, 1) = 1$ are usually termed normalized.*

The following result is at the very heart of the usual cocyclic test for Hadamard matrices [2,5]. However, we will rather state it and reproduce its proof explicitly, since both of them will be extensively used in the paper.

Lemma 2. *For every $g_i, g_j \in G$, the dot product of rows indexed by g_i and g_j in M_ψ consists of:*

$$\sum_{g_k \in G} \psi(g_i, g_k) \psi(g_j, g_k) = \psi(g_i g_j^{-1}, g_j) \sum_{g_k \in G} \psi(g_i g_j^{-1}, g_k).$$

Proof. Actually, this is an alternative way to read the usual cocyclic Hadamard test of [5]. From (1), taking $a = g_i g_j^{-1}$, $b = j$ and $c = g_k$, it follows that:

$$\psi(g_i g_j^{-1}, g_j) \cdot \psi(g_i g_j^{-1}, g_j g_k) = \psi(g_i, g_k) \cdot \psi(g_j, g_k).$$

Therefore, the dot product of rows indexed by g_i and g_j in M_ψ consists of:

$$\sum_{g_k \in G} \psi(g_i, g_k) \psi(g_j, g_k) = \sum_{g_k \in G} \psi(g_i g_j^{-1}, g_j) \psi(g_i g_j^{-1}, g_j g_k) = \psi(g_i g_j^{-1}, g_j) \sum_{g_k \in G} \psi(g_i g_j^{-1}, g_k).$$

□

Lemma 3. *Assume that the matrix in (3) is Hadamard. Then $\sum_{g_k \in G} \alpha_{g_k} = \pm 1$.*

Proof. From Remark 4 we know that $\psi(g_k, 1)$ is constant (for both 1 and -1) for every $g_k \in G$. Therefore, the dot product of columns 1 and 2 of the matrix in (3) consists of:

$$0 = \pm 1 \pm \sum_{g_k \in G} \alpha_{g_k},$$

and the result follows. □

Lemma 4. *Assume that the matrix in (3) is Hadamard. Then $\sum_{g_k \in G} \psi(g_i, g_k) = -\psi(g_i, 1) \cdot \alpha_1 \cdot \alpha_{g_i}$, for every $g_i \in G \setminus \{1\}$.*

Proof. Taking $g_j = 1 \in G$ in Lemma 2, it follows that the dot product of rows indexed by g_i and 1 in (3) consists of:

$$0 = \alpha_{g_i} \cdot \alpha_1 + \psi(g_i, 1) \sum_{g_k \in G} \psi(g_i, g_k),$$

from which the asserted result derives at once. □

Lemma 5. *Assume that the matrix in (3) is Hadamard. Then $\psi(g_i, g_j) = \psi(g_i, 1) \cdot \alpha_1 \cdot \alpha_{g_i} \cdot \alpha_{g_j} \cdot \alpha_{g_i g_j}$, for every $g_i, g_j \in G$.*

Proof. From Lemma 2, the dot product of the rows indexed by $g_i g_j$ and g_j in (3) consists of:

$$0 = \alpha_{g_i g_j} \cdot \alpha_{g_j} + \psi(g_i, g_j) \sum_{g_k \in G} \psi(g_i, g_k).$$

Consequently, taking into account Lemma 4,

$$0 = \alpha_{g_i g_j} \cdot \alpha_{g_j} - \psi(g_i, 1) \cdot \alpha_1 \cdot \alpha_{g_i} \psi(g_i, g_j),$$

so that $\psi(g_i, g_j) = \psi(g_i, 1) \cdot \alpha_1 \cdot \alpha_{g_i} \cdot \alpha_{g_j} \cdot \alpha_{g_i g_j}$. □

In the circumstances above, the following results may be straightforwardly derived.

Corollary 1. ψ is completely characterized as a 2-coboundary $\psi(g_i, g_j) = \phi(g_i)\phi(g_j)\phi(g_ig_j)$, for $\phi: G \to \{-1, 1\}$ defined as $\phi(g_i) = \phi(g_1) \cdot \alpha_1 \cdot \alpha_{g_i}$, $\phi(g_1) = \pm 1$.

Remark 5. Notice that it is irrelevant whether one fixes $\phi(g_1)$ to be either 1 or -1. This just has to be with the (un)normalized character of the related 2-cocycle, as noted in Remark 4.

Corollary 2. $\sum_{g_j \in G} \alpha_{g_j} \alpha_{g_i g_j} = -1$, for every $g_i \in G$.

Proof. From Lemma 5, $\psi(g_i, g_j) = \alpha_1 \alpha_{g_i} \alpha_{g_j} \alpha_{g_i g_j}$. Adding as g_j runs on G, we obtain:

$$-\alpha_1 \alpha_{g_i} = \sum_{g_j \in G} \psi(g_i, g_j) = \alpha_1 \alpha_{g_i} \sum_{g_j \in G} \alpha_{g_j} \alpha_{g_i g_j},$$

from which the result derives at once. □

Lemma 6. Assume that (α_{g_k}) and M_ψ are given so that rows from 2 to $4w$ in (3) are pairwise orthogonal. Then this matrix may be completed to a full Hadamard matrix, in essentially one way (up to negation of the row).

Proof. Let $(s_1, s_2, \ldots, s_{4w})$ be the unknown entries of the first row of (3).

Lemma 1 guarantees that the first column in M_ψ consists of a common constant, $\psi(1, 1)$. Take $s_2 = \psi(1, 1)$, so that the second column of (3) consists of a common constant.

From the orthogonality law, the dot product of column $i \neq 2$ with the second column has to be zero. Consequently, since the second column is formed by a common constant, the summation of each column $i \neq 2$ of (3) has to be zero, as well. This characterizes uniquely the first row of the matrix (once s_2 has been fixed). □

We can now prove Theorem 2.

Proof. We first prove the sufficient condition.

Assume that a Hadamard matrix of the form (3) exists, with a cocyclic core consisting of M_ψ.

In these circumstances, notice that (α_{g_k}) defines a *generalized* perfect sequence, in the sense that:

- It is balanced, as Lemma 3 indicates.
- A generalized autocorrelation function for (α_{g_i}) may be defined, so that shift g_t depends on the right action of g_t by means of the group law of G: $c_t(\alpha_{g_k}) = \sum_{g_k \in G} \alpha_{g_k} \alpha_{g_k g_t}$.
- Corollary 2 shows that (α_{g_k}) is perfect.

In these circumstances, the set $D = \{g_k : \alpha_{g_k} = 1\}$ defines a difference set, as noted in Remark 2.

Since the sequence is balanced, it follows that $|D| = 2w$ or $|D| = 2w - 1$. Furthermore, it may be straightforwardly checked that $|D \cap D \cdot g_t| = |D| - w$. No matter what the concrete value of $|D|$ is, a couple of complementary difference sets with parameters $(4w - 1, 2w, w)$ and $(4w - 1, 2w - 1, w - 1)$ are thus defined (see Remark 1).

Conversely, starting from such a difference set, as noted in Remark 2, the process works the other way around, and the proof ends, as soon as the matrix so obtained may be extended to a full Hadamard matrix, attending to Lemma 6. □

Example 1. Consider the multiplicative cyclic group of order 3, $G = (C_3, \cdot) = \langle a : a^3 = 1 \rangle$, endowed with the natural ordering $\{1, a, a^2\}$.

The subset $D = \{a, a^2\}$ defines a $(3, 2, 1)$-difference set in G, since $a \cdot a^{-2} = a^2$ and $a^2 \cdot a^{-1} = a$.

Let us consider the sequence $\alpha = (\alpha_g)_{g \in D} = (-1, 1, 1)$, such that $\alpha_g = 1$ if $g \in D$, and $\alpha_g = -1$ otherwise.

By construction, (α_g) defines a perfect sequence. Actually:

- $\alpha_1 \cdot \alpha_{1 \cdot a} + \alpha_a \cdot \alpha_{a \cdot a} + \alpha_{a^2} \cdot \alpha_{a^2 \cdot a} = -1$.
- $\alpha_1 \cdot \alpha_{1 \cdot a^2} + \alpha_a \cdot \alpha_{a \cdot a^2} + \alpha_{a^2} \cdot \alpha_{a^2 \cdot a^2} = -1$.

Consider the map $\phi : (C_3, \cdot) \to \{-1, 1\}$ defined as $\phi(1) = 1$, $\phi(a) = \alpha_1 \cdot \alpha_a = -1$, $\phi(a^2) = \alpha_1 \cdot \alpha_{a^2} = -1$. Let $\psi : C_3 \times C_3 \to \{-1, 1\}$ be the 2-coboundary defined as $\psi(i, j) = \phi(i)\phi(j)\phi(i \cdot j)$, so that M_ψ reads as:

$$\begin{pmatrix} 1 & 1 & 1 \\ 1 & -1 & 1 \\ 1 & 1 & -1 \end{pmatrix}.$$

Plugging this matrix in (3), we get:

$$\left(\begin{array}{c|ccc} ? & ? & ? & ? \\ \hline -1 & 1 & 1 & 1 \\ 1 & 1 & -1 & 1 \\ 1 & 1 & 1 & -1 \end{array}\right).$$

This matrix may be completed to form a full Hadamard matrix, as soon as one takes its first row to be $(-1, 1, -1, -1)$, attending to Lemma 6.

Remark 6. Notice that if one negates both of the third and fourth rows and columns of the Hadamard matrix of Example 1, one obtains the Hadamard equivalent matrix:

$$\left(\begin{array}{c|ccc} -1 & 1 & 1 & 1 \\ \hline -1 & 1 & -1 & -1 \\ -1 & -1 & -1 & 1 \\ -1 & -1 & 1 & -1 \end{array}\right),$$

which is indeed a Hadamard matrix with a back-circulant core. This may be transformed into a Hadamard equivalent matrix consisting of a usual circulant core, as soon as rows are permuted accordingly. This is not a casual fact, as the following result asserts.

Proposition 1. *Any Hadamard matrix with a circulant core is Hadamard equivalent to a Hadamard matrix with a cocyclic core.*

Proof. As noted in Remark 3 (see [11] for details), any $4w \times 4w$ Hadamard matrix H with a circulant core H_C is in one-to-one correspondence with the cyclic $(4w, 2w, w)$-difference set $D = \{a^i : H_C(1, i - 1) = 1\} \subset (C_{4w-1}, \cdot)$, consisting of the elements that correspond to the positions at which the 1s of the first row of H_C are located.

As illustrated in Example 1, starting from such a cyclic difference set, application of the constructive proof of Theorem 2 provides a Hadamard matrix with a cocyclic core M_ψ. Furthermore, Corollary 1 shows that the map ϕ underlying M_ψ, as defined, provides a cocyclic core, which is Hadamard equivalent to the initial circulant core. To check this, it suffices to negate both the sets of rows and columns indexed by the elements in D, and reorder the rows from bottom to top. □

A question arises in a natural way: is there any advantage in looking for Hadamard matrices with cocyclic cores instead of Hadamard matrices with circulant cores?

Proposition 2. *Hadamard matrices with cocyclic cores strictly include Hadamard matrices with one circulant core.*

Proof. Hadamard matrices of order $4w$ with a circulant core are in one-to-one correspondence with cyclic $(4w - 1, 2w - 1, w - 1)$-difference sets.

However, Hadamard matrices or order $4w$ with a cocyclic core are in one-to-one correspondence with $(4w - 1, 2w - 1, w - 1)$-difference sets, which are not necessarily cyclic.

Actually, there are orders $4w$ for which no such cyclic difference sets exist, but as yet, general difference sets do exist. □

Example 2. *Consider the case $4w = 28$, for instance.*

On the one hand, Theorem 2 in [11] states that there are no 28×28 Hadamard matrices with a circulant core. Consequently, no cyclic $(27, 13, 6)$-different set can exist.

On the other hand, $(27, 13, 6)$-difference sets do exist: as noted in [19],

$$D = \{1, a, a^2, b, ab, b^2, c, ac, bc, ac^2, a^2bc^2, b^2c^2, a^2b^2c^2\}$$

constitutes a $(27, 13, 6)$-difference set in $G = (C_3 \times C_3 \times C_3, \cdot) = \langle a, b, c : a^3 = b^3 = c^3 = 1 \rangle$, with ordering $a^{i_1}b^{j_1}c^{k_1} < a^{i_2}b^{j_2}c^{k_2}$ if and only if $k_1 < k_2$, or $k_1 = k_2$ and $j_1 < j_2$, or $(j_1, k_1) = (j_2, k_2)$ and $i_1 < i_2$.

Let us consider the sequence $\alpha = (\alpha_g)_{g \in D}$, such that $\alpha_g = 1$ if $g \in D$, and $\alpha_g = -1$ otherwise.

Since $\alpha_1 = 1$, consider the map $\phi : G \to \{-1, 1\}$ defined as $\phi(g) = \alpha_g$, for $g \in G$. Let $\psi : G \times G \to \{-1, 1\}$ be the 2-coboundary defined as $\psi(i, j) = \phi(i)\phi(j)\phi(i \cdot j)$. Plugging (α_g) and M_ψ in (3) and completing with regards to Lemma 6 leads to a 28×28 Hadamard matrix with a cocyclic core.

3. Hadamard Matrices with a $(4w - 2) \times (4w - 2)$ Cocyclic Core

Hadamard matrices with two circulant cores [3,12,13] come from a new "plug-in" technique, which extends the underlying idea applied when constructing Hadamard matrices with one circulant core. In this occasion, properly fixing two rows and columns, a full Hadamard matrix may be constructed as soon as two $(2w - 1) \times (2w - 1)$ circulant matrices A and B exist, satisfying the constraint:

$$AA^T + BB^T = 4wI_{2w-1} - 2J_{2w-1},$$

in which case the matrix:

$$\begin{pmatrix} -1 & -1 & 1 & 1 \\ -1 & 1 & 1 & -1 \\ 1 & 1 & A & B \\ 1 & -1 & B^T & -A^T \end{pmatrix} \quad (4)$$

would be Hadamard.

As commented in Section 1, this is the case if and only if the first rows of A and B, (a_i) and (b_i), define two balanced almost perfect sequences with $c_t(a_i) + c_t(b_i) = -2$, for $0 < t \leq w - 1$.

In this section we study the conditions under which a cocyclic matrix M_ψ (for ψ as in (1)) may be plugged in a structure of the type:

$$\begin{pmatrix} ? & ? & ? \\ \alpha & \beta & M_\psi \end{pmatrix}, \quad (5)$$

in order to provide a Hadamard matrix as well, for $\alpha = (\alpha_{g_0}, \ldots, \alpha_{g_{4w-3}})$ and $\beta = (\beta_{g_0}, \ldots, \beta_{g_{4w-3}})$, given an ordering $\{g_0 = 1, \ldots, g_{4w-3}\}$ of G.

As noted in Section 1, as soon as the rows from 3 to $4w$ are pairwise orthogonal, the matrix can be completed to a full Hadamard matrix [18]. Therefore we will focus on the rows from 3 to $4w$ in (5).

In what follows, the notation used in Section 2 still applies, so that the rows from 3 to $4w$ in (5) will be indexed by the corresponding elements in G. In particular, it is remarkable that the row indexed by $1 \in G$ corresponds to the third row in (5).

Furthermore, attending to Hadamard equivalence, up to negation of columns 1 or 2 in (5), without loss of generality we may assume that $\alpha_1 = \beta_1 = \psi(1, 1)$, so that the third row in (5) (that is indexed by $1 \in G$) consists of the constant vector $\psi(1, 1) \cdot \mathbf{1}$.

We now determine a collection of necessary and sufficient conditions for (5) being a Hadamard matrix with a cocyclic core.

Lemma 7. *Assume that (5) is a Hadamard matrix with a cocyclic core M_ψ. Then $\sum_{g \in G} \psi(h, g) \in \{-2, 0, 2\}$, for all $h \in G \setminus \{1\}$. Moreover,*

- $\sum_{g \in G} \psi(h, g) = 0$ *if and only if* $(\alpha_h, \beta_h) = (-1, 1) \cdot s_h$, *for some (undetermined by now)* $s_h \in \{1, -1\}$.
- $0 \neq \sum_{g \in G} \psi(h, g) = \pm 2$ *if and only if* $(\alpha_h, \beta_h) = (-1, -1) \cdot s_h$, *for* $s_h = \frac{1}{2} \sum_{g \in G} \psi(h, g)$.

Proof. Let $h \in G \setminus \{1\}$.

Taking into account the orthogonality constraint, it follows that the dot product $\langle \text{row } h, \text{row } 1 \rangle$ of rows indexed by h and $1 \in G$ in (5) must be zero. Therefore, from Lemma 2,

$$0 = \alpha_h \alpha_1 + \beta_h \beta_1 + \psi(h, 1) \cdot \sum_{g \in G} \psi(h, g).$$

Since $\alpha_1 = \beta_1 = \psi(1, 1) = \psi(h, 1)$, we get $\sum_{g \in G} \psi(h, g) = -\alpha_h - \beta_h$ and the result follows. □

Corollary 3. *Assume that (5) is a Hadamard matrix with a cocyclic core M_ψ, such that $\sum_{g \in G} \psi(h, g) \in \{-2, 2\}$, for all $h \in G \setminus \{1\}$. Then ψ is a 2-coboundary and $w = 1$.*

Proof. For every $g, h \in G$, attending to Lemma 2, the dot product of rows indexed by gh and h is:

$$0 = 2s_{gh}s_h + \psi(g, h)s_g,$$

so that $\psi(g, h) = -s_g s_h s_{gh}$ is actually a 2-coboundary ($\psi(g, h) = \phi(g)\phi(h)\phi(gh)$, for $\phi: G \to \{1, -1\}$ defined as $\phi(g) = -s_g$).

Furthermore, the summation of the row indexed by g in M_ψ is $2s_g = \sum_{h \in G} \psi(g, h) = -s_g \sum_{h \in G} s_h s_{gh}$, so that $\sum_{h \in G} s_h s_{gh} = -2$ and $(s_g)_{g \in G}$ defines a perfect sequence. It is known (see [10] for instance) that the only difference set corresponding to a perfect sequence of this type is the trivial $(2, 1, 0)$-difference set, and hence $w = 1$. □

Remark 7. *Consequently, from now on, we assume that there are elements $h \in G$ for which $\sum_{g \in G} \psi(h, g) = 0$. Actually, in these circumstances, notice that ψ becomes a quasi-orthogonal cocycle, as introduced in [20].*

Lemma 8. *In the circumstances above, the elements in $G \setminus \{1\}$ may be organized into two subsets, $S_0 = \{h \in G \setminus \{1\} : \sum_{g \in G} \psi(h, g) = 0$, and $\overline{S}_0 = (G \setminus \{1\}) \setminus S_0$, such that:*

1. $h \in S_0 \iff h^{-1} \in S_0$. *Accordingly,* $h \in \overline{S}_0 \iff h^{-1} \in \overline{S}_0$.
2. *For all* $g \in S_0$, $g \cdot S_0 \subseteq G \setminus S_0$. *Therefore,* $|S_0| \leq |G \setminus S_0|$.
3. *For all* $g \in G \setminus S_0$, $g \cdot (G \setminus S_0) \subseteq G \setminus S_0$. *Therefore,* $|G \setminus S_0| \leq |S_0|$.
4. *For all* $g \in S_0$, $g \cdot (G \setminus S_0) \subseteq S_0$ *and* $(G \setminus S_0) \cdot g \subseteq S_0$.

Proof. We proceed with the demonstration point by point.

1. For every $h \in G\setminus\{1\}$, since $\langle \text{row } 1, \text{row } h\rangle = \langle \text{row } h, \text{row } 1\rangle$. Therefore $\psi(h^{-1}, h)\sum_{g\in G}\psi(h^{-1}, g) = \psi(h, 1)\sum_{g\in G}\psi(h, g)$, and the result follows.

2. Let $g, h \in S_0$. Then $h^{-1} \in S_0$ as well. Now:
$$0 = \langle \text{row } g, \text{row } h^{-1}\rangle = \alpha_g\alpha_{h^{-1}} + \alpha_g\alpha_{h^{-1}} + \psi(gh, h)\cdot \sum_{k\in G}\psi(gh, k).$$
Therefore $gh \in G\setminus S_0$.

3. Let $g, h \in G\setminus S_0$. Then $h^{-1} \in G\setminus S_0$ as well. Now:
$$0 = \langle \text{row } g, \text{row } h^{-1}\rangle = \alpha_g\alpha_{h^{-1}} + \alpha_g\alpha_{h^{-1}} + \psi(gh, h)\cdot \sum_{k\in G}\psi(gh, k).$$
Therefore $gh \in G\setminus S_0$.

4. Let $g \in S_0$ and $h \in G\setminus S_0$. Then $h^{-1} \in G\setminus S_0$ as well. Now:
$$0 = \langle \text{row } g, \text{row } h^{-1}\rangle = \alpha_g\alpha_{h^{-1}} - \alpha_g\alpha_{h^{-1}} + \psi(gh, h)\cdot \sum_{k\in G}\psi(gh, k).$$
Therefore, $gh \in S_0$. □

Corollary 4. *In the circumstances above, $|S_0| = |G\setminus S_0| = 2w - 1$, $G\setminus S_0$ is a normal subgroup of G and $G/(G\setminus S_0) \simeq C_2$.*

Proof. This is a straightforward consequence of Lemma 8. □

Remark 8. *In the circumstances above, one may define a new ordering for the elements in G, such that the last $2w - 1$ elements correspond to S_0. For instance, when any $g \in S_0$ are fixed, such an ordering would be $\{1 = n_1, \ldots, n_{2w-1}, g, gn_2, \ldots, gn_{2w-1}\}$.*

Corollary 5. *In the circumstances above, for $h \in \overline{S}_0$ and $g \in G$, $\psi(h, g) = -s_h s_g s_{hg}$. Furthermore, $\sum_{g\in G} s_g s_{hg} = -2$.*

Proof. Let $h \in \overline{S}_0$ and $g \in G$. Consider the dot product of rows indexed by hg and g in (5). From Lemma 8, depending on whether:

- $g \in G\setminus S_0$, then $hg \in G\setminus S_0$. Attending to Lemma 7, then:
$$0 = \langle \text{row } hg, \text{row } g\rangle = 2s_{hg}s_g + \psi(h, g)\sum_{k\in G}\psi(h, k) = 2s_{hg}s_g + 2s_h\psi(h, g).$$

- $g \in S_0$, then $hg \in S_0$. Attending to Lemma 7, then:
$$0 = \langle \text{row } hg, \text{row } g\rangle = 2s_{hg}s_g + \psi(h, g)\sum_{k\in G}\psi(h, k) = 2s_{hg}s_g + 2s_h\psi(h, g).$$

Whichever is the case, for $h \in \overline{S}_0$ and $g \in G$, it is satisfied that $\psi(h, g) = -s_h s_g s_{hg}$. Taking a summation as g runs in G, we get $2s_h = \sum_{g\in G}\psi(h, g) = -s_h\sum_{g\in G}s_g s_{hg}$. The result follows immediately. □

We next summarize these results.

Theorem 3. *Let (5) be a matrix with a cocyclic core M_ψ over G. Then it is Hadamard if and only if the following conditions are satisfied:*

- G contains a normal subgroup N such that $G/N \simeq C_2$.
- There is a binary sequence $(s_g)_{g \in G}$ such that:
  - For every $h \in N$, $\psi(h,g) = -s_h s_g s_{hg}$, and $\sum_{g \in G} s_g s_{hg} = -2$.
  - For every $k \in G \setminus N$, $\psi(k,g) = -s_k s_g s_{kg} \varphi(k,g)$ (for some 2-cocycle $\varphi : G \times G \to \{1,-1\}$ such that $\varphi(h,g) = 1$ for all $h \in N$), and $\sum_{g \in G} s_g s_{kg} \varphi(g,k) = 0$.

Even though it might seem difficult to meet the hypothesis described in Theorem 3 altogether, we next describe a family of Hadamard matrices with a cocyclic core.

Proposition 3. *Hadamard matrices with two circulant cores are Hadamard equivalent to Hadamard matrices with a cocyclic core over D_{4w-2}.*

Proof. Consider the group $D_{4w-2} = \langle a,b : a^{2w-1} = b^2 = (ab)^2 = 1 \rangle$, with ordering $G = \{1, a, \ldots, a^{2w-2}, b, \ldots, a^{2w-2}b\}$. Notice that $N = \langle a \rangle$ is a normal subgroup of G, and that every element $k \in G \setminus N$ is of order 2, that is $k^2 = 1$. Consider the 2-cocycle $\varphi : G \times G \to \{1,-1\}$ defined as $\varphi(h,g) = -1$ if and only if both $h,g \in G \setminus N$, and 1 otherwise.

Attending to the description of cocyclic matrices over D_{4w-2} developed in [21,22], it may be straightforwardly derived that the two-circulant core structure of (2) is Hadamard equivalent to a cocyclic matrix over D_{4w-2}.

More concretely, consider two balanced sequences (a_i) and (b_i) such that $\sum a_i \cdot a_{i+t} + \sum b_i \cdot b_{i+t} = -2$, for $0 < t \leq w-1$. Take $s_{a^i} = -a_i$ and $s_{a^i b} = -b_i$, for $0 \leq i \leq 2w-2$.

Now, consider the subset $C \subset G$ of indices at which the positive entries of the sequence (s_i) (i.e., negative entries of $((a_i)|(b_i))$) occur, and select the corresponding subset of elementary coboundaries ∂_c, so that $\psi = \varphi \cdot \prod_{c \in C} \partial_c$. For the sake of convenience, it might be appropriate to recall that these elementary coboundaries are commonly defined as $\partial_g(h,k) = \delta_g(h) \delta_g(k) \delta_g(hk)$, for $\delta_i(j) = -1$ if and only if $i = j$, and 1 otherwise.

Actually, as indicated in [21,22], the process of successively negating the row and column indexed by $c \in C$ in M_ψ, ends in a Hadamard equivalent matrix with two back circulant cores similar to (2). Permuting the rows accordingly, the proper core of the matrix (2) may be obtained.

Now, consider the conditions $\sum a_i \cdot a_{i+t} + \sum b_i \cdot b_{i+t} = -2$, for $0 < t \leq w-1$, which guarantee the orthogonal constraint of (2) in [12,13]. These are straightforwardly translated to the conditions $\sum_{g \in G} s_g s_{hg} = -2$, for every $h \in N$, of Theorem 3.

Notice that, as defined, the constraints $\sum_{g \in G} s_g s_{kg} \varphi(g,k) = 0$, for every $k \in G \setminus N$, are naturally satisfied. Actually,

$$\sum_{g \in G} s_g s_{kg} \varphi(g,k) = \sum_{h \in N} s_h s_{kh} - \sum_{g \in G \setminus N} s_g s_{kg} = 0,$$

since there is a one-to-one correspondence from N to $kN = G \setminus N$, taking $h \in N$ on $g_h = kh$; so that each term $s_h s_{kh}$ on the left-hand side of the equation cancels with the corresponding term on the right-hand side, as $-s_{g_h} s_{kg_h} = -s_{kh} s_{k^2 h} = -s_{kh} s_h$. □

Example 3. *For instance, consider the 8×8 Hadamard matrix with two circulant cores of the form (2), which arises from the sequences $(a_i) = (b_i) = (1,1,-1)$, with $a_0 a_1 + a_1 a_2 + a_2 a_0 = -1$:*

$$H = \begin{pmatrix} -1 & -1 & 1 & 1 & 1 & 1 & 1 & 1 \\ -1 & 1 & 1 & 1 & 1 & -1 & -1 & -1 \\ 1 & 1 & 1 & 1 & -1 & 1 & 1 & -1 \\ 1 & 1 & -1 & 1 & 1 & -1 & 1 & 1 \\ 1 & 1 & 1 & -1 & 1 & 1 & -1 & 1 \\ 1 & -1 & 1 & -1 & 1 & -1 & 1 & -1 \\ 1 & -1 & 1 & 1 & -1 & -1 & -1 & 1 \\ 1 & -1 & -1 & 1 & 1 & 1 & -1 & -1 \end{pmatrix}.$$

Consider the dihedral group $D_6 = \langle a, b : a^3 = b^2 = (ab)^2 = 1 \rangle$, with ordering $\{1, a, a^2, b, ab, a^2b\}$, normal subgroup $N = \{1, a, a^2\}$ and the subset $S_0 = \{b, ab, a^2b\}$. Let $C = \{a^2, a^2b\}$ and consider the 2-cocycle $\psi : D_6 \times D_6 \to \{1, -1\}$ given by $\psi = \phi\varphi$, for $\phi = \partial_{a^2}\partial_{a^2b}$ and $\varphi(g, h) = -1$ if and only if both $g, h \in S_0$. The related cocyclic matrix is then:

$$M_\psi = \begin{pmatrix} 1 & 1 & 1 & 1 & 1 & 1 \\ 1 & -1 & -1 & 1 & -1 & -1 \\ 1 & -1 & 1 & 1 & -1 & 1 \\ 1 & -1 & -1 & -1 & 1 & 1 \\ 1 & 1 & 1 & -1 & -1 & -1 \\ 1 & -1 & 1 & -1 & 1 & -1 \end{pmatrix}.$$

Since $\phi = \partial_{a^2}\partial_{a^2b}$, we define $s_1 = -1$, $s_a = -1$, $s_{a^2} = 1$, $s_b = -1$, $s_{ab} = -1$, $s_{a^2b} = 1$, which is consistent with Lemma 7 and Proposition 3.

We may therefore extend M_ψ to a full Hadamard matrix of the form (5) with a cocyclic core M_ψ, as soon as one takes $\alpha = (-s_1, -s_a, -s_{a^2}, -s_b, -s_{ab}, -s_{a^2b}) = (1, 1, -1, 1, 1, -1)$ and $\beta = (-s_1, -s_a, -s_{a^2}, s_b, s_{ab}, s_{a^2b}) = (1, 1, -1, -1, -1, 1)$:

$$H_\psi = \begin{pmatrix} 1 & -1 & 1 & 1 & -1 & 1 & 1 & -1 \\ -1 & 1 & 1 & 1 & -1 & -1 & -1 & 1 \\ 1 & 1 & 1 & 1 & 1 & 1 & 1 & 1 \\ 1 & 1 & 1 & -1 & -1 & 1 & -1 & -1 \\ -1 & -1 & 1 & -1 & 1 & 1 & -1 & 1 \\ 1 & -1 & 1 & -1 & -1 & -1 & 1 & 1 \\ 1 & -1 & 1 & 1 & 1 & -1 & -1 & -1 \\ -1 & 1 & 1 & -1 & 1 & -1 & 1 & -1 \end{pmatrix}.$$

Notice that starting from H_ψ and negating both rows and columns 5 (indexed by a^2) and 8 (indexed by a^2b), and then permuting rows (4,5) to be ordered as (5,4), ends with the matrix H above, as claimed in Proposition 3.

Nevertheless, Hadamard matrices with a cocyclic core strictly include those Hadamard matrices with a circulant core. For the sake of completeness, we conclude the paper by describing an example of a Hadamard matrix with a cocyclic core over a group not isomorphic to any dihedral group, which supports this claim.

Example 4. *Consider the group $G = C_3 \times C_2 = \langle a, b : a^3 = b^2 = 1 \rangle$. The subgroup $N = \langle a \rangle$ is normal in G.*

Take $(s_i)_{i \in G} = (-1, -1, 1, -1, -1, 1)$. It may be readily checked that:

- $\sum_{g \in G} s_g s_{a \cdot g} = s_1 s_a + s_a s_{a^2} + s_{a^2} s_1 + s_b s_{ab} + s_{ab} s_{a^2b} + s_{a^2b} s_b = -2.$

- $\sum_{g \in G} s_g s_{a^2 \cdot g} = s_1 s_{a^2} + s_a s_1 + s_{a^2} s_a + s_b s_{a^2b} + s_{ab} s_b + s_{a^2b} s_{ab} = -2.$

- $\sum_{g \in G} s_g s_{b \cdot g} = s_1 s_b + s_a s_{ab} + s_{a^2} s_{a^2b} - s_b s_1 - s_{ab} s_a - s_{a^2b} s_{a^2} = 0.$

- $\sum_{g \in G} s_g s_{ab \cdot g} = s_1 s_{ab} + s_a s_{a^2b} + s_{a^2} s_b - s_b s_a - s_{ab} s_{a^2} - s_{a^2b} s_1 = 0.$

- $\sum_{g\in G} s_g s_{a^2b\cdot g} = s_1 s_{a^2b} + s_a s_b + s_{a^2} s_{ab} - s_b s_{a^2} - s_{ab} s_1 - s_{a^2b} s_a = 0.$

Accordingly, consider the 2-cocycle $\psi = \varphi \cdot \partial_{a^2} \partial_{a^2 b}$, *for* $\varphi(g,h) = -1$ *if and only if both* $g, h \in G \setminus N$. *By construction, the matrix* M_ψ *may be extended to a full Hadamard matrix with a cocyclic core,*

$$\begin{pmatrix} 1 & -1 & 1 & 1 & -1 & -1 & -1 & 1 \\ -1 & -1 & 1 & 1 & -1 & 1 & 1 & -1 \\ 1 & 1 & 1 & 1 & 1 & 1 & 1 & 1 \\ 1 & 1 & 1 & -1 & -1 & 1 & -1 & -1 \\ -1 & -1 & 1 & -1 & 1 & 1 & -1 & 1 \\ -1 & 1 & 1 & 1 & 1 & -1 & -1 & -1 \\ -1 & 1 & 1 & -1 & -1 & -1 & 1 & 1 \\ 1 & -1 & 1 & -1 & 1 & -1 & 1 & -1 \end{pmatrix}.$$

4. Conclusions and Further Work

In this paper we have explored the notion of Hadamard matrices with a cocyclic core, inspired by a series of papers [3,11–13] on Hadamard matrices with circulant cores.

Actually, we have described two new "plug-in" techniques for constructing Hadamard matrices, which strictly include those based on circulant cores. They depend on the existence of certain (almost) perfect sequences and (almost) difference sets, which will be our concern in the future.

Author Contributions: Conceptualization, software and writing—original draft preparation, V.Á.; methodology, formal analysis and writing—review and editing, J.A.A. and F.G.; validation, resources, data curation, visualization, supervision and project administration, M.D.F., M.B.G. and A.O.; investigation, V.Á. and J.A.A.; funding acquisition, J.A.A. All authors have read and agreed to the published version of the manuscript.

Funding: This work is partially supported by the Research Project FQM-016 from Junta de Andalucía.

Institutional Review Board Statement: Not applicable.

Informed Consent Statement: Not applicable.

Data Availability Statement: Not applicable.

Acknowledgments: We would like to thank the anonymous reviewers for their suggestions and comments, which have contributed to an improvement of the paper. We also would like to thank the Guest Editor of this special volume for giving us the opportunity of contributing with this paper.

Conflicts of Interest: The authors declare no conflict of interest.

References

1. Hadamard, J. Résolution d'une question relative aux determinants. *Bull. Sci. Math.* **1893**, *17*, 240–246.
2. Horadam, K.J. *Hadamard Matrices and Their Applications*; Princeton University Press: Princeton, NJ, USA, 2007.
3. Kotsireas, I.S. Structured Hadamard Conjecture, Number Theory and Related Fields. In *Springer Proceedings in Mathematics and Statistics*; Borwein, J., Shparlinski, I., Zudilin, W., Eds.; Springer: Berlin/Heidelberg, Germany, 2013; Volume 43, pp. 215–217.
4. Horadam, K.J.; de Launey, W. Cocyclic development of designs. *J. Algebraic Combin.* **1993**, *2*, 267–290; Erratum. *J. Algebraic Combin.* **1994**, *3*, 129. [CrossRef]
5. Horadam, K.J.; de Launey, W. Generation of cocyclic Hadamard matrices. *Math. Appl.* **1995**, *325*, 279–290.
6. Ó Catháin, P.; Röder, M. The cocyclic Hadamard matrices of order less than 40. *Des. Codes Cryptogr.* **2011**, *58*, 73–88. [CrossRef]
7. De Launey, W.; Flannery, D. *Algebraic Design Theory*; American Mathematical Society: Providence, RI, USA, 2011.
8. Álvarez, V.; Falcón, R.M.; Frau, M.D.; Gudiel, F.; Güemes, M.B. Cocyclic Hadamard matrices over Latin rectangles. *Eur. J. Comb.* **2019**, *79*, 74–96. [CrossRef]
9. Falcón, R.M.; Álvarez, V.; Frau, M.D.; Gudiel, F.; Güemes, M.B. Pseudococyclic partial Hadamard matrices over Latin rectangles. *Mathematics* **2021**, *9*, 113. [CrossRef]
10. Arasu, K.T. Sequences and arrays with desirable correlation properties. In *Information Security, Coding Theory and Related Combinatorics*; Crnković, D., Tonchev, V., Eds.; IOS Press: Amsterdam, The Netherlands, 2011; pp. 136–171.

11. Kotsireas, I.S.; Koukouvinos, C.; Seberry, J. Hadamard ideals and Hadamard matrices with circulant core. *J. Comb. Math. Comb. Comput.* **2006**, *57*, 47–63. [CrossRef]
12. Fletcher, R.J.; Gysin, M.; Seberry, J. Application of the discrete Fourier transform to the search for generalised Legendre pairs and Hadamard matrices. *Australas. J. Combin.* **2001**, *23*, 75–86.
13. Kotsireas, I.S.; Koukouvinos, C.; Seberry, J. Hadamard ideals and Hadamard matrices with two circulant cores. *Eur. J. Combin.* **2006**, *27*, 658–668. [CrossRef]
14. Goethals, J.M.; Seidel, J.J. Orthogonal matrices with zero diagonal. *Can. J. Math.* **1967**, *19*, 1001–1010. [CrossRef]
15. Ó Catháin, P. Group Actions on Hadamard Matrices. Master's Thesis, National University of Ireland, Galway, Ireland, 2008.
16. Álvarez, V.; Armario, J.A., Falcón, R.M.; Frau, M.D.; Gudiel, F.; Güemes, M.B.; Osuna, A. On cocyclic Hadamard matrices over Goethals–Seidel loops. *Mathematics* **2020**, *8*, 24. [CrossRef]
17. De Launey, W.; Flannery, D.L.; Horadam, K.J. Cocyclic Hadamard matrices and difference sets. *Discrete Appl. Math.* **2000**, *102*, 47–61. [CrossRef]
18. Verheiden, E. Integral and rational completions of combinatorial matrices. *J. Combin. Theory Ser. A* **1978**, *25*, 267–276. [CrossRef]
19. Kibler, R.E. A summary of noncyclic difference sets, $k < 20$. *J. Combin. Theory Ser. A* **1978**, *25*, 62–67.
20. Armario, J.A.; Flannery, D. On quasi-orthogonal cocycles. *J. Comb. Des.* **2018**, *26*, 401–411. [CrossRef]
21. Ãflvarez, V.; Armario, J.A.; Frau, M.D.; Real, P. A system of equations for describing cocyclic Hadamard matrices. *J. Comb. Des.* **2008**, *16*, 276–290. [CrossRef]
22. Ãflvarez, V.; Armario, J.A.; Frau, M.D.; Gudiel, F.; GÃƒÂ¼emes, M.B.; Osuna, A. On D_{4t}-cocyclic Hadamard matrices. *J. Comb. Des.* **2016**, *24*, 352–368. [CrossRef]

Article

Pseudococyclic Partial Hadamard Matrices over Latin Rectangles

Raúl M. Falcón *, Víctor Álvarez, María Dolores Frau, Félix Gudiel and María Belén Güemes

Department of Applied Mathematics I, University of Seville, 41004 Sevilla, Spain; valvarez@us.es (V.Á.); mdfrau@us.es (M.D.F.); gudiel@us.es (F.G.); bguemes@us.es (M.B.G.)
* Correspondence: rafalgan@us.es

Abstract: The classical design of cocyclic Hadamard matrices has recently been generalized by means of both the notions of the cocycle of Hadamard matrices over Latin rectangles and the pseudococycle of Hadamard matrices over quasigroups. This paper delves into this topic by introducing the concept of the pseudococycle of a partial Hadamard matrix over a Latin rectangle, whose fundamentals are comprehensively studied and illustrated.

Keywords: Hadamard matrix; Latin rectangle; pseudocoboundary; pseudococycle; quasigroup

MSC: 05B20; 05B15; 20N05

1. Introduction

A (binary) Hadamard matrix is a square matrix H of order n with entries in the set $\{-1, 1\}$ such that $HH^t = nI_n$. As such, all its rows (equivalently, columns) are pairwise orthogonal, and hence, its order must be 1, 2, or a multiple of 4. The Hadamard conjecture [1] ensures the existence of Hadamard matrices for every order multiple of 4. It has remained open for more than a century [2].

In 1993, as a new way for generating combinatorial designs that generalizes the group development method, in combinatorial design theory, Horadam and de Launey [3] (see also [4,5]) introduced the fundamentals of the so-called cocyclic development over finite groups. In this context, a matrix with entries in the set $\{-1, 1\}$ is said to be cocyclic over a finite group $(G, \cdot)$ if there exists a map $\phi : G \times G \to \{-1, 1\}$ satisfying the so-called cocycle equation:

$$\phi(i \cdot j, k) \, \phi(i, j) \phi(j, k) \, \phi(i, j \cdot k) = 1, \tag{1}$$

for all $i, j, k \in G$, so that the matrix under consideration is Hadamard equivalent to the cocyclic matrix $M_\phi := (\phi(i, j))_{i,j \in G}$. That is, they are equal up to permutation or negation of rows and columns. The map ϕ is a cocycle [3,6] over the group. A cocyclic matrix necessarily has a constant row and a constant column. According to the cocyclic test [6], it is Hadamard whenever the summation of all the entries of each row is zero, except for the ones in its constant row. As such, determining whether a cocyclic matrix is Hadamard is computationally much faster than checking the definition of a Hadamard matrix.

In 1995, Horadam and de Launey [6] proved that this cocyclic framework provides an excellent structural approach for dealing with the Hadamard conjecture, which would be a consequence of the so-called cocyclic Hadamard conjecture [3], for which a cocyclic Hadamard matrix of order $4t$ exists for every positive integer t. It is so that many known families of Hadamard matrices are cocyclic over certain groups: Sylvester matrices [7], Paley matrices [1], Williamson matrices [8], or Ito's type Q matrices [9] (see also [2,10–14] for some constructions in this regard). Nevertheless, the cocyclic framework turned out to fail [12] for two of the most prolific families of Hadamard matrices: the two-circulant core Hadamard matrices [15] and the Goethals–Seidel arrays [16].

Very recently, a new approach introduced by the authors of [17] has successfully dealt with a cocyclic development of Goethals–Seidel arrays, not over a group, but over a family of Moufang loops. This approach is comprehended in the new theory of cocyclic development over quasigroups and Latin rectangles, which has also recently been introduced by the authors in [18]. More specifically, a cocycle ϕ over a quasigroup $(Q, \cdot)$ is a map $\phi: Q \times Q \to \{-1, 1\}$ satisfying the cocycle Equation (1) for all $i, j, k \in Q$. If an ordering of the elements of Q is established, then the cocycle ϕ is uniquely represented by the cocyclic matrix $M_\phi := (\phi(i, j))_{i,j \in Q}$. In particular, the quasigroup $(Q, \cdot)$ must be a loop whenever the matrix M_ϕ is Hadamard. Moreover, the cocyclic Hadamard test also holds in this case.

The main aspect of this new approach is the fact that associativity is no longer a necessary condition for dealing with any of the concepts and results that are usually involved in the cocyclic development over finite groups. It is so that the existence of coboundaries over non-associative loops has already been proved [17]. In this regard, we remind the reader that a cocycle ϕ over a quasigroup $(Q, \cdot)$ is called a coboundary if there exists a map $\partial: Q \to \{-1, 1\}$ such that

$$\phi(i, j) = \partial(i)\partial(j)\partial(ij), \text{ for all } i, j \in Q. \quad (2)$$

This coboundary ϕ is said to be elementary if there exists an element $h \in Q$ such that $\partial = \partial_h$, where $\partial_h(i) = -1$, if $i = h$, and $\partial_h(i) = 1$ otherwise. From the cocycle equation, it is equivalent to say that

$$i(jk) = h \Leftrightarrow (ij)k = h,$$

holds for all $i, j, k \in Q$. It is straightforwardly satisfied in the case where $(Q, \cdot)$ is a group. Moreover, the cocycle equation has turned out not to be necessary in the quasigroup development theory. In this regard, a pseudocoboundary over the quasigroup $(Q, \cdot)$ is defined as any map $\psi_h: Q \times Q \to Q$ with $h \in Q$, satisfying Equation (2) for some ∂_h described as above. By extension, a pseudococycle is any map $\psi = (\prod_{h \in H \subseteq Q} \psi_h)\phi$ that is obtained as the product of some pseudocoboundaries ψ_h with $h \in H \subseteq Q$ and a cocycle ϕ, all of them over a given quasigroup $(Q, \cdot)$. It is represented by the pseudococyclic matrix $M_\psi := (\psi(i, j))_{i,j \in Q}$. If it is Hadamard equivalent to a given matrix, then the latter is called a pseudococyclic Hadamard matrix. Unlike the cocyclic framework over finite groups, every Goethals–Seidel array constitutes a pseudococyclic Hadamard matrix over a Moufang loop [17].

This last assertion corroborates the relevant role that non-associative quasigroups play in the generalization of the cocyclic framework over groups. This paper delves into this topic by focusing on the fundamentals of the pseudococyclic framework not only over quasigroups, but also over Latin rectangles. It enables us to generalize the classical notion of the cocycle of Hadamard matrices over groups to that of the pseudococycle of partial Hadamard matrices over Latin rectangles. We remind the reader in this regard that a partial Hadamard matrix is an $r \times n$ (binary) matrix H with $r \leq n$ such that $HH^t = nI_r$. The recent implementation of these types of matrices in cryptography [19], experimental design [20], and quantum information [21] has awakened the interest in describing different ways of constructing them [22–25]. In addition, Latin rectangles may be implemented in Internet of Things (IoT) studies [26], coding theory [27,28], and modern 5G wireless networks [29]. Of particular interest in our study, the relevant role that quasigroups with few associative triples play in cryptography [30,31] is remarkable. It is so that quasigroups with a high amount of non-associative triples are receiving particular attention [32–36].

The paper is organized as follows. In Section 2, we review some preliminary concepts and results on quasigroups and Latin rectangles that are used throughout the paper. In Section 3, we introduce and illustrate the notions of both the pseudocoboundary and pseudococycle over Latin rectangles. Then, we deal with the following two open problems concerning the pseudocoboundary framework over Latin rectangles. Both of them are completely answered in Section 4.

Problem 1. *Under which conditions may we ensure the existence of a partial Hadamard matrix that is a pseudocoboundary over a given Latin rectangle?*

Problem 2. *Under which conditions is a given partial Hadamard matrix a pseudocoboundary over a Latin rectangle?*

We also deal with the problem of determining under which conditions we may ensure the existence of a partial Hadamard matrix that is pseudococyclic over a given Latin rectangle. In this regard, Sections 5 and 6 focus respectively on the pseudococyclic framework associated with trivial cocycles and the pseudococyclic framework related to non-trivial cocycles. Finally, since this paper has a high dependence on notation, a glossary of symbols is shown in Appendix A.

2. Preliminaries

Let us review some of the basic concepts and results on quasigroups and Latin rectangles that are used throughout the paper. We refer the reader to [18,37] for more details about these topics.

A quasigroup [38] of order n is a pair $(Q, \cdot)$ formed by a finite set Q of n elements that is endowed with a product $\cdot$ so that any two of the three elements $i, j, k \in Q$ in the equation $i \cdot j = k$ uniquely determine the third element. That is to say, the product $\cdot$ makes possible both the left and the right division in Q. A loop is a quasigroup $(Q, \cdot)$ with a unit element e such that $i \cdot e = e \cdot i = i$ for all $i \in Q$. Every associative quasigroup is a group.

The Cayley table of a quasigroup of order n constitutes a Latin square of the same order; that is, an $n \times n$ array with entries in a set of n distinct symbols so that each symbol occurs exactly once per row and exactly once in each column. The removal of at least one row of a Latin square constitutes a Latin rectangle. More specifically, an $r \times n$ Latin rectangle, with $r \leq n$, is an $r \times n$ array with entries in a set of n distinct symbols so that each symbol occurs exactly once per row and at most once in each column. From here on, let $\mathcal{R}_{r,n}$ denote the set of $r \times n$ Latin rectangles with entries in the set $[n] := \{1, \ldots, n\}$. Further, $L[i, j]$ denotes the symbol contained in the cell (i, j) of a Latin rectangle $L \in \mathcal{R}_{r,n}$.

Let $L \in \mathcal{R}_{r,n}$. If one defines the subset of symbols

$$\mathcal{S}(L) := [r] \cup \{L[i,j] \mid 1 \leq i, j \leq r\} \subseteq [n],$$

then a cocycle over L is any function $\phi \colon \mathcal{S}(L) \times [n] \to \{-1, 1\}$ satisfying the cocycle equation

$$\phi(L[i,j], k)\phi(i,j)\phi(j,k)\phi(i, L[j,k]) = 1, \tag{3}$$

for all positive integers $i, j \leq r$ and $k \leq n$. It is termed trivial if $\phi(i,j) = 1$ for all $(i,j) \in \mathcal{S}(L) \times [n]$. Notice that the negation $-\phi$ of a cocycle ϕ over L is also a cocycle over L. Further, every cocycle ϕ over L is uniquely represented by the cocyclic matrix

$$M_\phi := (\phi(i,j))_{(i,j) \in \mathcal{S}(L) \times [n]}.$$

The following example illustrates all these concepts. From here on, we represent, respectively, the symbols -1 and 1 in any given binary array with the symbols $+$ and $-$.

Example 1. *Let us consider the 2×4 Latin rectangle*

$$L \equiv \begin{array}{|c|c|c|c|} \hline 1 & 2 & 4 & 3 \\ \hline 3 & 1 & 2 & 4 \\ \hline \end{array}$$

where we have highlighted those cells that are used to define the subset of symbols $\mathcal{S}(L) = \{1, 2, 3\}$. There exist exactly four cocycles over the Latin rectangle L: the trivial one and the function $\phi : \mathcal{S}(L) \times [4] \to \{-1, 1\}$, which are represented by the following matrix, together with their respective negations.

$$M_\phi \equiv \begin{array}{|c|c|c|c|} \hline + & + & + & + \\ \hline + & + & + & - \\ \hline + & + & - & + \\ \hline \end{array}$$

In particular, let us check that the function ϕ satisfies the cocycle Equation (3).

- If $i = 1$, then $L[i,j] = j$ for all $j \in \{1,2\}$, and hence, the cocycle equation holds readily from the fact that the first row of the matrix M_ϕ is constant.
- If $(i,j) = (2,1)$, then $\phi(3,k)\phi(2,1)\phi(1,k)\phi(2,L[1,k]) = \phi(3,k)\phi(2,L[1,k]) = 1$ for all $k \leq 4$.
- If $(i,j) = (2,2)$, then $\phi(1,k)\phi(2,2)\phi(2,k)\phi(2,L[2,k]) = \phi(2,k)\phi(2,L[2,k]) = 1$ for all $k \leq 4$.

3. Pseudocoboundaries and Pseudococycles over Latin Rectangles

In this section, we introduce the notions of both the pseudocoboundary and pseudo-cocycle over a Latin rectangle as a natural generalization of the similar concepts described over quasigroups in [17] by keeping in mind, to this end, the concepts introduced in [18]. Firstly, let us define the types of Latin rectangles where such a generalization is feasible.

Let r and n be two positive integers such that $r \leq n$, and let $L \in \mathcal{R}_{r,n}$ be such that

$$L[L[i,j],k] \neq L[i,L[j,k]], \tag{4}$$

for some triple $(i,j,k) \in [r] \times [r] \times [n]$ such that $L[i,j] \leq r$. We apply the term "non-associative" to any such triple satisfying Condition (4). Let $NS(L)$ denote from here on the set of such non-associative triples within the Latin rectangle L. The cardinality of this set is the index of non-associativity of L, which is denoted by $ns(L)$. If $r = n$, then Condition (4) implies that the associative property does not hold for the triple (i,j,k) in the non-associative quasigroup with L as its Cayley table. In this case, the index $ns(L)$ measures the associativity of that quasigroup. This index has been studied for different types of algebraic structures [39–42] since it was introduced in 1947 by Climescu [43] for any given multiplicative system. Particularly, it is easily verified [44] that $ns(L) \leq n^3 - n$ for every Latin square L of order n. This upper bound has recently been proved [32] to be sharp for order $n > 1$. Furthermore, it is also known [45] that $16n - 64 \leq ns(L)$ for every Latin square of even order $n \geq 168$. The reader is also referred to [46,47] for some other studies dealing with the number of non-associative triples of a Latin square.

In this paper, we are interested in the Latin rectangles $L \in \mathcal{R}_{r,n}$ such that $ns(L) > 0$. The following lemma characterizes the case of $r = 1$.

Lemma 1. Let $L \in \mathcal{R}_{1,n}$. Then, $ns(L) > 0$ if and only if $L[1,1] = 1$ and there exists a positive integer $k \leq n$ such that $L[1,k] \neq k$.

Proof. Notice from Condition (4) that every non-associative triple of the $1 \times n$ Latin rectangle L would be of the form $(1,1,k)$ for some positive integer $k \leq n$ satisfying that $L[L[1,1],k] \neq L[1,L[1,k]]$. In addition, Condition (4) also implies that $L[1,1] = 1$ and, hence, $L[1,k] \neq L[1,L[1,k]]$. As a consequence, $L[1,k] \neq k$. □

Let $L \in \mathcal{R}_{r,n}$ be such that $ns(L) > 0$. Every non-associative triple $(i,j,k) \in NS(L)$ is related to two distinct positive integers $h_1, h_2 \leq n$ such that $h_1 = L[L[i,j],k] \neq L[i,L[j,k]] = h_2$. From here on, let $\mathcal{H}(L)$ denote the set of positive integers $h \leq n$ such that

$$\{h\} \subset \{L[L[i,j],k], L[i,L[j,k]]\}, \tag{5}$$

for some $(i,j,k) \in NS(L)$. It is readily verified that $ns(L) = 0$ whenever $n \leq 2$. So, from now on, we suppose that $n > 2$ throughout the paper. Notice also that every Latin square in $\mathcal{R}_{n,n}$ with $ns(L) > 0$ is the Cayley table of a non-associative quasigroup of order n. The case $r < n$ is illustrated by the following example.

Example 2. *Let us consider the Latin rectangle L that is described in Example 1. Then,*

$$NS(L) = \{(1,1,3), (1,1,4), (1,2,1), (1,2,4), (2,2,1), (2,2,2), (2,2,3), (2,2,4)\}.$$

Hence, $ns(L) = 8$. In addition, $\mathcal{H}(L) = [4]$. To prove it, take, for instance, the triples $(2,2,1)$ and $(1,2,1)$ in $NS(L)$.

Let $L \in \mathcal{R}_{r,n}$ be such that $ns(L) > 0$ and let $h \in \mathcal{H}(L)$. We define the h-pseudocoboundary over the Latin rectangle L as the map $\psi_{L;h} \colon [r] \times [n] \to \{-1,1\}$, which is described so that

$$\psi_{L;h}(i,j) := \partial_h(i)\, \partial_h(j)\, \partial_h(L[i,j]), \qquad (6)$$

for all positive integers $i \leq r$ and $j \leq n$, where

$$\partial_h(k) := \begin{cases} -1, & \text{if } k = h, \\ 1, & \text{otherwise.} \end{cases}$$

In addition, we apply the term "h-pseudocoboundary matrix" over L to the $r \times n$ matrix $M_{\psi_{L;h}} := (\psi_{L;h}(i,j))_{(i,j) \in [r] \times [n]}$. When we want to refer to any h-pseudocoboundary (matrix) over L, we omit the prefix h. As such, the concept of the pseudocoboundary over a Latin rectangle constitutes a generalization of that over a quasigroup [17], which arises when $r = n$. In any case, the following result establishes that the pseudococyclic framework over Latin rectangles is not included in the cocyclic framework over such arrays. Hence, it constitutes a new proposal that has to be independently studied.

Lemma 2. *Let $L \in \mathcal{R}_{r,n}$ be such that $ns(L) > 0$ and let $h \in \mathcal{H}(L)$. The h-pseudococycle $\psi_{L;h}$ is not a cocycle over L.*

Proof. Let us see that the h-pseudococycle $\psi_{L;h}$ does not hold the cocycle Equation (3). To this end, let $(i,j,k) \in NS(L)$ be such that Condition (5) holds. Then,

$$\psi_{L;h}(L[i,j],k)\psi_{L;h}(i,j)\psi_{L;h}(j,k)\psi_{L;h}(i,L[j,k]) = \partial_h(L[L[i,j],k])\partial_h(L[i,L[j,k]]) = -1.$$

□

Let us illustrate all of these concepts with a series of examples.

Example 3. *Let L be the Latin rectangle described in Example 1. According to Example 2, we can define four pseudocoboundaries over L, which are represented by the following matrices.*

$$M_{\psi_{L;1}} \equiv \begin{array}{|c|c|c|c|} \hline - & - & - & - \\ \hline - & - & + & + \\ \hline \end{array} \qquad M_{\psi_{L;2}} \equiv \begin{array}{|c|c|c|c|} \hline + & + & + & + \\ \hline - & + & + & - \\ \hline \end{array}$$

$$M_{\psi_{L;3}} \equiv \begin{array}{|c|c|c|c|} \hline + & + & - & - \\ \hline - & + & - & + \\ \hline \end{array} \qquad M_{\psi_{L;4}} \equiv \begin{array}{|c|c|c|c|} \hline + & + & - & - \\ \hline + & + & + & + \\ \hline \end{array}$$

The following example enables us to ensure that, unlike the cocyclic development over quasigroups, there exist Hadamard matrices that are pseudocoboundary matrices over quasigroups that are not loops.

Example 4. *Let us consider the Latin square*

$$L \equiv \begin{array}{|c|c|c|c|} \hline 1 & 2 & 4 & 3 \\ \hline 2 & 1 & 3 & 4 \\ \hline 3 & 4 & 1 & 2 \\ \hline 4 & 3 & 2 & 1 \\ \hline \end{array}.$$

We have that $ns(L) = 32$ and $\mathcal{H}(L) = [4]$. In order to prove this last end, take, for instance, the subset $\{(1,1,3), (1,3,3)\} \subset NS(L)$. It is simply verified that every h-pseudocoboundary matrix of L with $1 \leq h \leq 4$ is Hadamard.

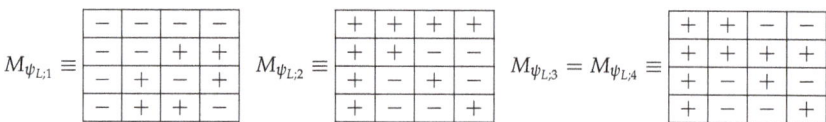

Observe that all the pseudocoboundary matrices shown in Examples 3 and 4 constitute (partial) Hadamard matrices. Proposition 2 described in Section 4 enables us to ensure that this condition does not hold in general. Finally, the following example enables us to ensure the existence of Hadamard matrices that are not cocyclic over any Latin rectangle, but that are pseudocoboundary matrices over a Latin square.

Example 5. *It is known ([18] Example 41) that the following Hadamard matrix is not cocyclic over any Latin rectangle.*

$$M \equiv \begin{pmatrix} + & + & + & + \\ - & + & + & - \\ - & - & + & + \\ + & - & + & - \end{pmatrix}$$

Nevertheless, it constitutes a 2-pseudocoboundary matrix over the Latin square

$$L \equiv \begin{array}{|c|c|c|c|} \hline 1 & 2 & 3 & 4 \\ \hline 3 & 4 & 2 & 1 \\ \hline 2 & 1 & 4 & 3 \\ \hline 4 & 3 & 1 & 2 \\ \hline \end{array}.$$

Let us finish this section by introducing the notion of a pseudococycle over a Latin rectangle as a generalization of both the concepts of a cocycle over a Latin rectangle [18] and a pseudococycle over a quasigroup [17]. To this end, we take into account the previously described notion of a pseudocoboundary over Latin rectangles. Thus, we define a pseudococycle over a given Latin rectangle $L \in \mathcal{R}_{r,n}$ with $ns(L) > 0$ as any map

$$\psi = \left(\prod_{h \in S \subseteq \mathcal{H}(L)} \psi_h \right) \phi$$

that is obtained as the product of some h-pseudocoboundaries with $h \in S \subseteq \mathcal{H}(L)$ and a cocycle ϕ, all of them over the Latin rectangle L. It is represented by the pseudococyclic matrix $M_\psi := (\psi(i,j))_{(i,j) \in [r] \times [n]}$. In particular, notice from this definition that every pseudocoboundary over a Latin rectangle is a pseudococycle over the latter by means of the trivial cocycle. Further, if $S = \emptyset$, then all of these concepts refer to the cocyclic framework over Latin rectangles, whose fundamentals were comprehensively studied in [18].

In a similar way, if $r = n$, then they refer to the pseudococyclic framework over quasigroups, which has only been briefly dealt with in [17]. This paper focuses, therefore, on the fundamentals of the case $S \neq \emptyset$, whatever the positive integer $r \leq n$ is. The following example illustrates this case.

Example 6. Let L be the Latin rectangle described in Example 1. Then, the following assertions are readily verified from the cocyclic matrix M_ϕ described in that example, together with the pseudocoboundary matrices $M_{\psi_{L;3}}$ and $M_{\psi_{L;4}}$ described in Example 3.

- The pseudococyclic matrix over L that is associated with the pseudococycle $\psi_{L;3}\psi_{L;4}$ is partial Hadamard.

$$M_{\psi_{L;3}\psi_{L;4}} \equiv \begin{array}{|c|c|c|c|} \hline + & + & + & + \\ \hline - & + & - & + \\ \hline \end{array}$$

- The pseudococyclic matrix over L that is associated with the pseudococycle $\psi_{L;3}\psi_{L;4}\phi$ is not a pseudococyclic partial Hadamard matrix.

$$M_{\psi_{L;3}\psi_{L;4}\phi} \equiv \begin{array}{|c|c|c|c|} \hline + & + & + & + \\ \hline - & + & - & - \\ \hline \end{array}$$

4. Pseudocoboundary Partial Hadamard Matrices over Latin Rectangles

Let us start our study by dealing with Problem 1 concerning the conditions under which we can ensure the existence of pseudocoboundary partial Hadamard matrices over a given Latin rectangle $L \in \mathcal{R}_{r,n}$ with $ns(L) > 0$. Firstly, we focus on the case $r = 1$.

Proposition 1. There always exists a pseudocoboundary partial Hadamard matrix over a Latin rectangle $L \in \mathcal{R}_{1,n}$ satisfying that $ns(L) > 0$.

Proof. Let $L \in \mathcal{R}_{1,n}$ be such that $ns(L) > 0$. From Lemma 1, it must be $L[1,1] = 1$ and $L[1,j] = h$ for some positive integers $j, h \leq n$ such that $1 \neq j \neq h \neq 1$. Hence, the Latin rectangle condition of no repetition of symbols in each row implies that $L[L[1,1], j] = h \neq L[1, h] = L[1, L[1,j]]$. Thus, $(1,1,j) \in NS(L)$ and $h \in \mathcal{H}(L)$. The matrix $\psi_{L;h}$ is trivially partial Hadamard over L. □

Let us focus now on the case $r > 1$. Since $ns(L) = 0$ for all $L \in \mathcal{R}_{2,2}$, we also suppose that the number $n \geq r$ of columns is a multiple of 4. We start with a preliminary lemma that describes the entries within each row and column of any pseudocoboundary partial Hadamard matrix over a given Latin rectangle. Particularly, it characterizes the rows and columns that are uniformly signed.

Lemma 3. Let r and n be two positive integers such that $2 \leq r \leq n$. Further, let $\psi_{L;h}$ be the h-pseudocoboundary over a Latin rectangle $L \in \mathcal{R}_{r,n}$ with $ns(L) > 0$ and $h \in \mathcal{H}(L)$. Then, the following assertions hold.

1. Let $i \leq r$ be such that $L[i, h] \neq h$. Then,

$$\psi_{L;h}(i,j) = \begin{cases} -\partial_h(i), & \text{if either } j = h \text{ or } L[i,j] = h, \\ \partial_h(i), & \text{otherwise.} \end{cases}$$

2. Let $j \leq n$. Then,

$$\psi_{L;h}(i,j) = \begin{cases} -\partial_h(j), & \text{if } \begin{cases} h \leq r, L[h,j] \neq h \text{ and either } i = h \text{ or } L[i,j] = h, \\ h > r \text{ and } L[i,j] = h, \end{cases} \\ \partial_h(j), & \text{otherwise.} \end{cases}$$

3. The ith row of the h-pseudocoboundary matrix $M_{\psi_{L;h}}$ with $i \leq r$ is uniformly signed if and only if $L[i, h] = h$. In such a case, $\psi_{L;h}(i,j) = \partial_h(i)$ for all $j \leq n$. As a consequence, there always exists at most one uniformly signed row.

4. Let $j \leq n$. If $h > r$, then the jth column of M_{ψ_h} is uniformly signed if and only if $L[i,j] \neq h$ for every positive integer $i \leq r$. Otherwise, if $h \leq r$, then the jth column of M_{ψ_h} is uniformly signed if $L[h,j] = h$. If $r > 2$, then this sufficient condition is also necessary. In any case,

$\psi_{L;h}(i,j) = \partial_h(j)$ for all $i \leq r$. Furthermore, there exists exactly one uniformly signed column if $h \leq r$ and $r > 2$.

Proof. The first two assertions and the sufficient conditions of the last two assertions follow from the Definition (6). Let us focus now on the proof of the necessary condition of the third assertion (that one of the four statements follows similarly). Thus, let us suppose the existence of a positive integer $i \leq r$ such that the ith row of the h-pseudocoboundary matrix $M_{\psi_{L;h}}$ is uniformly signed. Then, the mentioned Definition (6) implies that either $\partial_h(L[i,j]) = \partial_h(j)$ or $\partial_h(L[i,j]) = -\partial_h(j)$ for all $j \leq n$. Nevertheless, since $n > 2$, the definition of the map ∂_h, together with the Latin rectangle condition of no repetitions of symbols per row, implies that the second option is not possible. Hence, it must be $L[i,h] = h$. The final consequence described in the third assertion holds straightforwardly from the Latin rectangle condition of no repetitions of symbols in each column.

Concerning the last sentence of the fourth assertion, the definition of the map ∂_h, together with (6) and the Latin rectangle condition of no repetitions of symbols per row, implies the existence of exactly one uniformly signed column when $r > 2$. □

Example 7. *Let L be the Latin rectangle described in Example 1. The third assertion of Lemma 3 explains, for instance, the uniformity of signs of the first row of both matrices $M_{\psi_{L;1}}$ and $M_{\psi_{L;2}}$, and also of the second row of the matrix $M_{\psi_{L;4}}$, all of them described in Example 3. In addition, it also explains that there does not exist any uniformly signed row in the matrix $M_{\psi_{L;3}}$.*

The fourth assertion of Lemma 3 explains, for instance, the uniformity of signs of the first column of $M_{\psi_{L;1}}$ and the third column of $M_{\psi_{L;2}}$. It also explains the two uniformly signed columns of both matrices $M_{\psi_{L;3}}$ and $M_{\psi_{L;4}}$. Nevertheless, this fourth assertion of Lemma 3 does not explain the uniformity of signs of the second columns of $M_{\psi_{L;1}}$ and $M_{\psi_{L;2}}$, which follows indeed from the second assertion of this lemma. It illustrates, in particular, the exceptional case $r = 2$ that was discarded therein. The case $r > 2$ is illustrated by the existence of exactly one uniformly signed column in any of the Latin squares described in Examples 4 and 5.

The following result characterizes the Latin rectangles over which a pseudocoboundary partial Hadamard matrix exists. As such, it constitutes, together with Proposition 1, the answer to Problem 1.

Proposition 2. *Let r and n be two positive integers such that $2 \leq r \leq n$. Further, let $\psi_{L;h}$ be the h-pseudocoboundary over a Latin rectangle $L \in \mathcal{R}_{r,n}$ with $ns(L) > 0$ and $h \in \mathcal{H}(L)$. Then, the pseudocoboundary matrix $M_{\psi_{L;h}}$ is partial Hadamard if and only if $n = 4$.*

Proof. Lemma 3 enables us to ensure that the h-pseudocoboundary $\psi_{L;h}$ has at least $r - 2$ rows with precisely two negative entries. Hence, the pseudocoboundary matrix $M_{\psi_{L;h}}$ cannot be Hadamard if $n > 4$. Concerning the case $n = 4$, let us remind the reader that there exist 576 Latin squares of order four, from which only 16 of them constitute the Cayley table of an associative quasigroup. A simple and exhaustive computation enables us to ensure that $\mathcal{H}(L) = [4]$ for all of the 560 remaining Latin squares $L \in \mathcal{R}_{4,4}$, and also that all of their related h-pseudocoboundary matrices are partial Hadamard, whatever the positive integer $h \leq 4$ is. As a consequence, every h-pseudocoboundary matrix of an $r \times 4$ Latin rectangle is partial Hadamard, whatever the two positive integers $h, r \leq 4$ are. □

For Latin squares of any given order, the following result holds as an immediate consequence of Lemma 3, once it is noticed that its two last assertions always hold in the case of L being a Latin square. It is illustrated by any of the pseudocoboundary matrices described in Examples 4 and 5.

Proposition 3. *Let $\psi_{L;h}$ be the h-pseudocoboundary over a Latin square of order $n > 2$ with $ns(L) > 0$ and $h \in \mathcal{H}(L)$. Then, the h-pseudocoboundary matrix $M_{\psi_{L;h}}$ contains exactly one uniformly signed row and exactly one uniformly signed column.*

Let us finish this section by focusing on Problem 2 concerning the conditions under which a given partial Hadamard matrix is a pseudocoboundary over some Latin rectangle $L \in \mathcal{R}_{r,n}$ with $ns(L) > 0$. From Proposition 2, we may assume $n = 4$. Firstly, we focus on the case $r = 1$. Notice in this regard that every $1 \times n$ binary array trivially constitutes a partial Hadamard matrix by itself.

Lemma 4. *Let $M = (m_{1j})$ be a 1×4 partial Hadamard matrix. It is a pseudocoboundary matrix over a Latin rectangle if and only if $m_{11} = 1$ and it contains exactly two negative entries.*

Proof. In order to prove the necessary condition, let us suppose that the partial Hadamard matrix M is an h-pseudocoboundary over a Latin rectangle $L \in \mathcal{R}_{1,4}$ with $h \in \mathcal{H}(L) \neq \emptyset$. From Lemma 1, it must be $L[1,1] = 1$, and then, the Latin rectangle condition of no repetitions of symbols in each row implies that $(1,1,1) \notin NS(L)$ and $1 \notin \mathcal{H}(L)$. Hence, $h \neq 1$ and $m_{11} = 1$. In addition, since every non-associative triple in $NS(L)$ is of the form $(1,1,k)$ with $k \in \{2,3,4\}$ and $h \in \mathcal{H}(L)$, it should be $\{h\} \subset \{L[L[1,1],k_0], L[1,L[1,k_0]]\} = \{L[1,k_0], L[1,L[1,k_0]]\}$ for some positive integer $k_0 \in \{2,3,4\}$. If $k_0 = h$, then we get $\{h\} \subset \{h\}$, which is a contradiction. So, $L[1,h] \neq h$, and hence, the matrix M contains exactly two negative entries. More specifically, $m_{1k_0} = m_{1h} = -1$.

Now, in order to prove the sufficient condition, let us suppose that $m_{11} = 1$ and let $h, i, j \in [4] \setminus \{1\}$ be three distinct positive integers such that $m_{1,h} = m_{1,i} = -1$ and $m_{1,j} = 1$. Then, let $L \in \mathcal{R}_{1,4}$ be defined so that $L[1,1] = 1$, $L[1,h] = j$, $L[1,i] = h$, and $L[1,j] = i$. Then, $L[L[1,1],h] = j \neq i = L[1,L[1,h]]$. Hence, $(1,1,h) \in NS(L)$ and $h \in \mathcal{H}(L)$. It is straightforwardly verified that the partial Hadamard matrix M is an h-pseudocoboundary over L. □

Let us focus now on the case $2 \leq r \leq 4$. The following preliminary lemma holds straightforwardly from the definition (6) of a pseudocoboundary.

Lemma 5. *Let $r \in \{2,3,4\}$ and let $M = (m_{ij})$ be an $r \times 4$ partial Hadamard matrix such that there exists a Latin rectangle $L \in \mathcal{R}_{r,4}$ with $ns(L) > 0$, over which M is an h-pseudocoboundary matrix for some $h \in \mathcal{H}(L)$. The following assertions hold.*

1. *The ith row of the partial Hadamard matrix M with $i \leq r$ is uniformly signed if and only if $L[i,h] = h$. In such a case, $m_{ij} = \partial_h(i)$ for all $j \leq 4$.*
2. *If $h \leq r$ and $L[h,h] = h$, then $m_{ih} = -1$ for all $i \leq r$. Moreover, if $m_{ij} = -1$ with $i \neq h \neq j$ then $L[i,j] = h$.*
3. *If $L[i,h] = h$ for some $i \in [r] \setminus \{h\}$, then $m_{jh} = -\partial_h(j)$ for all $j \in [r] \setminus \{i\}$. Moreover, if $m_{jk} = -\partial_h(j)$ for some $j \in [r] \setminus \{i\}$ and $k \in [4] \setminus \{h\}$, then $L[j,k] = h$.*

Example 8. Let us consider the following four partial Hadamard matrices.

$$M_1 \equiv \begin{array}{|c|c|c|c|} \hline - & - & - & - \\ \hline + & - & - & + \\ \hline \end{array} \qquad M_2 \equiv \begin{array}{|c|c|c|c|} \hline - & - & - & - \\ \hline - & - & + & + \\ \hline \end{array}$$

$$M_3 \equiv \begin{array}{|c|c|c|c|} \hline + & + & + & + \\ \hline + & + & - & - \\ \hline \end{array} \qquad M_4 \equiv \begin{array}{|c|c|c|c|} \hline + & + & + & + \\ \hline - & + & - & + \\ \hline \end{array}$$

Let $N = (n_{ij}) \in \{M_1, M_2\}$. The first statement of Lemma 5 enables us to ensure that, if the matrix N were an h-pseudocoboundary over some Latin rectangle $L \in \mathcal{R}_{2,4}$ with $h \in \mathcal{H}(L) \neq \emptyset$, then it should be $h = 1$ and $L[1,1] = 1$. However, then, the second statement of the mentioned lemma implies that $n_{2,1} = -1$, which is not the case when $N = M_1$. As a consequence, the partial Hadamard matrix M_1 is not a pseudocoboundary over any Latin rectangle. Further, concerning the case $N = M_2$, the second statement of Lemma 5 also enables us to ensure that $L[2,2] = 1$. Thus, for instance, it is readily verified that the matrix M_2 is a 1-pseudocoboundary over the Latin rectangle

$$L \equiv \begin{array}{|c|c|c|c|} \hline 1 & 4 & 2 & 3 \\ \hline 2 & 1 & 3 & 4 \\ \hline \end{array}.$$

In particular, $(2,1,3) \in NS(L) = \{(1,1,2), (1,1,3), (1,1,4), (2,1,2), (2,1,3), (2,1,4), (2,2,2), (2,2,3), (2,2,4)\}$ and $1 \in \mathcal{H}(L) = [4]$. More specifically, $L[L[2,1],3] = 3 \neq 1 = L[2, L[1,3]]$.

Notice also that the partial Hadamard matrices M_3 and M_4 are, respectively, 2-pseudocoboundaries over the Latin rectangles

$$L' \equiv \begin{array}{|c|c|c|c|} \hline 3 & 2 & 1 & 4 \\ \hline 2 & 4 & 3 & 1 \\ \hline \end{array} \quad \text{and} \quad L'' \equiv \begin{array}{|c|c|c|c|} \hline 1 & 2 & 3 & 4 \\ \hline 3 & 1 & 4 & 2 \\ \hline \end{array}.$$

In particular, $(2,1,3) \in NS(L') = \{(1,2,3), (1,2,4), (2,1,1), (2,1,3)\}$ and $2 \in \mathcal{H}(L') = \{1,2,3\}$. More specifically, $L'[L'[2,1],3] = 3 \neq 2 = L'[2, L'[1,3]]$. Further, concerning the Latin rectangle L'', we have that $(2,2,2) \in NS(L'') = \{(2,2,1), (2,2,2), (2,2,3), (2,2,4)\}$ and $2 \in \mathcal{H}(L'') = [4]$. In fact, $L''[L''[2,2],2] = 2 \neq 3 = L''[2, L''[2,2]]$.

The following result characterizes the partial Hadamard matrices that have a uniformly signed row with all its entries being negative, which are pseudocoboundaries over a Latin rectangle. Its constructive proof is illustrated by the matrix M_2 and the Latin rectangle L described in Example 8.

Proposition 4. *Let $M = (m_{ij})$ be an $r \times 4$ partial Hadamard matrix with $r > 1$ such that $m_{hj} = -1$ for some $h \leq r$ and all $j \leq 4$. It is a pseudocoboundary matrix over a Latin rectangle if and only if $m_{ih} = -1$ for all $i \leq r$.*

Proof. The necessary condition follows from Lemma 5. Now, in order to prove the sufficient condition, let $i \in [r] \setminus \{h\}$ and $j \in [4] \setminus \{h\}$ be such that $m_{ij} = -1$. It always exists because M is an $r \times 4$ partial Hadamard matrix with $r > 1$. In addition, let $k \in [4] \setminus \{h\}$ be such that $i \neq k \neq j$. Finally, let L be any $r \times 4$ Latin rectangle satisfying that $L[h,h] = L[i,j] = h$, $L[h,k] = j$, $L[i,h] = i$, and $L[i,k] = k$. Moreover, it must be $L[i',j'] = h$ for all $i' \in [r] \setminus \{h\}$ and $j' \in [4] \setminus \{h\}$ such that $m_{i'j'} = -1$. In particular, $L[L[i,h],k] = k \neq h = L[i, L[h,k]]$. Hence, $(i,h,k) \in NS(L)$ and $h \in \mathcal{H}(L)$. It is simply verified that the partial Hadamard matrix M is h-pseudocoboundary over L. □

In a similar way, the next result characterizes the partial Hadamard matrices have a uniformly signed row with all its entries being positive, which are pseudocoboundaries over a Latin rectangle. The two subcases described in its constructive proof are respectively illustrated by the matrices M_3 and M_4, together with the Latin rectangles L' and L'', which are described in Example 8.

Proposition 5. *Let $M = (m_{ij})$ be an $r \times 4$ partial Hadamard matrix with $r > 1$ such that $m_{ij} = 1$ for some positive integer $i \leq r$ and all $j \leq 4$. It is a pseudocoboundary matrix over a Latin rectangle if and only if there exists a positive integer $h \in [r] \setminus [i]$ such that $m_{jh} = -\partial_h(j)$ for all $j \in [r] \setminus \{i\}$.*

Proof. Again, the necessary condition follows from Lemma 5. Now, in order to prove the sufficient condition, let $j \in [4] \setminus \{h\}$ be such that $m_{hj} = 1$. It always exists because M is an $r \times 4$ partial Hadamard matrix with $r > 1$. The following two cases arise.

- If $j = i$, then let $k \in [4] \setminus \{h, i\}$ and let L be any $r \times 4$ Latin rectangle satisfying that $L[i,h] = L[h,i] = h$, $L[i,k] = i$ and $L[h,k] = k$. In addition, it must be $L[i',j'] = h$ for all $i' \in [r] \setminus \{i\}$ and $j' \in [4] \setminus \{h\}$ such that $m_{i'j'} = -\partial_h(i')$. Then, $L[L[h,i],k] = k \neq h = L[h, L[i,k]]$.

- If $j \neq i$, then let L be any $r \times 4$ Latin rectangle satisfying that $L[i,h] = L[h,j] = h$, $L[h,h] = i$, and $L[h,i] = j$. Again, we also impose that $L[i',j'] = h$ for all $i' \in [r] \setminus \{i\}$ and $j' \in [4] \setminus \{h\}$ such that $m_{i'j'} = -\partial_h(i')$. Then, $L[L[h,h],h] = h \neq j = L[h,L[h,h]]$.

In any case, $h \in \mathcal{H}(L)$, and thus, the partial Hadamard matrix M is an h-pseudocoboundary over L. □

Finally, in order to give a complete answer to Problem 2, the following result characterizes the $r \times 4$ partial Hadamard matrices with $r > 1$ and without uniformly signed rows, which are pseudocoboundaries over a Latin rectangle. Example 9 illustrates its constructive proof.

Proposition 6. *Let $M = (m_{ij})$ be an $r \times 4$ partial Hadamard matrix with $r > 1$ and without uniformly signed rows. Then, the following assertions hold.*

1. *If $r = 4$, then the matrix M is not a pseudocoboundary over any Latin square of order four.*
2. *If $r \in \{2,3\}$, then the matrix M is pseudocoboundary over an $r \times 4$ Latin rectangle if and only if the following two conditions hold.*
   (a) *There exists a positive integer $h \leq 4$ such that $m_{ih} = -\partial_h(i)$ for all $i \leq r$.*
   (b) *For each positive integer $i \leq r$, there exists exactly one positive integer $j_i \in [4] \setminus \{h\}$ such that $m_{i,j_i} = m_{i,h}$. Moreover, the set $\{j_1, \ldots, j_r\}$ is formed by r distinct positive integers.*

If this is the case, then the matrix M is indeed an h-pseudocoboundary over an $r \times 4$ Latin rectangle.

Proof. Let us suppose that the partial Hadamard matrix M is an h-pseudocoboundary over a Latin rectangle $L \in \mathcal{R}_{r,4}$ with $ns(L) > 0$ and $h \in \mathcal{H}(L)$. From the first assertion of Lemma 5, the non-existence of uniformly signed rows within M implies that $L[i,h] \neq h$ for every positive integer $i \leq r$. It constitutes a contradiction when $r = 4$ because of the Latin rectangle condition of no repetitions of symbols per column. Hence, the first assertion holds. Further, if $r \in \{2,3\}$, then $m_{ih} = \psi_{L;h}(i,h) = \partial_h(i)\partial_h(h)\partial_h(L[i,h]) = -\partial_h(i)$ for every positive integer $i \leq r$. Similarly, it is readily proven that the elements j_i described in Condition (2b) refer to the columns in which the symbol h appears in the ith row of L. That is, $L[i,j_i] = h$ for all $i \leq r$. Notice that all these columns are pairwise distinct from the Latin rectangle condition of no repetition of symbols in each column.

In order to prove the sufficient condition of the second assertion, let us suppose that both Conditions (2a) and (2b) hold. Then, let L be any $r \times 4$ Latin rectangle satisfying that $L[i,h] \neq h = L[i,j_i]$ for every positive integer $i \leq r$. The following two cases arise.

- If $h \leq r$, then let us consider a positive integer $i \in [r] \setminus \{h\}$. It exists because $r \geq 2$. The following two subcases arise.
  - If $i = j_i$, then let us impose that $L[i,j_h] = j_h$. Then, $L[L[i,i],j_h] = h \neq j_h = L[i,L[i,j_h]]$.
  - If $i \neq j_i$, then let us impose that $L[i,h] = i$, $L[i,j_h] = j_i$ and $L[h,j_i] = j_h$. Under such assumptions, we have that $L[L[i,h],j_i] = h \neq j_i = L[i,L[h,j_i]]$.
- If $h > r$, then let us consider a pair of distinct positive integers $i_1, i_2 \leq r$. Notice again to this end that $r \geq 2$. Similarly to the previous case, the following two subcases arise.
  - Firstly, let us suppose the existence of a positive integer $i \in \{i_1, i_2\}$ such that $i = j_i$. Without loss of generality, we can suppose that $i_1 = j_{i_1}$. Then, let us impose that $L[i_2, i_1] = i_1$ and $L[i_2, h] = i_2$. Under such assumptions, we have that $L[L[i_2, i_1], i_1] = h \neq i_2 = L[i_2, L[i_1, i_1]]$.
  - Otherwise, let us suppose that $i_1 \neq j_{i_1}$ and $i_2 \neq j_{i_2}$. Then, let us impose that $L[i_1, i_1] = i_1$ and $L[i_1, h] = i_2$. Under such assumptions, we have that $L[L[i_1, i_1], j_{i_1}] = h \neq i_2 = L[i_1, L[i_1, j_{i_1}]]$.

In any case, $h \in \mathcal{H}(L)$, and thus, the partial Hadamard matrix M is an h-pseudocoboundary over L. □

Example 9. Let us consider the following six partial Hadamard matrices.

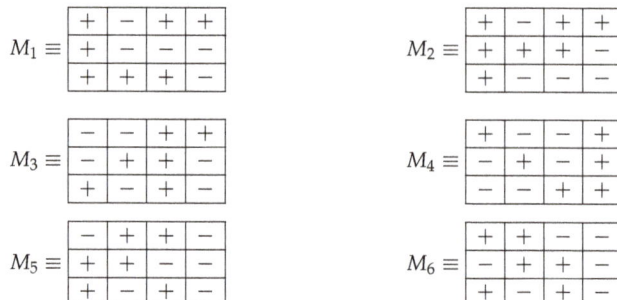

Condition (2a) in Proposition 6 implies that M_1 is not a pseudocoboundary over any 3×4 Latin rectangle. It also enables us to ensure that the only possibility to get M_2 to be an h-pseudocoboundary over some 3×4 Latin rectangle for some positive integer $h \leq 4$ is by considering $h = 2$. However, then, Condition (2b) implies that it neither is an option because, for instance, the first row only contains one negative sign.

On the other hand, the partial Hadamard matrix M_3 is a 2-pseudocoboundary over the Latin rectangle

$$L \equiv \begin{array}{|c|c|c|c|} \hline 2 & 1 & 3 & 4 \\ \hline 1 & 4 & 2 & 3 \\ \hline 4 & 3 & 1 & 2 \\ \hline \end{array}.$$

Here, $ns(L) = 20$, $(1,1,3) \in NS(L)$, and $2 \subset \mathcal{H}(L) = [4]$. More specifically, $L[L[1,1],3] = 2 \neq 3 = L[1, L[1,3]]$.

Further, the partial Hadamard matrices M_4 and M_5 are, respectively, 2- and 4-pseudocoboundaries over the Latin rectangle

$$L' \equiv \begin{array}{|c|c|c|c|} \hline 4 & 1 & 2 & 3 \\ \hline 1 & 3 & 4 & 2 \\ \hline 2 & 4 & 3 & 1 \\ \hline \end{array}.$$

In particular, $ns(L') = 16$, $\{(1,2,3), (2,1,1)\} \subset NS(L')$, and $\{2,4\} \subset \mathcal{H}(L') = [4]$. More specifically, $L'[L'[1,2],3] = 2 \neq 3 = L'[1, L'[2,3]]$ and $L'[L'[2,1],1] = 4 \neq 2 = L'[2, L'[1,1]]$.

Finally, the partial Hadamard matrix M_6 is a 4-pseudocoboundary over the Latin rectangle

$$L'' \equiv \begin{array}{|c|c|c|c|} \hline 1 & 3 & 4 & 2 \\ \hline 4 & 1 & 2 & 3 \\ \hline 2 & 4 & 3 & 1 \\ \hline \end{array}.$$

Particularly, $ns(L'') = 18$, $(1,1,3) \in NS(L)$, and $4 \in \mathcal{H}(L'') = [4]$. More specifically, $L''[L''[1,1],3] = 4 \neq 2 = L''[1, L''[1,3]]$.

5. Pseudococyclic Partial Hadamard Matrices Associated with the Trivial Cocycle

Let us focus now on the characterization of the Latin rectangles $L \in \mathcal{R}_{r,n}$ with $ns(L) > 0$ over which there exists a pseudococyclic partial Hadamard matrix. As a first stage, we focus in this section on the pseudococycles associated with the trivial cocycle; that is, on the pseudococycles of the form $\prod_{h \in S \subseteq \mathcal{H}(L)} \psi_{L;h}$. Of course, the case $|S| = 1$ corresponds to the pseudocoboundary framework that has already been studied in the previous subsection. It is so that we start with a generalization of Lemma 3 that describes the rows and columns of the pseudococyclic matrix associated with one such pseudococycle. To this end, for each given subset $S \subseteq \mathcal{H}(L)$ and each pair of positive integers $i \leq r$ and $j \leq n$, we previously define the sets

$$\mathcal{D}_L^-(S,i) := \{k \in [n]\colon L[i,k] \in S\} \quad \text{and} \quad \mathcal{D}_L^+(S,j) := \{k \in [r]\colon L[k,j] \in S\}.$$

If $r = n$, then the sets $\mathcal{D}_L^-(S,i)$ and $\mathcal{D}_L^+(S,i)$ constitute, respectively, the left division of S by i and the right division of S by j, both of them within the quasigroup with the Latin square L as its Cayley table. In addition, for all $r \leq n$, the Latin rectangle condition of no repetitions of symbols per row implies that $|\mathcal{D}_L^-(S,i)| = |S|$. Further, let $A \Delta B$ denote from here on the symmetric difference between two given sets A and B.

Lemma 6. *Let $\psi = \prod_{h \in S \subseteq \mathcal{H}(L)} \psi_{L;h}$ be a pseudococycle over a Latin rectangle $L \in \mathcal{R}_{r,n}$ with $ns(L) > 0$. Then, the following assertions hold.*

1. *Let $i \in [r]$. Then,*

$$\psi(i,j) = \begin{cases} -\prod_{h \in S} \partial_h(i), & \text{if } j \in S \Delta \mathcal{D}_L^-(S,i), \\ \prod_{h \in S} \partial_h(i), & \text{otherwise.} \end{cases}$$

2. *Let $j \in [n]$. Then,*

$$\psi(i,j) = \begin{cases} -\prod_{h \in S} \partial_h(j), & \text{if } i \in (S \cap [r]) \Delta \mathcal{D}_L^+(S,i), \\ \prod_{h \in S} \partial_h(j), & \text{otherwise.} \end{cases}$$

3. *Let $i \in [r]$. The ith row of the pseudococyclic matrix M_ψ is uniformly signed if and only if one of the following two conditions hold.*
   (a) *$S \Delta \mathcal{D}_L^-(S,i) = \emptyset$, in whose case, $\psi(i,j) = \prod_{h \in S} \partial_h(i)$, for all $j \leq n$.*
   (b) *$S \Delta \mathcal{D}_L^-(S,i) = [n]$, in whose case, $\psi(i,j) = -\prod_{h \in S} \partial_h(i)$, for all $j \leq n$.*

4. *Let $j \in [n]$. The jth column of the pseudococyclic matrix M_ψ is uniformly signed if and only if one the following two conditions hold.*
   (a) *$(S \cap [r]) \Delta \mathcal{D}_L^+(S,i) = \emptyset$, in which case $\psi(i,j) = \prod_{h \in S} \partial_h(j)$ for all $i \leq r$.*
   (b) *$(S \cap [r]) \Delta \mathcal{D}_L^+(S,i) = [r]$, in which case $\psi(i,j) = -\prod_{h \in S} \partial_h(j)$ for all $i \leq r$.*

Proof. The first two assertions and both sufficient conditions of the last two assertions follow readily from the definition (6). So, let us focus on the necessary condition of the third statement (that one of the last statements follows similarly). Thus, let us suppose the existence of a positive integer $i \leq r$ such that the ith row of the pseudococyclic matrix M_ψ is uniformly signed. Then, the mentioned definition (6) implies that either $\prod_{h \in S} \partial_h(j) = \prod_{h \in S} \partial_h(L[i,j])$ or $\prod_{h \in S} \partial_h(j) = -\prod_{h \in S} \partial_h(L[i,j])$ for all $j \leq n$. In the first case, $j \in S$ if and only if $L[i,j] \in S$, and hence, Condition (3a) holds. In the second case, $j \in S$ if and only if $L[i,j] \notin S$, and hence, Condition (3b) holds. In any case, the result follows then from the Latin rectangle condition of no repetitions of symbols in each row. □

Example 10. *Let L be the Latin rectangle described in Example 1. The third assertion of Lemma 6 explains, for instance, the uniformity of signs of the first row of the pseudococyclic matrix $M_{\psi_{L;3}\psi_{L;4}}$ appearing in Example 6. More specifically, if we consider the subset $S = \{3,4\}$, then $\mathcal{D}_L^-(S,1) = S$. That is, the the first row of L satisfies the condition described in Lemma 6. (3a).*

The third assertion of Lemma 6 also implies that $S = [4]$ is the only way to get a pseudococyclic matrix related to a pseudococycle $\psi = \prod_{h \in S \subseteq [4]} \psi_{L;h}$ of L, whose rows are all uniformly signed. In such a case, all the signs within M_ψ are negative.

Further, the fourth assertion of Lemma 6 explains, for instance, the uniformly signed columns of the following two pseudococyclic matrices.

$$M_{\psi_{L;1}\psi_{L;2}} \equiv \begin{array}{|c|c|c|c|} \hline - & - & - & - \\ \hline + & - & + & - \\ \hline \end{array} \qquad M_{\psi_{L;2}\psi_{L;3}} \equiv \begin{array}{|c|c|c|c|} \hline + & + & - & - \\ \hline + & + & - & - \\ \hline \end{array}$$

Thus, concerning the first pseudococyclic matrix, we have that, if $S = \{1,2\}$, then $\mathcal{D}_L^+(S,2) = S$ and $\mathcal{D}_L^+(S,4) = \emptyset$. Concerning the second pseudococyclic matrix, we have that, if $S = \{2,3\}$, then $\mathcal{D}_L^+(S,1) = \mathcal{D}_L^+(S,3) = \{2\} = S \cap [2]$ and $(S \cap [2]) \cap \mathcal{D}_L^+(S,2) = (S \cap [2]) \cap \mathcal{D}_L^+(S,3) = \emptyset$.

Finally, the last statement of the fourth assertion of Lemma 6 explains, for instance, the uniformity of signs of the second and fourth columns of the pseudococyclic matrix $M_{\psi_{L;3}} M_{\psi_{L;4}}$, which is described in Example 6. Here, if $S = \{3,4\}$, then $\mathcal{D}_L^+(S,2) = \emptyset$ and $\mathcal{D}_L^+(S,4) = \{1,2\}$.

The following result characterizes the Latin rectangles $L \in \mathcal{R}_{r,n}$ with $r > 1$ and $ns(L) > 0$ over which a pseudococycle $\prod_{h \in S \subseteq \mathcal{H}(L)} \psi_{L;h}$ exists, so that its related pseudococyclic matrix is partial Hadamard.

Proposition 7. *Let $\psi = \prod_{h \in S \subseteq \mathcal{H}(L)} \psi_{L;h}$ be a pseudococycle over a Latin rectangle $L \in \mathcal{R}_{r,n}$ with $r > 1$ and $ns(L) > 0$. The pseudococyclic matrix M_ψ is partial Hadamard if and only if, for each pair of distinct positive integers $i_1, i_2 \leq r$,*

$$|\mathcal{D}_L^-(S,i_1) \Delta \mathcal{D}_L^-(S,i_2)| = \frac{n}{2}.$$

Proof. Since the pseudococyclic matrix M_ψ is partial Hadamard, all its rows are pairwise orthogonal and, hence, $\sum_{j \leq n} \psi(i_1,j) \psi(i_2,j) = 0$. Then, the first statement of Lemma 6 implies that

$$\left|(S \Delta \mathcal{D}_L^-(S,i_1)) \cap (S \Delta \mathcal{D}_L^-(S,i_2))\right| + \left|([n] \setminus (S \Delta \mathcal{D}_L^-(S,i_1))) \cap ([n] \setminus (S \Delta \mathcal{D}_L^-(S,i_2)))\right| = \frac{n}{2}.$$

Equivalently, after all the set operations are done and simplified, we have that

$$\left|[n] \setminus (\mathcal{D}_L^-(S,i_1) \Delta \mathcal{D}_L^-(S,i_2))\right| = \frac{n}{2}$$

and the result follows straightforwardly. □

The worst-case complexity of the implicit algorithm described in Proposition 7 corresponds to a Latin square of order n. Thus, the time complexity of this algorithm is $\mathcal{O}(n^4)$, which is required for the computation of all the difference sets under consideration (notice that the computation of all the sets $\mathcal{D}_L^-(S,i)$ with $i \leq n$ only requires a time complexity of $\mathcal{O}(n^3)$).

Example 11. *Let L be the Latin rectangle defined in Example 1, and let us consider the pseudococyclic matrix associated with the pseudococycle $M_{\psi_{L;2}} M_{\psi_{L;4}}$, which is partial Hadamard.*

$$M_{\psi_{L;2}} M_{\psi_{L;4}} \equiv \begin{array}{|c|c|c|c|} \hline + & + & - & - \\ \hline - & + & + & - \\ \hline \end{array}$$

If we consider the subset $S = \{2,4\}$, then we have that $\mathcal{D}_L^-(S,1) = \{2,3\}$ and $\mathcal{D}_L^-(S,2) = \{3,4\}$. Hence, $\mathcal{D}_L^-(S,1) \Delta \mathcal{D}_L^-(S,2) = \{2,4\}$, which is formed by two elements, as is required by Proposition 7.

Proposition 7 establishes a lower bound of the cardinality of $\mathcal{H}(L)$ for any $r \times n$ Latin rectangle L with $r > 1$ over which a pseudococyclic partial Hadamard matrix associated with the trivial cocycle exists.

Theorem 1. *Let $\psi = \prod_{h \in S \subseteq \mathcal{H}(L)} \psi_{L;h}$ be a pseudococycle over a Latin rectangle $L \in \mathcal{R}_{r,n}$ with $r > 1$ and $ns(L) > 0$ such that $|\mathcal{H}(L)| < \frac{n}{4}$. Then, the pseudococyclic matrix M_ψ is not partial Hadamard.*

Proof. For each positive integer $i \leq r$, we have already indicated that $|\mathcal{D}_L^-(S,i)| = |S|$. As a consequence, $|\mathcal{D}_L^-(S,i_1) \Delta \mathcal{D}_L^-(S,i_2)| \leq 2 \cdot |S| \leq 2 \cdot |\mathcal{H}(L)| < \frac{n}{2}$ for all $i_1, i_2 \leq r$. Then, the result follows straightforwardly from Proposition 7. □

The following example illustrates how the bound described in Theorem 1 does not constitute a necessary condition for ensuring the non-existence of pseudococyclic partial Hadamard matrices associated with the trivial cocycle.

Example 12. *Let us consider the following 2×12 Latin rectangle.*

$$L \equiv \begin{array}{|c|c|c|c|c|c|c|c|c|c|c|c|} \hline 1 & 2 & 4 & 3 & 5 & 6 & 7 & 8 & 9 & 10 & 11 & 12 \\ \hline 2 & 4 & 3 & 1 & 6 & 5 & 8 & 7 & 10 & 9 & 12 & 11 \\ \hline \end{array}$$

It is easily verified that $NS(L) = \{(1,1,3), (1,1,4), (1,2,2), (1,2,3), (2,1,3), (2,1,4)\}$, and $\mathcal{H}(L) = \{1,3,4\}$. In addition, we have that

$\mathcal{D}_L^-(\{1\},1) \Delta \mathcal{D}_L^-(\{1\},2) = \{1,4\}$, $\quad\quad \mathcal{D}_L^-(\{3\},1) \Delta \mathcal{D}_L^-(\{3\},2) = \{3,4\}$,
$\mathcal{D}_L^-(\{4\},1) \Delta \mathcal{D}_L^-(\{4\},2) = \{2,3\}$, $\quad\quad \mathcal{D}_L^-(\{1,3\},1) \Delta \mathcal{D}_L^-(\{1,3\},2) = \{1,3\}$,
$\mathcal{D}_L^-(\{1,4\},1) \Delta \mathcal{D}_L^-(\{1,4\},2) = \{1,2,3,4\}$, $\quad\quad \mathcal{D}_L^-(\{3,4\},1) \Delta \mathcal{D}_L^-(\{3,4\},2) = \{2,4\}$

and $\mathcal{D}_L^-(\{1,3,4\},1) \Delta \mathcal{D}_L^-(\{1,3,4\},2) = \{1,2\}$. Thus, $|\mathcal{D}_L^-(S,1) \Delta \mathcal{D}_L^-(S,2)| \neq 6$ for all $S \subseteq \mathcal{H}(L)$, and hence, no pseudococyclic partial Hadamard matrix associated with the trivial cocycle over L exists.

The next result deals with the pseudococyclic partial Hadamard matrices that have a uniformly signed row.

Theorem 2. *Let $\psi = \prod_{h \in S \subseteq \mathcal{H}(L)} \psi_{L;h}$ be a pseudococycle over a Latin rectangle $L \in \mathcal{R}_{r,n}$ with $ns(L) > 0$ so that the pseudococyclic matrix M_ψ is partial Hadamard. Then, there exists at most one positive integer $i \leq r$ such that $S \Delta \mathcal{D}_L^-(S,i) \in \{\emptyset, [n]\}$. If it exists, then $|S \Delta \mathcal{D}_L^-(S,i')| = \frac{n}{2}$ for all $i' \in [r] \setminus \{i\}$. Moreover, $\frac{n}{4} \leq |S| \leq \frac{3n}{4}$, and hence, $|\mathcal{H}(L)| \geq \frac{n}{4}$.*

Proof. Since the partial Hadamard matrix M_ψ can only have at most one uniformly signed row, the third statement of Lemma 6 implies the existence of at most one positive integer $i \leq r$ such that $S \Delta \mathcal{D}_L^-(S,i) \in \{\emptyset, [n]\}$. Thus, $\mathcal{D}_L^-(S,i) \in \{S, [n] \setminus S\}$. Now, let us consider a positive integer $i' \in [r] \setminus \{i\}$. The following two cases arise.

- If $\mathcal{D}_L^-(S,i) = S$, then Proposition 7 implies that

$$\frac{n}{2} = |\mathcal{D}_L^-(S,i) \Delta \mathcal{D}_L^-(S,i')| = |S \Delta \mathcal{D}_L^-(S,i')|.$$

- If $\mathcal{D}_L^-(S,i) = [n] \setminus S$, then Proposition 7 implies that

$$\frac{n}{2} = |\mathcal{D}_L^-(S,i) \Delta \mathcal{D}_L^-(S,i')| = |([n] \setminus S) \Delta \mathcal{D}_L^-(S,i')| = n - |S \Delta \mathcal{D}_L^-(S,i')|.$$

Hence, $|S \Delta \mathcal{D}_L^-(S,i')| = \frac{n}{2}$. The rest of the result follows easily from the fact that the Latin rectangle condition of no repetitions of symbols per row implies that $|\mathcal{D}_L^-(S,i)| = |S|$. □

The worst-case complexity of the implicit algorithm in Theorem 2 corresponds to a Latin square of order n. Thus, the time complexity of this algorithm is $\mathcal{O}(n^3)$, which is required for computing all the sets $\mathcal{D}_L^-(S,i)$ with $i \leq n$, and also for computing all the difference sets under consideration.

The following example illustrates the sharpness of both bounds concerning the cardinality of the subset S in Theorem 2.

Example 13. *Let L be the Latin rectangle defined in Example 1. In order to illustrate that the upper bound described in Theorem 2 is sharp, it is enough to consider the pseudococyclic matrix over L*

$$M_{\psi_{L;1}\psi_{L;2}\psi_{L;3}} \equiv \begin{array}{|c|c|c|c|} \hline - & - & + & + \\ \hline - & - & - & - \\ \hline \end{array}.$$

Thus, if we consider the subset $S = \{1,2,3\}$, then $\mathcal{D}_L^-(S,2) = S$, and hence, $S\Delta\mathcal{D}_L^-(S,2) = \emptyset$. In addition, $\mathcal{D}_L^-(S,1) = \{1,2,4\}$, and thus, $S\Delta\mathcal{D}_L^-(S,1) = \{3,4\}$. That is, $|S\Delta\mathcal{D}_L^-(S,1)| = 2$.

Now, in order to illustrate the sharpness of the lower bound described in Theorem 2, we can make use of any of the h-pseudocoboundary matrices over L with $h \in \{1,2,4\}$ that are described in Example 3. Thus, for instance, if we consider $S = \{1\}$, then $\mathcal{D}_L^-(S,1) = S$ and $S\Delta\mathcal{D}_L^-(S,2) = \{1,2\}$.

In order to illustrate the sharpness of this lower bound, but now avoiding the purely pseudocoboundary framework, let us consider the following 2×8 Latin rectangle.

$$L' \equiv \begin{array}{|c|c|c|c|c|c|c|c|} \hline 1 & 2 & 3 & 4 & 5 & 6 & 7 & 8 \\ \hline 4 & 3 & 1 & 2 & 6 & 5 & 8 & 7 \\ \hline \end{array}$$

It is easily verified that $NS(L') = \{(1,1,3), (1,1,4), (1,2,1), (1,2,2)\}$, and $\mathcal{H}(L') = \{3,4\}$. If we consider the subset $S = \{3,4\}$, then we have that $\mathcal{D}_{L'}^-(S,1) = S$ and $S\Delta\mathcal{D}_{L'}^-(S,2) = \{1,2,3,4\}$. Then, the pseudococyclic matrix over L' associated with the pseudococycle $\psi_{L';3}\psi_{L';4}$ is partial Hadamard.

$$M_{\psi_{L';3}\psi_{L';4}} \equiv \begin{array}{|c|c|c|c|c|c|c|c|} \hline + & + & + & + & + & + & + & + \\ \hline - & - & - & - & + & + & + & + \\ \hline \end{array}$$

6. Pseudococyclic Partial Hadamard Matrices Associated with Non-Trivial Cocycles

Let us finish our study by focusing on the pseudococycles $\prod_{h \in S \subseteq \mathcal{H}(L)} \psi_{L;h}\phi$ over a given Latin rectangle $L \in \mathcal{R}_{r,n}$ with $ns(L) > 0$ where the cocycle ϕ over L is not trivial. The following result generalizes Proposition 7 by characterizing the Latin rectangles over which one such pseudococycle exists so that its related pseudococyclic matrix is partial Hadamard.

Proposition 8. *Let $\psi = \prod_{h \in S \subseteq \mathcal{H}(L)} \psi_{L;h}\phi$ be a pseudococycle over a Latin rectangle $L \in \mathcal{R}_{r,n}$ with $ns(L) > 0$ for some cocycle ϕ over L. The pseudococyclic matrix M_ψ is partial Hadamard if and only if, for each pair of positive integers $i_1, i_2 \leq r$, the set*

$$\{j \in \mathcal{D}_L^-(S,i_1)\Delta\mathcal{D}_L^-(S,i_2) \colon \phi(i_1,j) = \phi(i_2,j)\} \cup \{j \notin \mathcal{D}_L^-(S,i_1)\Delta\mathcal{D}_L^-(S,i_2) \colon \phi(i_1,j) = -\phi(i_2,j)\} \quad (7)$$

has cardinality $\frac{n}{2}$.

Proof. The result follows in a similar way to the proof of Proposition 7, once it is observed that $\sum_{j \leq n} \psi(i_1,j)\psi(i_2,j) = 0$ if and only if

$$\sum_{j \in \mathcal{D}_L^-(S,i_1)\Delta\mathcal{D}_L^-(S,i_2)} \phi(i_1,j)\phi(i_2,j) = \sum_{j \notin \mathcal{D}_L^-(S,i_1)\Delta\mathcal{D}_L^-(S,i_2)} \phi(i_1,j)\phi(i_2,j).$$

□

Keeping in mind the observation made just after Proposition 7, the time complexity of the implicit algorithm described in Proposition 8 is $\mathcal{O}(n^5)$, which corresponds once more to the Latin square case.

Example 14. *Let L be the Latin rectangle defined in Example 1 and let us consider the pseudococyclic matrix $M_{\psi_{L_2;3}\psi_{L_2;4}\phi_2}$ described in Example 6, which is not partial Hadamard. If we again take $S = \{3,4\}$, then we have that $\mathcal{D}_L^-(S,1) = \{3,4\}$ and $\mathcal{D}_L^-(S,2) = \{1,4\}$. Hence, $\mathcal{D}_L^-(S,1)\Delta\mathcal{D}_L^-(S,2) = \{1,3\}$. In this case, the set defined in (7) concerning the pseudococycle $\psi_{L;3}\psi_{L;4}\phi_2$ is the set $\{2,3,4\}$, which is not formed by two elements, as is required by Proposition 8.*

Example 15. Let us consider the Latin rectangle $L \in \mathcal{R}_{2,12}$ that is described in Example 12, and let us define the cocycle ϕ over L that is represented by the matrix

$$M_\phi \equiv \begin{array}{|c|c|c|c|c|c|c|c|c|c|c|c|} \hline + & + & + & + & + & + & + & + & + & + & + & + \\ \hline + & + & + & + & - & - & + & + & + & + & + & + \\ \hline + & + & + & + & + & + & + & + & + & + & + & + \\ \hline \end{array}$$

Notice here that the third row of this cocyclic matrix corresponds to the positive integer $4 \in \mathcal{S}(L) = \{1, 2, 4\}$. The pseudococyclic matrix associated with the pseudococycle $\psi_{L;1}\psi_{L;4}\phi$ is

$$M_{\psi_{L;1}\psi_{L;4}\phi} \equiv \begin{array}{|c|c|c|c|c|c|c|c|c|c|c|c|} \hline - & - & + & + & - & - & - & - & - & - & - & - \\ \hline - & - & + & + & - & - & + & + & + & + & + & + \\ \hline \end{array}$$

which is partial Hadamard. If we consider the subset $S = \{1, 4\}$, then we have that $\mathcal{D}_L^-(S, 1) \Delta \mathcal{D}_L^-(S, 2) = \{4\}$. Moreover, the set defined in (7) concerning the pseudococycle $\psi_{L;1}\psi_{L;4}\phi$ is the set $\{1, 2, 3, 4, 5, 6\}$, which is formed by six elements, as is required by Proposition 8.

The pseudococyclic partial Hadamard matrix in Example 15 shows that Theorem 1 cannot be generalized for pseudococycles associated with non-trivial cocycles. Concerning the possible generalization of Theorem 2, the following result deals with the case of a pseudococycle related to a non-trivial cocycle whose pseudococyclic partial Hadamard matrix contains a uniformly signed row.

Proposition 9. Let $\psi = \prod_{h \in S \subseteq \mathcal{H}(L)} \psi_{L;h}\phi$ be a pseudococycle over a Latin rectangle $L \in \mathcal{R}_{r,n}$ with $ns(L) > 0$ for some cocycle ϕ over L. If the pseudococyclic matrix M_ψ is partial Hadamard, then there exists at most one positive integer $i \leq r$ and an integer $a \in \{-1, 1\}$ such that

$$\phi(i, j) = \begin{cases} a, & \text{if } j \in S \Delta \mathcal{D}_L^-(S, i), \\ -a, & \text{if } j \notin S \Delta \mathcal{D}_L^-(S, i). \end{cases}$$

Proof. Since the pseudococyclic matrix M_ψ is partial Hadamard, it can only have at most one uniformly signed row. Hence, there exists at most one positive integer $i \leq r$ such that $\psi(i, j_1) = \psi(i, j_2)$ for all pairs of positive integers $j_1, j_2 \leq n$. The result then follows from the third statement of Lemma 6, together with the definition of the cocycle ϕ. □

Example 16. Let us consider the Latin rectangle $L \in \mathcal{R}_{2,12}$ that is described in Example 12 and let us consider the cocycle ϕ over L that is represented by the matrix

$$M_\phi \equiv \begin{array}{|c|c|c|c|c|c|c|c|c|c|c|c|} \hline - & - & + & + & - & - & - & - & - & - & - & - \\ \hline + & + & - & - & - & - & - & - & - & - & - & - \\ \hline + & + & + & + & + & + & + & + & + & + & + & + \\ \hline \end{array}$$

Further, let us consider the subset $S = \{1, 4\}$. Then, $S \Delta \mathcal{D}_L^-(S, 1) = \{3, 4\}$ and $S \Delta \mathcal{D}_L^-(S, 2) = \{1, 2\}$. According to Proposition 9, the pseudococyclic matrix $M_{\psi_{L;1}\psi_{L;4}\phi}$ over L is not partial Hadamard. In fact,

$$M_{\psi_{L;1}\psi_{L;4}\phi} \equiv \begin{array}{|c|c|c|c|c|c|c|c|c|c|c|c|} \hline + & + & + & + & + & + & + & + & + & + & + & + \\ \hline - & - & - & - & - & - & - & - & - & - & - & - \\ \hline \end{array}.$$

7. Conclusions and Further Work

In this paper, we have introduced the concepts of both the pseudocoboundary and pseudococycle over a Latin rectangle (see Section 3) as a natural generalization of the similar notions recently described in [17] over quasigroups. To this end, we have made use of the cocyclic framework over Latin rectangles previously introduced by the authors in [18]. Both cocyclic and pseudococyclic developments over Latin rectangles together constitute a much more general framework than the classical cocyclic framework over groups. Its potential has already been illustrated in the mentioned papers by means of examples of (pseudo)cocyclic Hadamard matrices over quasigroups that are not cocyclic over any group. This paper constitutes a step forward in this regard. Thus, for instance, Example 5 illustrates a pseudocoboundary Hadamard matrix over a Latin square that is not cocyclic over any Latin rectangle.

Let us remark that this paper is conceived as an introductory stage concerning the fundamentals of both the pseudocoboundary and the pseudococyclic frameworks over Latin rectangles. Particularly, in Section 4, we completely answered both Problems 1 and 2 concerning the conditions under which we may ensure either the existence of a partial Hadamard matrix that is a pseudocoboundary over a given Latin rectangle or, reciprocally, the existence of a Latin rectangle over which a given partial Hadamard matrix is a pseudocoboundary. More specifically, Propositions 1 and 2 give the answer of the first question, whereas the second one is answered by Lemma 1, together with Propositions 4–6.

Furthermore, we have also dealt with the problem of determining under which conditions we may ensure the existence of a partial Hadamard matrix that is pseudococyclic over a given Latin rectangle. To this end, we have distinguished two distinct frameworks (see Sections 5 and 6), depending on whether we make use of trivial cocycles or not. The reciprocal problem concerning the conditions under which we may ensure the existence of a Latin rectangle over which a given partial Hadamard matrix is pseudococyclic is established as future work. Once this last question is solved, the next natural stage would be the construction of pseudococyclic partial Hadamard matrices of higher dimensions in order to deal with the Hadamard conjecture described in the introductory section, which indeed constitutes the keystone of the theory of Hadamard matrices.

The following open questions are also established as future work. They generalize similar ones described for the cocyclic development of Hadamard matrices over Latin rectangles [18].

Problem 3. *Let M be an $r \times n$ partial Hadamard matrix that is not pseudococyclic over any Latin rectangle. Does there exist, however, a partial Hadamard equivalent matrix in the same equivalence class of M for which one such Latin rectangle can be found?*

Problem 4. *Let us consider an equivalence class of Hadamard matrices such that none of them are cocyclic over any finite group. Does there exist, however, a Hadamard matrix within such a class that is pseudococyclic over a Latin rectangle?*

Pseudococycles over Latin rectangles have been introduced in this paper as the product of a cocycle with some pseudocoboundaries. A possible generalization of this notion consists of enabling the product of a cocycle not only with pseudocoboundaries (related to non-associative triples), but also with elementary coboundaries (related to associative triples). This would constitute a more general framework that puts together both cocyclic and pseudococyclic frameworks over Latin rectangles. Its formal description and characterization is also proposed as future work.

Finally, another question to take into consideration for further study is the following one. Both the pseudocoboundary and the pseudococyclic frameworks over Latin rectangles described in this paper are based on the existence of non-associative triples within a Latin rectangle. As was already indicated in the introductory section and in Section 3, the study of this type of triple in the case of dealing with Latin squares has received particular attention in the recent literature [32–36] because of its possible application in different areas as cryptography [30,31]. A comprehensive study of non-associative triples in the case of dealing with Latin rectangles instead of Latin squares is established, therefore, as natural further work.

Author Contributions: Conceptualization, V.Á., R.M.F. and F.G.; Data curation, M.D.F., F.G. and M.B.G.; Formal analysis, V.Á., R.M.F. and F.G.; Investigation, V.Á. and R.M.F.; Methodology, R.M.F., M.D.F. and M.B.G.; Software, V.Á. and R.M.F.; Supervision, F.G.; Validation, M.D.F. and M.B.G.; Writing—original draft, R.M.Falcón; Writing—review & editing, V.Á., R.M.F., M.D.F. and F.G. All authors have read and agreed to the published version of the manuscript.

Funding: This research received no external funding.

Institutional Review Board Statement: Not applicable.

Informed Consent Statement: Not applicable.

Acknowledgments: This work was partially supported by the Research Project FQM-016 from Junta de Andalucía. In addition, the authors want to express their gratitude to the anonymous referees for the comprehensive reading of the paper and their pertinent comments and suggestions, which helped improve the manuscript. Particularly, we are grateful to the anonymous referee who suggested to us the more general framework described in the conclusion section concerning the product of a cocycle with both types of pseudocoboundaries and elementary coboundaries of a given Latin rectangle.

Conflicts of Interest: The authors declare no conflict of interest.

Appendix A. Glossary of Symbols

$\mathcal{H}(L)$ — The set of positive integers satisfying Condition (5).
$M_{\psi_{L;h}}$ — The h-pseudocoboundary matrix associated to a Latin rectangle $L \in \mathcal{R}_{r,n}$, with $h \in \mathcal{H}(L)$.
$[n]$ — The set $\{1, \ldots, n\}$.
$ns(L)$ — The non-associative index of a Latin rectangle L.
$NS(L)$ — The set of non-associative triples of a Latin rectangle L.
$\mathcal{R}_{r,n}$ — The set of $r \times n$ Latin rectangles with entries in $[n]$.
$\mathcal{S}(L)$ — The subset of symbols describing the rows of a cocyclic matrix over a Latin rectangle L.
$\psi_{L;h}$ — The h-pseudocoboundary over a Latin rectangle L, with $h \in \mathcal{H}(L)$.

References

1. Paley, R.E.A.C. On orthogonal matrices. *J. Math. Phys.* **1933**, *12*, 311–320. [CrossRef]
2. Horadam, K.J. *Hadamard Matrices and Their Applications*; Princeton University Press: Princeton, NJ, USA, 2007.
3. Horadam, K.J.; de Launey, W. Cocyclic development of designs. *J. Algebr. Comb.* **1993**, *2*, 267–290; Erratum: *J. Algebr. Comb.* **1994**, *3*, 129. [CrossRef]
4. de Launey, W. On the construction of n-dimensional designs from 2-dimensional designs. *Australas. J. Comb.* **1990**, *1*, 67–81.
5. de Launey, W.; Horadam, K.J. A weak difference set construction for higher dimensional designs. *Des. Codes Cryptogr.* **1993**, *3*, 75–87. [CrossRef]
6. Horadam, K.J.; de Launey, W. Generation of cocyclic Hadamard matrices. *Math. Appl.* **1995**, *325*, 279–290.
7. Sylvester, J.J. LX. Thoughts on inverse orthogonal matrices, simultaneous sign-successions, and tessellated pavements in two or more colours, with applications to Newton's rule, ornamental tile-work, and the theory of numbers. *Lond. Edinb. Dublin Philos. Mag. J. Sci.* **1867**, *34*, 461–475. [CrossRef]
8. Williamson, J. Hadamard's determinant theorem and the sum of four squares. *Duke Math. J.* **1944**, *11*, 65–81. [CrossRef]
9. Ito, N. On Hadamard groups III. *Kyushu J. Math.* **1997**, *51*, 369–379. [CrossRef]
10. de Launey, W.; Flannery, D.L.; Horadam, K.J. Cocyclic Hadamard matrices and difference sets. *Discret. Appl. Math.* **2000**, *102*, 47–61. [CrossRef]
11. de Launey, W.; Smith, M.J. Cocyclic orthogonal designs and the asymptotic existence of cocyclic Hadamard matrices and maximal size relative difference sets with forbidden subgroup of size 2. *J. Comb. Theory Ser. A* **2001**, *93*, 37–92. [CrossRef]
12. Catháin, P. Group Actions on Hadamard Matrices. Master's Thesis, National University of Ireland, Galway, Ireland, 2008.
13. de Launey, W.; Flannery, D. *Algebraic Design Theory*; American Mathematical Society: Providence, RI, USA, 2011.
14. Egan, R.; Flannery, D.L. Automorphisms of generalized Sylvester Hadamard matrices. *Discret. Math.* **2017**, *340*, 516–523. [CrossRef]
15. Fletcher, R.J.; Gysin, M.; Seberry, J. Application of the discrete Fourier transform to the search for generalised Legendre pairs and Hadamard matrices. *Australas. J. Comb.* **2001**, *23*, 75–86.
16. Goethals, J.M.; Seidel, J.J. Orthogonal matrices with zero diagonal. *Can. J. Math.* **1967**, *19*, 1001–1010. [CrossRef]
17. Álvarez, V.; Armario, J.A.; Falcón, R.M.; Frau, M.D.; Gudiel, F.; Güemes, M.B.; Osuna, A. On cocyclic Hadamard matrices over Goethals-Seidel loops. *Mathematics* **2020**, *8*, 1–22. [CrossRef]
18. Álvarez, V.; Falcón, R.M.; Frau, M.D.; Gudiel, F.; Güemes, M.B. Cocyclic Hadamard matrices over Latin rectangles. *Eur. J. Comb.* **2019**, *79*, 74–96. [CrossRef]

19. Craigen, R.; Faucher, G.; Low, R.; Wares, T. Circulant partial Hadamard matrices. *Linear Algebra Appl.* **2013**, *439*, 3307–3317. [CrossRef]
20. Kao, M.H. Universally optimal fMRI designs for comparing hemodynamic response functions. *Stat. Sin.* **2015**, *25*, 499–506. [CrossRef]
21. Shi, F; Zhang, X.; Guo, Y. Constructions of unextendible entangled bases. *Quantum Inf. Process.* **2019**, *18*, 14.
22. Banica, T.; Skalski, A. The quantum algebra of partial Hadamard matrices. *Linear Algebra Appl.* **2015**, *469*, 364–380. [CrossRef]
23. Lin, Y.L.; Phoa, F.K.H.; Kao, M.H. Circulant partial Hadamard matrices: construction via general difference sets and its application to fMRI experiments. *Stat. Sin.* **2017**, *27*, 1715–1724.
24. Banica, T.; Özteke, D.; Pittau, L. Isolated partial Hadamard matrices and related topics. *Open Syst. Inf. Dyn.* **2018**, *25*, 27. [CrossRef]
25. Álvarez, V.; Armario, J.A.; Falcón, R.M.; Frau, M.D.; Gudiel, F.; Güemes, M.B.; Osuna, A. Generating binary partial Hadamard matrices. *Discret. Appl. Math.* **2019**, *263*, 2–7. [CrossRef]
26. Boucetta, C.; Nour, B.; Moungla, H.; Lahlou, L. An IoT scheduling and interference mitigation scheme in TSCH using Latin rectangles. In Proceedings of the 2019 IEEE Global Communications Conference (GLOBECOM), Waikoloa, HI, USA, 9–13 December 2019; pp. 1–6.
27. Chang, C. Reliable and Secure Storage with Erasure Codes for OpenStack Swift in PyECLib. Master's Thesis, KTH Royal Institute of Technology, Stockholm, Sweden, 2016.
28. Stones, R.J. K-plex 2-erasure codes and Blackburn partial Latin squares. *IEEE Trans. Inform. Theory* **2020**, *66*, 3704–3713 [CrossRef]
29. Gligoroski, D.; Kralevska, K. Expanded combinatorial designs as tool to model network slicing in 5G. *IEEE Access* **2019**, *7*, 54879–54887. [CrossRef]
30. Dénes, J.; Keedwell, A.D. A new authentication scheme based on Latin squares. *Discret. Math.* **1992**, *106/107*, 157–161. [CrossRef]
31. Grošek, O.; Horák, P. On quasigroups with few associative triples. *Des. Codes Cryptogr.* **2012**, *64*, 221–227. [CrossRef]
32. Drápal, A.; Lisoněk, P.. Maximal nonassociativity via nearfields. *Finite Fields Appl.* **2020**, *62*, 27. [CrossRef]
33. Artamonov, V.A.; Chakrabarti, S.; Pal, S.K. Characterizations of highly non-associative quasigroups and associative triples. *Quasigroups Relat. Syst.* **2017**, *25*, 1–19.
34. Drápal, A.; Valent, V. Few associative triples, isotopisms and groups. *Des. Codes Cryptogr.* **2018**, *86*, 555–568. [CrossRef]
35. Drápal, A.; Valent, V. High nonassociativity in order 8 and an associative index estimate. *J. Comb. Des.* **2019**, *27*, 205–228. [CrossRef]
36. Drápal, A.; Valent, V. Extreme nonassociativity in order nine and beyond. *J. Comb. Des.* **2020**, *28*, 33–48. [CrossRef]
37. Bruck, R.H. *A Survey of Binary Systems*; Springer: New York, NY, USA, 1958.
38. Moufang, R. Zur Struktur von Alternativkörpern. *Math. Ann.* **1935**, *110*, 416–430. [CrossRef]
39. Gavrilov, M.; Čobanov, I. The index of non-associativity of multiplicative structures. *Annu. Univ. Sofia Fac. Sci. Phys. Math. Livre 1 Math.* **1963**, *56*, 23–26.
40. Drápal, A.; Kepka, T. Sets of associative triples. *Eur. J. Comb.* **1985**, *6*, 227–231. [CrossRef]
41. Kepka, T.; Trch, M. Groupoids and the associative law. I. Associative triples. *Acta Univ. Carol. Math. Phys.* **1992**, *33*, 69–86.
42. Waldhauser, T. Almost associative operations generating a minimal clone. *Discuss. Math. Gen. Algebra Appl.* **2006**, *26*, 45–73. [CrossRef]
43. Climescu, A.C. Etudes sur la théorie des systèmes multiplicatifs uniformes I. L'indice de non-associativité. *Bull. Ecole Polytech. Jassy* **1947**, *2*, 347–371.
44. Ježek, J.; Kepka, T. Notes on the number of associative triples. *Acta Univ. Carol. Math. Phys.* **1990**, *31*, 15–19.
45. Drápal, A. On quasigroups rich in associative triples. *Discret. Math.* **1983**, *44*, 251–265. [CrossRef]
46. Dénes, J.; Keedwell, A.D. *Latin Squares and Their Applications*; Academic Press: New York, NY, USA; London, UK, 1974.
47. Drápal, A.; Kepka, T. Group distances of Latin squares. *Comment. Math. Univ. Carol.* **1985**, *26*, 275–283.

Article

A Discussion of a Cryptographical Scheme Based in ℑ-Critical Sets of a Latin Square [†]

Laura M. Johnson [1,*] and Stephanie Perkins [2]

[1] School of Mathematics and Statistics, University of St. Andrews, St Andrews KY16 9SS, UK
[2] School of Computing and Mathematics, University of South Wales, Pontypridd CF37 1DL, UK; stephanie.perkins@southwales.ac.uk
[*] Correspondence: lj68@st-andrews.ac.uk
[†] The work detailed in this short communication was undertaken as part of an MMath research module at the University of South Wales.

Abstract: This communication provides a discussion of a scheme originally proposed by Falcón in a paper entitled "Latin squares associated to principal autotopisms of long cycles. Applications in cryptography". Falcón outlines the protocol for a cryptographical scheme that uses the ℑ-critical sets associated with a particular Latin square to generate access levels for participants of the scheme. Accompanying the scheme is an example, which applies the protocol to a particular Latin square of order six. Exploration of the example itself, revealed some interesting observations about both the structure of the Latin square itself and the autotopisms associated with the Latin square. These observations give rise to necessary conditions for the generation of the ℑ-critical sets associated with certain autotopisms of the given Latin square. The communication culminates with a table which outlines the various access levels for the given Latin square in accordance with the scheme detailed by Falcón.

Keywords: ℑ-critical sets; Latin square; Latin subsquare; intercalate; secret sharing scheme

Citation: Johnson, L.M.; Perkins, S. A Discussion of a Cryptographical Scheme Based in ℑ-Critical Sets of a Latin Square [†]. *Mathematics* **2021**, *9*, 285. https://doi.org/10.3390/math9030285

Academic Editor: Carsten Schneider
Received: 30 November 2020
Accepted: 27 January 2021
Published: 31 January 2021

Publisher's Note: MDPI stays neutral with regard to jurisdictional claims in published maps and institutional affiliations.

Copyright: © 2021 by the authors. Licensee MDPI, Basel, Switzerland. This article is an open access article distributed under the terms and conditions of the Creative Commons Attribution (CC BY) license (https://creativecommons.org/licenses/by/4.0/).

1. Introduction and Preliminaries

A *Latin square* of order n is an $n \times n$ array comprising of n distinct elements, such that each element occurs exactly once in each row and column [1,2]. A *partial Latin square* is an $n \times n$ array with all entries of the array belonging to the set $\{0, 1, \ldots, n-1\}$. There can be blank entries within a *partial Latin square*, but each element of the set $\{0, 1, \ldots, n-1\}$ must only occur once in each row and column [3]. Partial Latin squares can be considered substructures of *Latin squares*, as such; a partial Latin square can be *completed* to form a Latin square by replacing the blank entries of the partial Latin square with elements of the set $\{0, 1, \ldots, n-1\}$ in such a way that each element in the set only occurs once in each row and column [3]. A *partial Latin square* is said to be *uniquely completable* if it only has one possible *completion* [3]. We consider two mechanisms by which a partial Latin square P can be (uniquely) completed to a Latin square L. A triple $(i, j; k) \in P$ denotes an entry within a partial Latin square such that i is the row component, j is the column component and k denotes the symbol in the cell (i, j). A triple $(i, j; k)$ in a partial Latin square P is *forced* if the cell (i, j) is the only empty cell in either the ith row or jth column and the symbol k is the only symbol not appearing in the respective row or column. Similarly a triple is forced if the symbol k appears in every row and column of L except the ith row and jth column [4].

The second mechanism considered is applying autotopisms to the set of triples of a partial Latin square P to generate a Latin square L, on occasion this may additionally require the application of forced moves. Before defining an autotopism, it is important to define the notion of a quasigroup; a set S is a *quasigroup* if there exists a binary operator $*$ such that $\forall a, b \in S$ $a * x = b$ and $y * a = b$ have exactly one solution. The multiplication table of a quasigroup forms a Latin square [1,2]. An autotopism is formally defined [1,2,5];

Definition 1. *Let $(B, \cdot)$ and $(C, *)$ be two quasigroups. An isotopism is an ordered triple of row, column and symbol permutations, $\theta = (\alpha, \beta, \gamma)$ that maps $(B, \cdot)$ onto $(C, *)$, providing that $\forall i, j \in B$, i, j denote a pair of row and column coordinates $(\alpha(i)) * (\beta(j)) = \gamma(i \cdot j)$. An autotopism is an isotopism that maps a quasigroup onto itself.*

Let Atop(L) denote the set of all autotopisms associated with a Latin square L. Atop(L) constitutes a group under the composition of permutations; this is know as the autotopism group of L [4]. As stated in [4], each autotopism $\theta = (\alpha, \beta, \gamma) \in$ Atop(L) generates a subgroup of Atop(L), denoted $\langle \theta \rangle$. This may be extended to the set generated by $\theta_1, .., \theta_q \in$ Atop(L), which will also form a subgroup of Atop(L), denoted $\langle \theta_1, \ldots, \theta_p \rangle$.

As in [4], let Ent(P) denote the set of non-empty cells of a partial Latin square P. Further, Reference [4] defines the θ-orbit of a triple $(i, j; k) \in$ Ent(L), for some autotopism $\theta = (\alpha, \beta, \gamma) \in$ Atop(L), as the set

$$\text{Orb}_\theta((i, j; k)) = \{(\alpha^m(i), \beta^m(j); \gamma^m(k) : m \geq 0\} \subseteq \text{Ent(L)}$$

This idea can be extended to $\mathfrak{F}$-orbits [4]. For a collection of autotopisms $\mathfrak{F} \subseteq$ Atop(L), the $\mathfrak{F}$-orbit of a triple $(i, j; k) \in$ Ent(L) is the set

$$\text{Orb}_\mathfrak{F}((i, j; k)) = \bigcup_{\theta \in \mathfrak{F}} \{(\alpha^m(i), \beta^m(j); \gamma^m(k) : m \geq 0\} \subseteq \text{Ent(L)}.$$

We are interested in using $\mathfrak{F}$-orbits to determine $\mathfrak{F}$-critical sets. A critical set is formally defined [5]:

Definition 2. *A critical set C in a Latin square, L, is a set*

$$C = \{(i, j; k) : i, j, k \in \{0, 1, \ldots, n-1\}\}$$

where:

1. *L is the only Latin square of order n which has the symbol k in the cell (i, j) for each $(i, j; k) \in C$.*
2. *No proper subset of C has property 1.*

Furthermore, we define a partial Latin square P to be $\mathfrak{F}$-completable to a Latin square L, with $\mathfrak{F} \subseteq$ Atop(P), if there exists a partial Latin square Q that is completable to L such that;

$$\text{Ent}(Q) = \bigcup_{t \in \text{Ent}(P)} \text{Orb}_\mathfrak{F}(t).$$

We can say that P is uniquely $\mathfrak{F}$-completable if L is unique, and moreover, P is an $\mathfrak{F}$-critical set of the Latin square L if no proper subset of Ent(P) is $\mathfrak{F}$-completable to L [4].

The paper by Falcón [6], on which this communication is based, looks at building a secret sharing scheme using $\mathfrak{F}$-critical sets.

A *secret sharing scheme* is a cryptographical scheme in which k participants are each given a part of a secret key K, called a share [7]. In secret sharing schemes, certain shares may be combined to generate the original secret key K. These are referred to as authorised groups. All unauthorised groups will be unable to recover the secret key K [6]. The *access structure* Γ defines the set of authorised groups of shares [6]. Throughout this communication, the term *access level* will be used to refer to each minimal authorised group.

A previous secret sharing scheme based on critical sets in Latin squares was proposed by Cooper et al [8]. In this secret sharing scheme, a particular Latin square K of order n is chosen as the secret key. The k shares distributed to participants in this scheme are triples of Ent(K). The access structure for this scheme is the set $\Gamma = \{S \mid \text{Ent}(C) \subseteq \text{Ent}(S) \subseteq \text{Ent}(K)$, where C is a critical set of K$\}$.

The scheme proposed by Falcón, seeks to extend the scheme proposed by Cooper et al. to $\mathfrak{F}$-critical sets of Latin squares. The secret key for the scheme proposed in [6] is also a Latin square K. However, in this scheme there are two types of shares that may be distributed to the k participants of the scheme; a group of the shares will be autotopisms $\theta \in \mathfrak{F}$, such that $\mathfrak{F} \subseteq$ Atop(K) and the remaining shares will be triples $T_i \in$ Ent(K). Formally, the access structure for the scheme is then the set $\Gamma = \{S \mid \text{Ent}(C) \subseteq \text{Ent}(S) \subseteq \text{Ent}(K)$, where C is an $\mathfrak{F}$-critical set of K$\}$.

Below, an overview of the scheme proposed in [6] is given:

Overview of the secret sharing scheme:

- A Latin Square K of order n is selected as the key for the scheme. The order n of the Latin Square K is made public, whilst K is kept private.
- A set of T triples, where Ent(T) $\subset$ Ent(K) is selected, along with a collection of $\mathfrak{F}$ autotopisms associated with K.
- The triples of Ent(T) and autotopisms in $\mathfrak{F}$ associated with K are distributed to the k participants in the secret sharing scheme in such a way that when a group of t participants come together, the union of whose shares form an $\mathfrak{F}$-critical set of K. They are thus able to combine their shares in order to find the key K.

In [6], Falcón provides an example to accompany the scheme, which demonstrates how the secret sharing scheme may be applied to a particular Latin square of order 6. The example is detailed below.

Example 1. *The Latin square K is chosen as the key for the secret sharing scheme, where;*

$$K = \begin{array}{|c|c|c|c|c|c|} \hline 0 & 1 & 2 & 3 & 4 & 5 \\ \hline 1 & 2 & 0 & 4 & 5 & 3 \\ \hline 2 & 0 & 1 & 5 & 3 & 4 \\ \hline 3 & 4 & 5 & 0 & 1 & 2 \\ \hline 4 & 5 & 3 & 1 & 2 & 0 \\ \hline 5 & 3 & 4 & 2 & 0 & 1 \\ \hline \end{array}$$

The k participants in the scheme will be assigned autotopisms belonging to $\mathfrak{F}$ and triples belonging to a partial Latin square T, where Ent(T) $\subset$ Ent(K). In this example, the set $\mathfrak{F}$ consists of the four autotopisms $\mathfrak{F}=\{\theta_1,\theta_2,\theta_3,\theta_4\}$ associated with the Latin square K. These are defined;

$$\theta_1 = ((012)(345), (0)(1)(2)(3)(4)(5), (021)(354))$$
$$\theta_2 = ((0)(1)(2)(3)(4)(5), (012)(345), (021)(354))$$
$$\theta_3 = ((03)(14)(25), (03)(14)(25), (0)(1)(2)(3)(4)(5))$$
$$\theta_4 = ((0)(1)(2)(3)(4)(5), (03)(14)(25), (03)(14)(25))$$

There are 11 triples in the partial Latin square T. Each triple in the set T=$\{T_1,...,T_{11}\}$ is defined;

$T_1 = (0,4;4), T_2 = (1,1;2), T_3 = (1,5;3), T_4 = (2,2;1), T_5 = (2,4;3), T_6 = (3,1;4), T_7 = (3,2;5), T_8 = (3,3;0),$
$T_9 = (4,0;4), T_{10} = (5,3;2), T_{11} = (5,5;1)$

The autotopisms and T triples are assigned to participants within the scheme in accordance with Table 1, where Table 1 provides examples of access levels for the autotopisms and T triples given in Example 1. Note that m in Table 1 denotes the number of shares within each access level. There has also been a change in notation from the original example in [6]; the notation $\langle \ldots \rangle$ has been used in Table 1 in place of the notation $\{\ldots\}$. This is to highlight more clearly that the autotopisms in each access level will generate a subgroup of Atop(K).

Table 1. Access level definitions in [6].

m	Permutations	Triples of P	m	Permutations	Triples of P
11	-	T	6	$\langle \theta_1, \theta_2 \rangle$	$\{T_1, T_2, T_6, T_8\}$
11	$\langle \theta_4 \rangle$	$T \setminus \{T_9\}$	6	$\langle \theta_1, \theta_4 \rangle$	$\{T_2, T_3, T_7, T_9\}$
10	$\langle \theta_3 \rangle$	$T \setminus \{T_1, T_{11}\}$	6	$\langle \theta_2, \theta_3 \rangle$	$\{T_3, T_6, T_8, T_{10}\}$
10	$\langle \theta_3, \theta_4 \rangle$	$T \setminus \{T_1, T_9, T_{11}\}$	6	$\langle \theta_1, \theta_3, \theta_4 \rangle$	$\{T_2, T_4, T_8\}$
9	$\langle \theta_1 \rangle$	$T \setminus \{T_5, T_7, T_{10}\}$	5	$\langle \theta_1, \theta_2, \theta_3 \rangle$	$\{T_1, T_2\}$
9	$\langle \theta_2 \rangle$	$T \setminus \{T_1, T_7, T_{10}\}$	5	$\langle \theta_2, \theta_3, \theta_4 \rangle$	$\{T_1, T_2\}$
7	$\langle \theta_1, \theta_3 \rangle$	$\{T_2, T_3, T_4, T_6, T_9\}$	5	$\langle \theta_1, \theta_2, \theta_4 \rangle$	$\{T_2, T_4\}$
7	$\langle \theta_2, \theta_4 \rangle$	$\{T_1, T_2, T_4, T_6, T_9\}$	5	$\langle \theta_1, \theta_2, \theta_3, \theta_4 \rangle$	$\{T_1\}$

To give an example of how these access levels work; take the set of shares θ_3 and $T \setminus \{T_1, T_{11}\}$. Table 1, shown above, states that the union of $\mathfrak{F}$-orbits for each triple in the set $T \setminus \{T_1, T_{11}\}$, should form an $\mathfrak{F}$-critical set, when $\mathfrak{F}$ is the subgroup of autotopisms generated by $\langle \theta_3 \rangle$. The autotopisms within this subgroup are;

$$Id = ((0)(1)(2)(3)(4)(5), (0)(1)(2)(3)(4)(5), (0)(1)(2)(3)(4)(5))$$
$$\theta_3 = ((03)(14)(25), (03)(14)(25), (0)(1)(2)(3)(4)(5))$$

This subgroup of Atop(K) will generate the following $\mathfrak{F}$-orbits for the shares $T \setminus \{T_1, T_{11}\}$;

$$Orb_{\mathfrak{F}}(T_2) = Orb_{\mathfrak{F}}((1,1;2)) = \{(1,1;2), (4,4;2)\}$$
$$Orb_{\mathfrak{F}}(T_3) = Orb_{\mathfrak{F}}((1,5;3)) = \{(1,5;3), (4,2;3)\}$$
$$Orb_{\mathfrak{F}}(T_4) = Orb_{\mathfrak{F}}((2,2;1)) = \{(2,2;1), (5,5;1)\}$$
$$Orb_{\mathfrak{F}}(T_5) = Orb_{\mathfrak{F}}((2,4;3)) = \{(2,4;3), (5,1;3)\}$$
$$Orb_{\mathfrak{F}}(T_6) = Orb_{\mathfrak{F}}((3,1;4)) = \{(3,1;4), (0,4;4)\}$$
$$Orb_{\mathfrak{F}}(T_7) = Orb_{\mathfrak{F}}((3,2;5)) = \{(3,2;5), (0,5;5)\}$$
$$Orb_{\mathfrak{F}}(T_8) = Orb_{\mathfrak{F}}((3,3;0)) = \{(3,3;0), (0,0;0)\}$$
$$Orb_{\mathfrak{F}}(T_9) = Orb_{\mathfrak{F}}((4,0;4)) = \{(4,0;4), (1,3;4)\}$$
$$Orb_{\mathfrak{F}}(T_{10}) = Orb_{\mathfrak{F}}((5,3;2)) = \{(5,3;2), (2,0;2)\}$$

$$\text{Ent}(Q_1) = \bigcup_{T_i \in T \setminus \{T_1, T_{11}\}} Orb_{\mathfrak{F}}(T_i).$$

Let $q_1 = \text{Ent}(Q_1)$ be a partial Latin square, where;

$$q_1 = \begin{array}{|c|c|c|c|c|c|}
\hline
0 &   &   &   & 4 & 5 \\ \hline
  & 2 &   & 4 &   & 3 \\ \hline
  2 &   & 1 &   & 3 &   \\ \hline
  & 4 & 5 & 0 &   &   \\ \hline
4 &   & 3 &   & 2 &   \\ \hline
  & 3 &   & 2 &   & 1 \\ \hline
\end{array}$$

Observe that the partial Latin square q_1 is uniquely completable, hence applying the subgroup of Atop(K) generated by $\langle \theta_3 \rangle$ to the set of triples $T \setminus \{T_1, T_{11}\}$ will give a uniquely $\mathfrak{F}$-completable set. Notice that the removal of any $\mathfrak{F}$-orbit of Ent(Q_1) will generate a partial Latin square $q_1 = \text{Ent}(Q_1)$ that is not uniquely completable to K. This demonstrates that $\mathfrak{F}$-orbits of $T \setminus \{T_1, T_{11}\}$ under the autotopism θ_3 form an $\mathfrak{F}$-critical set. As the set is a minimal collection of shares that combine to generate the secret key K, it is an access level for the scheme.

2. Interesting Observations about Uniquely Completable Partial Latin Squares and the Applications of These Observations to the Example

The Applications of These Observations to the Example in [6], In this section, we will consider further substructures of Latin squares and demonstrate how the existence of these substructures within a Latin square L informs how the $\mathfrak{F}$-critical sets of L may be constructed.

Definition 3. *[9] A Latin subsquare of a Latin square is an $m \times m$ submatrix of (not necessarily adjacent) entries that is itself a Latin square. Note that a Latin subsquare has order at least 2.*

Definition 4. *[9] An intercalate of order 2 is a Latin subsquare of order 2.*

Example 2. *Observe that the four quadrants of the Latin square K given in the example in [6] form four Latin subsquares of order 3, which will form a set $S = \{S_{(0,0)}, S_{(0,3)}, S_{(3,0)}, S_{(3,3)}\}$, where $S_{(i,j)} = \{(i,j;k), (i,j+1;k+1), (i,j+2;k+2), (i+1,j;k+1), (i+1,j+1;k+2), (i+1,j+2;k), (i+2,j;k+2), (i+2,j+1;k), (i+2,j+2;k+1)\}$ for $i,j,k \in \{0,3\}$. There are also nine intercalates of the form $I_{(i,j)} = \{(i,j;k), (i+3,j;k+3), (i,j+3;k+3), (i+3,j+3;k)\}$ for $i,j,k \leq 2$ within K. The set of intercalates will be denoted $I = \{I_{(0,0)}, I_{(0,1)}, I_{(0,2)}, I_{(1,0)}, I_{(1,1)}, I_{(1,2)}, I_{(2,0)}, I_{2,1)}, I_{(2,2)}\}$.*

Lemma 1. *All Latin squares of order $n \geq 2$ contain critical sets.*

Proof. Let L be a Latin square of order $n \geq 2$. Removing the triple $(i,j;k)$ from L will generate a partial Latin square P in which the cell (i,j) is empty, but all other cells within P are non-empty. Hence, P is a uniquely completable to the Latin square L and $P \subset L$.

The empty partial Latin square P' of order $n \geq 2$ is not uniquely completable to any Latin square of order n.

Therefore, every Latin square L of order n contains a non-empty partial Latin square P that is uniquely completable to L and a partial Latin square that is not uniquely completable to L. Therefore, there exists a minimal partial Latin square P^* that is uniquely completable to L, such that every subset of P^* is not uniquely completable to L. Hence, every Latin square of order $n \geq 2$ contains a critical set. □

Corollary 1. *For each Latin subsquare Q of order $m \geq 2$ there exists a partial Latin square A such that A is not uniquely completable to Q.*

Proof. A Latin subsquare Q is a Latin square of order m within a Latin square of order n. By Lemma 1, as Q has order $m \geq 2$, it has a critical set and hence there will be some partial Latin square A such that A is not uniquely completable to Q. □

Lemma 2. *Let Q be a Latin subsquare of order $m \geq 2$ contained within a Latin square L and let A be a partial Latin square that is not uniquely completable to the Latin subsquare Q. If a partial Latin square P contains A and no other elements of $Ent(Q)$, then P will not be uniquely completable to L.*

Proof. By Corollary 1, every Latin subsquare Q of order m, where $|m| \geq 2$, contains a partial Latin square A, where A is not uniquely completable to Q. Note, when Q is an intercalate, A is the empty partial Latin square. Let P denote a partial Latin square, such that $P \subset L$. If a partial Latin square P contains A and no other triples in $Ent(Q)$, then the partial Latin square P will not force the entries of the Latin subsquare Q. As $Q \subset L$ and the triples of Q are not forced from the triples of P, then P is not uniquely completable to L. □

Although Lemma 2 does not imply that a partial Latin square P will always be uniquely completable to a Latin square L if it contains a critical set of each Latin subsquare

$Q \in L$, it does imply that if this condition is not met, then P will not be uniquely completable to L.

To relate this to $\mathfrak{F}$-critical sets in the example in [6]; if the $\mathfrak{F}$-orbits for some partial Latin square P do not intersect with the critical sets of each Latin subsquare within $S_{(i,j)}$, $I_{(i,j)} \in K$, then the partial Latin square P will not be an $\mathfrak{F}$-critical set of K. Example 3 details the more specific implications of Lemma 2 to the example in [6].

Example 3. *In [4], it was demonstrated that the critical sets of Latin squares of order 3 either consist of two triples $(i_1, j_1; k_1)$ and $(i_2, j_2; k_2)$, where $i_1 \neq i_2, j_1 \neq j_2$ and $k_1 \neq k_2$, or a critical set of a Latin square of order 3 consists of a set of three triples such that each pair of triples in this set share exactly one common ith, jth or kth component. The key observation here is that critical sets of Latin squares of order 3 must contain entries in at least two distinct rows, two distinct columns and the critical sets contain two sets of distinct symbols. By Lemma 2, a partial Latin square P is not uniquely completable to the Latin square K if it does not contain a critical set of each Latin subsquare in K. This implies that if a partial Latin square P does not contain an entry in at least two distinct rows and columns of each order 3 Latin subsquare $S_{i,j} \in K$, or if each of the Latin subsquare $S_{i,j}$ in P does not contain at least two distinct symbols, then P will not be uniquely completable to K.*

Furthermore, the Latin square K contains nine intercalates, each denoted by $I_{(i,j)}$ for $i,j \leq 2$. Since order 2 Latin squares have a critical set of size 1, if a partial Latin square does not contain at least one entry in each intercalate $I_{(i,j)} \in K$, then P will not be uniquely completable to K.

3. Interesting Observations about the Autotopisms $\theta_1, \theta_2, \theta_3$ and θ_4 in the Example

Interesting Observations about the Autotopisms $\theta_1, \theta_2, \theta_3$ and θ_4 in the Example in [6]. Each individual autotopism $\theta \subseteq \text{Atop}(L)$ for some Latin square L will act differently on the triples of L. The actions of individual autotopisms on a Latin square L is important in determining the structure of $\mathfrak{F}$-critical sets of L. It is therefore worth examining the actions of the individual autotopisms $\theta_1, \theta_2, \theta_3, \theta_4 \subseteq \text{Atop}(K)$, where K is the Latin square in example [6], to determine the structure of each $\mathfrak{F}$-critical set associated with each subgroup of autotopisms in the group $\text{Atop}(K)$.

Example 4. *The autotopisms θ_1 and θ_2 permute the elements of some Latin subsquare of order 3 $S_i \in S$ to two other triples within the same Latin subsquare $S_{(i,j)}$. Both θ_1 and θ_2 map each triple T in some intercalate $I_{(i,j)}$ to some intercalate $I_{(i',j')}$, where $I_{(i,j)} \neq I_{(i',j')}$.*

The autotopisms θ_3 and θ_4 permute the sets {0,3}, {1,4} and {2,5}. They map triples of an intercalate $I_{(i,j)}$ to another triple within the same intercalate, and map triples in a particular Latin subsquare $S_{(i,j)}$ of order three to some Latin subsquare $S_{(i',j')}$ of order three, where $i \neq i'$ and $j \neq j'$.

4. Discussion of Example

Ref [6]. Not all autotopisms listed in example [6] are members of the autotopism group $\text{Atop}(K)$. Further to this, there are some minor errors in the access levels listed in Table 1 in Section 1. Lemma 2 and the observations about the autotopisms discussed in Section 3, make it possible to modify to the example. Each amendment will be discussed in detail within this section.

4.1. Discussion Regarding the Autotopisms θ_1 and θ_2

Discussion Regarding the Autotopisms θ_1 and θ_2 in [6]. The first two modifications are changes to some of the autotopisms associated with the Latin square K in [6]. Two of the autotopisms, θ_1 and θ_2, are not associated with the Latin square K. By definition, applying an autotopism to a Latin square that it is associated with should generate another element of that Latin square. However, applying the autotopisms θ_1 and θ_2 to any of the 11 chosen shares from the set $\{T_1, ..., T_{11}\}$ does not generate another element of K. To demonstrate this, θ_1 and θ_2 are applied to the share T_1;

$$T_1 = (0, 4; 4) \implies \theta_1(T_1) = (1, 4; 3), \theta_2(T_1) = (0, 5; 3)$$

Observe, applying θ_1 and θ_2 to T_1 does not generate elements of the original Latin square, L. Hence, these autotopisms are not associated with Atop(K). It is believed that the intended autotopisms for θ_1 and θ_2 should be;

$$\theta_1 = ((012)(345), (0)(1)(2)(3)(4)(5), (012)(345))$$
$$\theta_2 = ((0)(1)(2)(3)(4)(5), (012)(345), (012)(345))$$

From this point in the communication, when θ_1 and θ_2 are referred to, they refer to the autotopisms θ_1 and θ_2 given above and not the autotopisms given in [6].

All subsequent suggested amendments focus on the access levels.

4.2. Discussion Regarding the Access Level for the Autotopisms in the Subgroup $\langle \theta_4 \rangle$

Discussion Regarding the Access Level for the Autotopisms in the Subgroup $\langle \theta_4 \rangle$ in [6]. The access level generated by the autotopism subgroup $\langle \theta_4 \rangle$ was mis-recorded in [6]. According to the example in [6], combining the subgroup of Atop(K), $\langle \theta_4 \rangle$, with all triples in the set $T \setminus \{T_9\}$ should generate a uniquely completable partial Latin square. However, combining $\langle \theta_4 \rangle$ with the stated triples generates the following $\mathfrak{F}$-orbits;

$$Orb_\mathfrak{F}(T_1) = Orb_\mathfrak{F}((0,4;4)) = \{(0,4;4),(0,1;1)\}$$
$$Orb_\mathfrak{F}(T_2) = Orb_\mathfrak{F}((1,1;2)) = \{(1,1;2),(1,4;5)\}$$
$$Orb_\mathfrak{F}(T_3) = Orb_\mathfrak{F}((1,5;3)) = \{(1,5;3),(1,2;0)\}$$
$$Orb_\mathfrak{F}(T_4) = Orb_\mathfrak{F}((2,2;1)) = \{(2,2;1),(2,5;4)\}$$
$$Orb_\mathfrak{F}(T_5) = Orb_\mathfrak{F}((0,4;4)) = \{(2,4;3),(2,1;0)\}$$
$$Orb_\mathfrak{F}(T_6) = Orb_\mathfrak{F}((3,1;4)) = \{(3,1;4),(3,4;1)\}$$
$$Orb_\mathfrak{F}(T_7) = Orb_\mathfrak{F}((3,1;4)) = \{(3,2;5),(3,5;2)\}$$
$$Orb_\mathfrak{F}(T_8) = Orb_\mathfrak{F}((3,3;0)) = \{(3,3;0),(3,0;3)\}$$
$$Orb_\mathfrak{F}(T_{10}) = Orb_\mathfrak{F}((5,3;2)) = \{(5,3;2),(5,0;5)\}$$
$$Orb_\mathfrak{F}(T_{11}) = Orb_\mathfrak{F}((5,5;1)) = \{(5,5;1),(5,2;4)\}$$

The union of these $\mathfrak{F}$-orbits gives the partial Latin square P_1, where;

$$P_1 = \begin{array}{|c|c|c|c|c|c|} \hline * & 1 & * & * & 4 & * \\ \hline * & 2 & 0 & * & 5 & 3 \\ \hline * & 0 & 1 & * & 3 & 4 \\ \hline 3 & 4 & 5 & 0 & 1 & 2 \\ \hline * & * & * & * & * & * \\ \hline 5 & * & 4 & 2 & * & 1 \\ \hline \end{array}$$

This partial Latin square P_1 is not uniquely completable as it only uniquely completes to the partial Latin square P_2, where;

$$P_2 = \begin{array}{|c|c|c|c|c|c|} \hline 0 & 1 & 2 & 3 & 4 & 5 \\ \hline * & 2 & 0 & * & 5 & 3 \\ \hline 2 & 0 & 1 & 5 & 3 & 4 \\ \hline 3 & 4 & 5 & 0 & 1 & 2 \\ \hline * & 5 & 3 & * & 2 & 0 \\ \hline 5 & 3 & 4 & 2 & 0 & 1 \\ \hline \end{array}$$

Since there are no entries in the intercalate $I_{(1,0)}$, by Lemma 2, P_2 is not uniquely completable to L. In order for the partial Latin square P_1 to be uniquely completable to L, the share T_9 needs to be included within this access level so that there is an entry in the intercalate $I_{(1,0)}$.

It is also worth noting that $\mathfrak{F}$-critical sets are supposed to be minimal. As T_1 and T_6 are both members of the intercalate $I_{(0,1)}$ and similarly T_4 and T_{11} both belong to the intercalate $I_{(2,2)}$, this set is not minimal. By removing one element of each set $\{T_1, T_6\}$ and $\{T_4, T_{11}\}$, the access level becomes an $\mathfrak{F}$-critical set comprising of nine triples from the set T and the autotopism θ_4; giving ten individual shares in total. An example of a viable $\mathfrak{F}$-critical set is to take the $\mathfrak{F}$-orbits of the triples $\{T_1, T_2, T_3, T_4, T_5, T_7, T_8, T_9, T_{10}\}$, where $\mathfrak{F}$ is the subgroup of Atop(K) generated by the autotopism θ_4.

4.3. Discussion Regarding the Access Level for the Autotopisms in the Subgroup $\langle \theta_3, \theta_4 \rangle$

Discussion Regarding the Access Level for the Autotopisms in the Subgroup $\langle \theta_3, \theta_4 \rangle$ in [6]. Access levels can also be generated by $\mathfrak{F}$-orbits, where $\mathfrak{F}$ is a subgroup of the Atop(K) generated by more than one autotopism. The first access level to be generated by a set of multiple autotopisms, is the access level generated by the $\mathfrak{F}$-orbits of the subgroup of autotopisms $\langle \theta_3, \theta_4 \rangle$. This subgroup consists of the following non-trivial autotopisms;

$$\theta_3 = ((03)(14)(25), (03)(14)(25), (0)(1)(2)(3)(4)(5))$$
$$\theta_4 = ((0)(1)(2)(3)(4)(5), (03)(14)(25), (03)(14)(25))$$
$$\theta_3\theta_4 = ((03)(14)(25), (0)(1)(2)(3)(4)(5), (03)(14)(25))$$

The example in [6] (see Table 1 in Section 1) suggests that applying this subgroup of Atop(K) to the set of triples $\{T_2, T_3, T_4, T_5, T_6, T_7, T_8, T_{10}\}$ will generate an $\mathfrak{F}$-critical set. However, when $\mathfrak{F}$ is the subgroup of Atop(K) generated by $\langle \theta_3, \theta_4 \rangle$, the $\mathfrak{F}$-orbits of the set of triples $\{T_2, T_3, T_4, T_5, T_6, T_7, T_8, T_{10}\}$ forms a partial Latin square that is not uniquely completable, as the $\mathfrak{F}$-orbits do not contain an entry in the intercalate $I_{(1,0)}$. As above, if the triple T_9 is included within the set of triples for this access level, then the resultant partial Latin square is uniquely completable to the Latin square K. However, adding T_9 to this set means that this access level consists of nine triples from the set T and both autotopisms θ_3 and θ_4. This gives a total of eleven shares. As previously shown, the $\mathfrak{F}$-orbits of the triples $\{T_2, T_3, T_4, T_5, T_6, T_7, T_8, T_9, T_{10}\}$ under the subgroup of Atop(K), $\langle \theta_4 \rangle$, form an $\mathfrak{F}$-critical set of size 10. Hence, the autotopisms $\langle \theta_3, \theta_4 \rangle$ will generate a uniquely $\mathfrak{F}$-completable set that is not minimal, and therefore not an $\mathfrak{F}$-critical set. Therefore, the autotopisms θ_3 and θ_4 cannot be used in combination to generate an access level for this scheme.

4.4. Discussion Regarding the Access Level for for the Autotopisms in the Subgroup $\langle \theta_2, \theta_3, \theta_4 \rangle$

Discussion Regarding the Access Level for for the Autotopisms in the Subgroup $\langle \theta_2, \theta_3, \theta_4 \rangle$ in [6]. This access level uses the subgroup of Atop(K) generated by $\langle \theta_2, \theta_3, \theta_4 \rangle$. As θ_2 is an autotopism based upon length 3 cycles and θ_3 and θ_4 are based upon length 2 cycles, this subgroup of Atop(K) consists of eleven non-trivial autotopisms, these autotopisms are;

$$\theta_2 = ((0)(1)(2)(3)(4)(5), (012)(345), (012)(345))$$
$$\theta_2\theta_2 = ((0)(1)(2)(3)(4)(5), (021)(354), (021)(354))$$
$$\theta_3 = ((03)(14)(25), (03)(14)(25), (0)(1)(2)(3)(4)(5))$$
$$\theta_4 = ((0)(1)(2)(3)(4)(5), (03)(14)(25), (03)(14)(25))$$
$$\theta_2\theta_3 = ((03)(14)(25), (042315), (012)(345))$$
$$\theta_2\theta_2\theta_3 = ((03)(14)(25), (051324), (021)(354))$$
$$\theta_2\theta_4 = ((0)(1)(2)(3)(4)(5), (042315), (042315))$$
$$\theta_2\theta_2\theta_4 = ((0)(1)(2)(3)(4)(5), (051324), (051324))$$
$$\theta_3\theta_4 = ((03)(14)(25), (0)(1)(2)(3)(4)(5), (03)(14)(25))$$
$$\theta_2\theta_3\theta_4 = ((03)(14)(25), (012)(345), (042315))$$
$$\theta_2\theta_2\theta_3\theta_4 = ((03)(14)(25), (021)(354), (051324))$$

The example in [6] suggests that, when $\mathfrak{F}$ is generated by $\langle \theta_2, \theta_3, \theta_4 \rangle$, the union of the $\mathfrak{F}$-orbits Orb$_\mathfrak{F}(T_1)$ and Orb$_\mathfrak{F}(T_2)$ should be uniquely $\mathfrak{F}$-completable to K. However, combining these $\mathfrak{F}$-orbits generates the partial Latin square P_3, where;

$$P_3 = \begin{array}{|c|c|c|c|c|c|}\hline 0 & 1 & 2 & 3 & 4 & 5 \\\hline 1 & 2 & 0 & 4 & 5 & 3 \\\hline * & * & * & * & * & * \\\hline 3 & 4 & 5 & 0 & 1 & 2 \\\hline 4 & 5 & 3 & 1 & 2 & 0 \\\hline * & * & * & * & * & * \\\hline \end{array}$$

As the intercalates $I_{(2,0)}$, $I_{(2,1)}$ and $I_{(2,2)}$ are missing from P_3, it is not uniquely completable under the autotopism θ_2. A triple present in any one of these intercalates will generate an $\mathfrak{F}$-orbit that spans all three intercalates under the subgroup of Atop(K) generated by $\langle \theta_2, \theta_3, \theta_4 \rangle$. Hence, to make this an access level, one triple from the set $\{T_4, T_5, T_{10}, T_{11}\}$ should be included in the set of triples.

There are multiple $\mathfrak{F}$-critical sets that may be formed using this subgroup of Atop(K). As discussed in Section 3, each autotopism within the autotopism group Atop(K) has a unique action. When multiple autotopisms are combined in an $\mathfrak{F}$-critical set, each autotopism generated by the union of any subgroup of autotopisms will also take on a unique action. Observe that in combination, the subgroup of Atop(K) generated by autotopisms $\langle \theta_3, \theta_4 \rangle$ takes a triple $T_i \in I_{(i,j)}$ and maps it to every other triple within the same intercalate. The autotopism subgroup generated by $\langle \theta_2 \rangle$ maps each $T_{i'} = (i', j'; k') \in S_{(i,j)}$ to all other triples in the i'th row of the Latin subsquare $S_{(i,j)}$. This means that the combined action of the autotopism subgroup generated by $\langle \theta_2, \theta_3, \theta_4 \rangle$ takes a triple $T_{i'} \in K$ and maps $T_{i'} = (i', j'; k')$ to all triples in i'th and $i' + 3$ mod 6 row of K. Hence, any $\mathfrak{F}$-critical set under the subgroup of autotopisms $\langle \theta_2, \theta_3, \theta_4 \rangle$ must contain 3 triples, with one triple in either the 0th or 3rd row, one triple in either the 1st or 4th row and finally one triple in either the 2nd or 5th row. This ensures that the $\mathfrak{F}$-orbits contain a critical set of each intercalate $I_{(i,j)}$ and each Latin subsquare $S_{(i,j)}$.

Therefore, exactly one entry must be chosen from each of the following three sets; $\{T_1, T_6, T_7, T_8\}$, $\{T_2, T_3, T_9\}$ and $\{T_4, T_5, T_{10}, T_{11}\}$, as each individual set contains all entries of the ith and $i + 3$th rows, where $i \leq 2$.

4.5. Discussion Regarding the Access Level for for the Autotopisms in the Subgroup $\langle \theta_1, \theta_2, \theta_4 \rangle$

Discussion Regarding the Access Level for for the Autotopisms in the Subgroup $\langle \theta_1, \theta_2, \theta_4 \rangle$ in [6]. This access level uses the subgroup of Atop(K) generated by $\langle \theta_1, \theta_2, \theta_4 \rangle$. As θ_1 and θ_2 are both autotopisms based upon length 3 cycles, and θ_4 is an autotopism based upon length 2 cycle; this subgroup of Atop(K) will consist of 17 non-trivial autotopisms. Example 4 states that autotopism θ_1 maps a triple $T_i \in S_{(i,j)}$, where $T_i = (i, j; k)$ to the other two triples in the ith row of the Latin subsquare $S_{(i,j)} \in S$, while the autotopism θ_2 maps each triple $T_i \in S_{(i,j)}$ to the other two triples in the jth column of the Latin subsquare $S_{(i,j)} \in S$ and the autotopism θ_4 maps a triple $T_i \in I_{(i,j)}$, where $I_{(i,j)} \in I$, to the triple $I_{(i,j+3)}$ mod 6. This means that the subgroup of autotopisms generated by θ_1, θ_2 and θ_4 will map a triple $T_i \in S_{(i,j)}$, for $S_{(i,j)} \in S$ to all other triples in the Latin subsquare $S_{(i,j)}$, as well as all triples in the Latin subsquare $S_{(i,j+3)}$ mod $6 \in S$.

The access level in the example in [6] suggests that this subgroup of Atop(K) should be combined with the triples $\{T_1, T_2\}$ and from here it should be possible to generate the Latin square L. However, when $\mathfrak{F}$ is generated by $\langle \theta_1, \theta_2, \theta_4 \rangle$, $\text{Orb}_{\mathfrak{F}}(T_1) \cup \text{Orb}_{\mathfrak{F}}(T_2)$ is the partial Latin square P_4, where:

$$P_4 = \begin{array}{|c|c|c|c|c|c|}\hline 0 & 1 & 2 & 3 & 4 & 5 \\\hline 1 & 2 & 0 & 4 & 5 & 3 \\\hline 2 & 0 & 1 & 5 & 3 & 4 \\\hline * & * & * & * & * & * \\\hline * & * & * & * & * & * \\\hline * & * & * & * & * & * \\\hline \end{array}$$

The entries of the Latin subsquares $S_{(3,0)}$ and $S_{(3,3)}$ are missing from the partial Latin square P_4, hence by Lemma 2, P_4 is not uniquely completable to K. To amend this access level, either T_1 or T_2 should be removed and replaced with a triple from the set $\{T_6, T_7, T_8, T_9, T_{10}, T_{11}\}$.

There are multiple pairs of $\mathfrak{F}$-orbits that constitute an $\mathfrak{F}$-critical set when $\mathfrak{F}$ is the subgroup of Atop(K) generated by $\langle \theta_1, \theta_2, \theta_4 \rangle$. As an $\mathfrak{F}$-orbit of a triple T_i under these autotopisms will span two adjacent Latin subsquares $S_{(i,j)}$ and $S_{(i,j+3)}$ mod 6, when $T_i \in S_{(i,j)}$ each $\mathfrak{F}$-orbit contains a critical set of each intercalate $I_{(i,j)} \in I$. Therefore, a second $\mathfrak{F}$-orbit is only required to ensure that the union of $\mathfrak{F}$-orbits contains a critical set of the Latin subsquares $S_{(i+3,j)}$ mod 6 and $S_{(i+3,j+3)}$ mod 6. Hence, any two triples $T_i, T_j \in T$, where $T_i \neq T_j$ will generate an $\mathfrak{F}$-critical set under the autotopisms θ_1, θ_2 and θ_4 providing that if T_i is a triple in some Latin subsquare $S_{(i,j)} \in S$, then the triple T_j is either in the Latin subsquare $S_{(i+3,j)}$ or the Latin subsquare $S_{(i+3,j+3)}$. All triples in the set $\{T_1, T_2, T_3, T_4, T_5\}$ belong either to the Latin subsquare $S_{(0,0)}$ or the Latin subsquare $S_{(0,3)}$, while triples in the set $\{T_6, T_7, T_8, T_9, T_{10}, T_{11}\}$ belong either to the Latin subsquare $S_{(3,0)}$ or the Latin subsquare $S_{(3,3)}$. Therefore, if $T_i \in \{T_1, T_2, T_3, T_4, T_5\}$ and $T_j \in \{T_6, T_7, T_8, T_9, T_{10}, T_{11}\}$ then the union of the $\mathfrak{F}$-orbits $\text{Orb}_\mathfrak{F}(T_i) \cup \text{Orb}_\mathfrak{F}(T_j)$ will be an $\mathfrak{F}$-critical set, when $\mathfrak{F}$ is generated by $\langle \theta_1, \theta_2, \theta_4 \rangle$.

4.6. Discussion Regarding the Access Level for the Autotopisms in the Subgroup $\langle \theta_1, \theta_3 \rangle$

Discussion Regarding the Access Level for the Autotopisms in the Subgroup $\langle \theta_1, \theta_3 \rangle$ in [6]. Whereas other access levels given in the example in [6] contain too little information, the access level specified for the subgroup of Atop(K) generated by $\langle \theta_1, \theta_3 \rangle$ gives too much information.

The subgroup $\langle \theta_1, \theta_3 \rangle$ consists of 5 non-trivial autotopisms, these are autotopisms denoted by; $\theta_1, \theta_1\theta_1, \theta_3, \theta_1\theta_3$ and $\theta_1\theta_1\theta_3$. The example suggests that the $\mathfrak{F}$-orbits, where $\mathfrak{F}$ is generated $\langle \theta_1, \theta_3 \rangle$, for the triples $\{T_2, T_3, T_4, T_6, T_9\}$ should be an $\mathfrak{F}$-critical set. However, the union $\mathfrak{F}$-orbits of these triples is the partial Latin square P_5, where;

$$P_5 = \begin{array}{|c|c|c|c|c|c|} \hline * & 1 & 2 & 3 & 4 & 5 \\ \hline * & 2 & 0 & 4 & 5 & 3 \\ \hline * & 0 & 1 & 5 & 3 & 4 \\ \hline 3 & 4 & 5 & * & 1 & 2 \\ \hline 4 & 5 & 3 & * & 2 & 0 \\ \hline 5 & 3 & 4 & * & 0 & 1 \\ \hline \end{array}$$

Observe that P_5 is uniquely completable to L, however, access levels are supposed to provide the minimal amount of information required to generate the original key. Note that if either one of the shares T_3 or T_6 were to be removed from this access level, then one is still able to generate a uniquely $\mathfrak{F}$-completable partial Latin square, hence the specified set of triples is not an $\mathfrak{F}$-critical set when $\mathfrak{F}$ is generated by $\langle \theta_1, \theta_3 \rangle$. To amend this, each access level should be defined in such a way that only one triple from the set $\{T_3, T_6\}$ is included.

4.7. Summary of Findings

The above subsections discuss amendments to particular errors in the example in [6].

Following this, it is possible to generalise sets of triples of T that can be combined with each possible subgroup of the autotopism group Atop(K) generated by some collection of the autotopisms $\theta_1, \theta_2, \theta_3$ and θ_4. Using the results discussed in Sections 2 and 3, it is possible to generalise combinations of triples that form $\mathfrak{F}$-critical sets under the subgroups of Atop(K) defined by the autotopisms $\theta_1, \theta_2, \theta_3$ and θ_4. Table A1 in Appendix A details the combinations of triples that will generate a $\mathfrak{F}$-critical set when combined with the autotopisms stated in the same row of the table. Reasoning behind the constructions of certain $\mathfrak{F}$-critical sets in Table A1 in Appendix A is outlined in Section 4. Table A2 in

Appendix A provides an example of an $\mathfrak{F}$-critical set for each subgroup of autotopisms generated by elements of the set $\{\theta_1, \theta_2, \theta_3, \theta_4\}$.

5. Conclusions

In this correspondence, minor errors in the original definitions of the $\mathfrak{F}$-critical sets detailed within the paper [6] are amended. The importance of Lemma 2 in determining both critical sets and $\mathfrak{F}$-critical sets within a Latin square is highlighted.

Lemma 2 states that if a partial Latin square P does not contain a critical set for each Latin subsquare $Q \in L$, where L is a Latin square, P is not be uniquely completable to L. Further, let a partial Latin square $P \subset L$, where L is a Latin square and let $\mathfrak{F}$ denote a subgroup of the autotopism group of L. If the $\mathfrak{F}$-orbits of a partial Latin square P, do not contain a critical set for each Latin subsquare $Q \in L$, then the combination of these triples and autotopisms do not form an $\mathfrak{F}$-critical set. Lemma 2 can therefore be used to eliminate several partial Latin squares that are not $\mathfrak{F}$-critical sets of a Latin square L.

By considering $\mathfrak{F}$-orbits that satisfy Lemma 2, $\mathfrak{F}$-critical sets of a Latin square K can be generated, where:

$$K = \begin{array}{|c|c|c|c|c|c|} \hline 0 & 1 & 2 & 3 & 4 & 5 \\ \hline 1 & 2 & 0 & 4 & 5 & 3 \\ \hline 2 & 0 & 1 & 5 & 3 & 4 \\ \hline 3 & 4 & 5 & 0 & 1 & 2 \\ \hline 4 & 5 & 3 & 1 & 2 & 0 \\ \hline 5 & 3 & 4 & 2 & 0 & 1 \\ \hline \end{array}$$

The $\mathfrak{F}$-critical sets detailed within the correspondence use subgroups of the autotopism group of K to generate all possible combinations of the autotopisms $\theta_1, \theta_2, \theta_3$ and θ_4, where;

$\theta_1 = ((012)(345), (0)(1)(2)(3)(4)(5), (012)(345))$
$\theta_2 = ((0)(1)(2)(3)(4)(5), (012)(345), (012)(345))$
$\theta_3 = ((03)(14)(25), (03)(14)(25), (0)(1)(2)(3)(4)(5))$
$\theta_4 = ((0)(1)(2)(3)(4)(5), (03)(14)(25), (03)(14)(25))$

The $\mathfrak{F}$-critical sets generated by the $\mathfrak{F}$-orbits of the triples (0,4;4),(1,1;2),(1,5;3),(2,2;1), (2,4;3),(3,1;4),(3,2;5), (3,3;0),(4,0;4),(5,3;2),(5,5;1) $\subseteq$ Ent(K) are listed in Table A1 of Appendix A. For comparison, the suggested $\mathfrak{F}$-critical sets for the example in [6] are listed in Table 1 in Section 1.

If a partial Latin square P satisfies Lemma 2, this does not guarantee that P is uniquely completable to a Latin square L; however, Lemma 2 does provide a necessary condition, that if not met, means a partial Latin square P is not uniquely completable. Lemma 2 can then be applied to all partial Latin squares P of order n. In other words, by looking at all Latin subsquares of order m within a Latin square L of order n, where $m < n$, one can ascertain the critical sets of each Latin subsquare Q within L. Each partial Latin square P that is uniquely completable to L then contains some combination of critical sets of Latin subsquares of L, hence by determining the Latin subsquares of L, the problem of generating the critical sets of L is reduced in size. This approach may similarly be applied to θ-critical sets or $\mathfrak{F}$-critical sets.

Further work is needed to determine necessary conditions for ensuring that a partial Latin square P is a critical set of a Latin square L, but by the application of Lemma 2, it may be possible for larger Latin squares of order n to be analysed.

Author Contributions: This short communication was written as part of an MMath research project at the University of South Wales undertaken by L.M.J. and supervised by S.P. All authors have read and agreed to the published version of the manuscript.

Funding: This research received no external funding.

Institutional Review Board Statement: Not applicable.

Informed Consent Statement: Not applicable.

Data Availability Statement: Not applicable.

Acknowledgments: We would like to thank Raul Falcón for his advice about the original example, as well as his help with proof reading.

Conflicts of Interest: The authors declare no conflict of interest.

Appendix A

Table A1 details the newly defined access levels, generated by results in this communication. Note that m the number of individual shares in each access level.

Observe, that the access level defined by the autotopisms $\langle \theta_3, \theta_4 \rangle$ has been removed from Table A1, as it is shown that these autotopisms cannot form an $\mathfrak{F}$-critical set.

Table A2 gives specific examples of $\mathfrak{F}$-critical sets for the Latin square K under the autotopisms $\{\theta_1, \theta_2, \theta_3, \theta_4\}$. Each $\mathfrak{F}$-critical set is constructed in accordance with the specifications of Table A1.

Table A1. Redefined access levels based upon results of this communication.

m	Permutations	Triples of P
11	-	T
10	$\langle \theta_3 \rangle$	T exluding one entry from each of the sets $\{T_1,T_6\}$ and $\{T_4,T_{11}\}$
10	$\langle \theta_4 \rangle$	T exluding one entry from each of the sets $\{T_1,T_6\}$ and $\{T_4,T_{11}\}$
9	$\langle \theta_1 \rangle$	T excluding one entry from each of the sets $\{T_1,T_5\}$, $\{T_8,T_{10}\}$ and $\{T_6,T_7,T_9\}$
9	$\langle \theta_2 \rangle$	T excluding one entry from each of the sets $\{T_6,T_7\}$, $\{T_{10},T_{11}\}$ and $\{T_1,T_3,T_5\}$
7	$\langle \theta_2, \theta_4 \rangle$	Exactly one entry from five out of the following six sets; $\{T_1\},\{T_2,T_3\},\{T_4,T_5\}, \{T_6,T_7,T_8\},\{T_9\},\{T_{10},T_{11}\}$
6	$\langle \theta_1, \theta_3 \rangle$	To ensure that two distinct columns of $S_{(0,3)}$ and $S_{(3,0)}$ contain two entries, one triple should be selected from two of the following three sets $\{T_1, T_5, T_6\}, \{T_3, T_7\}, \{T_9\}$, to ensure two distinct columns of $S_{(0,0)}$ and $S_{(3,3)}$ contain entries, two of the three sets; $\{T_2\}, \{T_4, T_{11}\}, \{T_8, T_{10}\}$ should be selected. To ensure each intercalate contains at least one entry, at least one element from the following sets should be chosen; $\{T_1, T_2, T_5, T_6\}, \{T_3, T_4, T_7, T_{11}\}, \{T_8, T_9, T_{10}\}$
6	$\langle \theta_1, \theta_2 \rangle$	Exactly one entry should be chosen from each of the sets $\{T_1,T_3,T_5\}, \{T_2,T_4\}, \{T_6,T_7,T_9\}$ and $\{T_8,T_{10},T_{11}\}$.
6	$\langle \theta_1, \theta_4 \rangle$	To ensure that two distinct columns of $S_{(0,0)}$ and $S_{(0,3)}$ contain entries, one triple should be selected from both of the following sets $\{T_1, T_2, T_5\}, \{T_3, T_4\}$, to ensure two distinct columns of $S_{(0,0)}$ and $S_{(3,3)}$ contain entries, one entry from two of the sets; $\{T_6\}, \{T_7, T_{11}\}, \{T_8, T_9, T_{10}\}$ should be selected. To ensure each intercalate contains at least one entry, at least one element from the following sets should be chosen; $\{T_1, T_2, T_5, T_6\}, \{T_3, T_4, T_7, T_{11}\}, \{T_8, T_9, T_{10}\}$
6	$\langle \theta_2, \theta_3 \rangle$	To ensure that two distinct columns of $S_{(0,3)}$ and $S_{(3,0)}$ contain entries, one triple should be selected from two of the following three sets $\{T_1,T_6,T_7\} \{T_3,T_9\}, \{T_5\}$, to ensure two distinct columns of $S_{(0,0)}$ and $S_{(3,3)}$ contain entries, two of the three sets; $\{T_2\} \{T_4,T_{10},T_{11}\}, \{T_8\}$ should be selected. To ensure each intercalate contains at least one entry, at least one element from the following sets should be chosen; $\{T_1, T_6, T_7, T_8\}, \{T_2, T_3, T_9\}, \{T_4, T_5, T_{10}, T_{11}\}$
6	$\langle \theta_1, \theta_3, \theta_4 \rangle$	One entry from each of the sets $\{T_1,T_2,T_5,T_6\}, \{T_3,T_4,T_7,T_{11}\}$ and $\{T_8,T_9,T_{10}\}$
6	$\langle \theta_2, \theta_3, \theta_4 \rangle$	One entry from each of the sets $\{T_1,T_6,T_7,T_8\}, \{T_2,T_3,T_9\}$ and $\{T_4,T_5,T_{10},T_{11}\}$
5	$\langle \theta_1, \theta_2, \theta_3 \rangle$	One entry from each of the sets $\{T_1,T_3,T_5,T_6,T_7,T_9\}$ and $\{T_2,T_4,T_8,T_{10},T_{11}\}$
5	$\langle \theta_1, \theta_2, \theta_4 \rangle$	One entry from each of the sets $\{T_1,T_2,T_3,T_4,T_5\}$ and $\{T_6,T_7,T_8,T_9,T_{10},T_{11}\}$
5	$\langle \theta_1, \theta_2, \theta_3, \theta_4 \rangle$	One share of T

Table A2. Examples of access levels as outlined in Table A1.

m	Permutations	Triples of P	m	Permutations	Triples of P
11	-	T	6	$\langle\theta_1,\theta_4\rangle$	$\{T_1,T_4,T_6,T_{10}\}$
10	$\langle\theta_3\rangle$	$T\setminus\{T_1,T_4\}$	6	$\langle\theta_2,\theta_3\rangle$	$\{T_1,T_2,T_9,T_{10}\}$
10	$\langle\theta_4\rangle$	$T\setminus\{T_6,T_{11}\}$	6	$\langle\theta_1,\theta_3,\theta_4\rangle$	$\{T_1,T_3,T_{10}\}$
9	$\langle\theta_1\rangle$	$T\setminus\{T_5,T_7,T_{10}\}$	6	$\langle\theta_2,\theta_3,\theta_4\rangle$	$\{T_1,T_2,T_4\}$
9	$\langle\theta_2\rangle$	$T\setminus\{T_5,T_6,T_{11}\}$	5	$\langle\theta_1,\theta_2,\theta_3\rangle$	$\{T_1,T_2\}$
7	$\langle\theta_2,\theta_4\rangle$	$\{T_1,T_2,T_4,T_6,T_9\}$	5	$\langle\theta_1,\theta_2,\theta_4\rangle$	$\{T_1,T_6\}$
6	$\langle\theta_1,\theta_3\rangle$	$\{T_1,T_3,T_4,T_8\}$	5	$\langle\theta_1,\theta_2,\theta_3,\theta_4\rangle$	$\{T_7\}$
6	$\langle\theta_1,\theta_2\rangle$	$\{T_1,T_2,T_6,T_8\}$			

References

1. Laywine, C.F.; Mullen, G.L. *Discrete Mathematics Using Latin Squares*; Wiley-Interscience: New York, NY, USA, 1998.
2. Dénes, J.; Keedwell, A.D. *Latin Squares and Their Applications*; English Universities Press Limited Ltd.: London, UK, 1974.
3. Burton, B.A. Completion of Partial Latin Squares. Ph.D. Thesis, University of Queensland, Brisbane, Australia, 1996.
4. Falcón, R.M.; Johnson, L.; Perkins, S. A census of critical sets based on non-trivial autotopisms of Latin squares of order up to five. *AIMS Math.* **2020**, *6*, 261–295. [CrossRef]
5. Olsson, C. Discreet Discrete Mathematics: Secret Communication Using Latin Squares and Quasigroups. Independent Bachelor Thesis, Umeå University, Umeå, Sweden, 2017.
6. Falcón, R. Latin squares associated to principal autotopisms of long cycles. Applications in cryptography. In *Proceedings of Transgressive Computing 2006: A Conference in Honor of Jean Della Dora*; Universidad de Granada: Granada, Spain, 2006; pp. 213–230.
7. Piper, F.; Murphy, S. *Cryptography A Very Short Introduction*; Oxford University Press Inc.: New York, NY, USA, 2002.
8. Cooper, J.; Donovan, D.; Seberry, J. Secret Sharing Schemes Arising From Latin Squares. *Bull. ICA* **1994**, *12*, 33–43.
9. Wanless, I.M. Latin squares with one subsquare. *J. Comb. Des.* **2001**, *9*, 128–146. [CrossRef]

Article

Self-Orthogonal Codes Constructed from Posets and Their Applications in Quantum Communication

Yansheng Wu [1,2] and Yoonjin Lee [2,*]

1 School of Computer Science, Nanjing University of Posts and Telecommunications, Nanjing 210023, China; wysasd@163.com
2 Department of Mathematics, Ewha Womans University, Seoul 03760, Korea
* Correspondence: yoonjinl@ewha.ac.kr

Received: 3 August 2020; Accepted: 31 August 2020 ; Published: 3 September 2020

Abstract: It is an important issue to search for self-orthogonal codes for construction of quantum codes by *CSS construction* (Calderbank-Sho-Steane codes); in quantum error correction, *CSS codes* are a special type of stabilizer codes constructed from classical codes with some special properties, and the CSS construction of quantum codes is a well-known construction. First, we employ hierarchical posets with two levels for construction of binary linear codes. Second, we find some necessary and sufficient conditions for these linear codes constructed using posets to be self-orthogonal, and we use these self-orthogonal codes for obtaining binary quantum codes. Finally, we obtain four infinite families of binary quantum codes for which the minimum distances are three or four by CSS construction, which include binary quantum Hamming codes with length $n \geq 7$. We also find some (almost) "optimal" quantum codes according to the current database of Grassl. Furthermore, we explicitly determine the weight distributions of these linear codes constructed using posets, and we present two infinite families of some optimal binary linear codes with respect to the Griesmer bound and a class of binary Hamming codes.

Keywords: binary linear code; poset; weight distribution; self-orthogonal code; quantum code

MSC: 94B05; 81P70

1. Introduction

Quantum error-correcting codes have attracted wide attention in recent years due to their applications in quantum communications and quantum computations [1–3]. In quantum error correction, *CSS codes* (Calderbank-Sho-Steane) are a special type of stabilizer codes constructed from classical codes with some special properties, and the *CSS construction* of quantum codes is a well-known construction. As we can see from the CSS construction of quantum codes [1,3], self-orthogonal codes have been used for construction of quantum codes. Moreover, for construction of quantum codes, there have been some developments on non-stabilizer codes [4] and nonadditive quantum codes such as permutation-invariant quantum codes [5–8]; permutation-invariant quantum codes are constructed using the generator function method [5,6].

Recently, some optimal and minimal binary linear codes were constructed using simplicial complexes by Hyun et al. [9,10]. Then, Wu et al. [11,12] applied simplicial complexes to construct few-weight linear codes over $\mathbb{F}_p + u\mathbb{F}_p$ with $u^2 = 0$. Afterwards, the construction method was extended using arbitrary posets [13], and they presented some optimal and minimal binary linear codes not satisfying the condition of Ashikhmin–Barg [14]. Most recently, Wu and Lee [15] first used the difference of simplicial complexes for construction of binary linear complementary dual codes and binary self-orthogonal codes.

Note that, especially, anti-chains correspond to simplicial complexes. Inspired by the works mentioned as above, we focus on constructing binary self-orthogonal codes with new parameters and quantum codes using self-orthogonal codes. The main contributions of our paper are the following:

(1) We employ hierarchical posets with two levels for generating binary linear codes, and we explicitly determine the weight distributions of these codes (Theorem 1).

(2) We present some optimal binary linear codes (Corollary 1), and we find some necessary and sufficient conditions for the binary linear codes constructed from posets to be self-orthogonal (Theorem 3).

(3) We obtain four infinite families of binary quantum codes for which the minimum distances are three or four; this is achieved by construction of binary self-orthogonal codes (Theorem 4). We also find some (almost) optimal quantum codes; their optimality is based on the current database of Grassl.

(4) Furthermore, we obtain infinite families of binary quantum codes using these self-orthogonal codes, which include all binary quantum Hamming codes with length $n \geq 7$; some binary quantum codes with minimum distance three or four are obtained by using Theorem 4, and we confirm the optimality of the codes in the tables according to the database of Grassl [16].

As final remarks, we point out that all binary quantum Hamming codes for which the length is $n \geq 7$ (including the Steane code) are special cases of an infinite family of the binary quantum Hamming codes, which is one of the four infinite families of quantum codes in this paper (See Remark 2 for more details). Furthermore, in [17,18], the authors constructed many interesting binary quantum codes with a minimum distance of three or four. There are significant differences between our results and the results in [17,18]; in Remark 4, we compare our results with the results in [17,18].

The rest of this paper is organized as follows. In Section 2, we introduce some basic concepts and notations on hierarchical posets with two levels and the CSS construction of quantum codes. In Section 3, we determine the weight distributions of binary linear codes associated with order ideals in hierarchical posets with two levels, and we also discuss the minimum distances of their dual codes and find some optimal binary linear codes. In Section 4, we obtain some binary self-orthogonal codes, and we find four infinite families of binary quantum codes and some (almost) optimal binary quantum codes. Finally, we finish this paper with some remarks in Section 4 and a conclusion in Section 5.

2. Preliminaries

Let $\mathbb{F}_2$ be the finite field of order two. For positive integers $n, k,$ and d, an $[n, k, d]$ linear code $\mathcal{C}$ over $\mathbb{F}_2$ is just a k-dimensional subspace of $\mathbb{F}_2^n$ with the minimum Hamming distance d. The number of codewords in a linear code $\mathcal{C}$ with Hamming weight i is denoted by A_i. Then, the weight enumerator of the code $\mathcal{C}$ is defined by $1 + A_1 z + A_2 z^2 + \cdots + A_n z^n$. The sequence $(1, A_1, A_2, \ldots, A_n)$ is called the *weight distribution* of the linear code $\mathcal{C}$. We say that a code $\mathcal{C}$ is *t-weight* if the number of nonzero A_is in the sequence $(A_1, A_2, \ldots, A_n)$ is equal to t. We say that a linear code is *distance-optimal* if it has the highest minimum distance with a prescribed length and dimension. An $[n, k, d]$ linear code is called *almost optimal* if the code $[n, k, d+1]$ is optimal [19] (Section 2). For an $[n, k, d]$ binary linear code, the *Griesmer bound* (see [20]) could be stated as follows:

$$n \geq \sum_{i=0}^{k-1} \left\lceil \frac{d}{2^i} \right\rceil,$$

where $\lceil x \rceil$ is the ceiling function.

For a vector $\mathbf{v} \in \mathbb{F}_2^n$, the support $\mathrm{supp}(\mathbf{v})$ of $\mathbf{v}$ is defined by the set of nonzero coordinate positions. The Hamming weight $\mathrm{wt}(\mathbf{v})$ of $\mathbf{v} \in \mathbb{F}_2^n$ is defined by the cardinality of $\mathrm{supp}(\mathbf{v})$. Let $[n] = \{1, \ldots, n\}$ and $2^{[n]}$ denote the power set of $[n]$. There is a bijection between $\mathbb{F}_2^n$ and $2^{[n]}$, defined by $\mathbf{v} \mapsto \mathrm{supp}(\mathbf{v})$. In this paper, we always identify a vector in $\mathbb{F}_2^n$ with its support. For two sets A and B, the cardinality of A is denoted by $|A|$ and the set $\{x : x \in A \text{ and } x \notin B\}$ is denoted by $A \backslash B$.

2.1. Generic Construction of Linear Codes

Let D be a subset of $\mathbb{F}_q^*$, where q is a power of a prime number p. A linear code $\mathcal{C}_D$ of length $|D|$ over the finite field $\mathbb{F}_p$ is defined by

$$\mathcal{C}_D = \{c_D(\beta) = (\mathrm{Tr}(\beta\alpha))_{\alpha \in D} : \beta \in \mathbb{F}_q\},$$

where Tr is the trace function from $\mathbb{F}_q$ to $\mathbb{F}_p$. The code $\mathcal{C}_D$ is called a *trace code* over $\mathbb{F}_p$, and the set D is called the *defining set* of $\mathcal{C}_D$. This generic construction was first introduced by Ding et al. [21,22].

Zhou et al. [23] reconsidered the generic construction of linear codes as follows. Let $D = \{\mathbf{g_1}, \ldots, \mathbf{g_n}\} \subseteq \mathbb{F}_p^m$. We give a linear code $\mathcal{C}_D$ of length n over $\mathbb{F}_p$ as follows:

$$\mathcal{C}_D = \{c_{\mathbf{u}} = (\mathbf{u} \cdot \mathbf{g_1}, \mathbf{u} \cdot \mathbf{g_2}, \ldots, \mathbf{u} \cdot \mathbf{g_n}) : \mathbf{u} \in \mathbb{F}_p^m\}, \tag{1}$$

where $x \cdot y$ denotes the Euclidean inner product of $\mathbf{x} = (x_1, \ldots, x_m)$ and $\mathbf{y} = (y_1, \ldots, y_m)$ in $\mathbb{F}_p^m$. From the defining set D, we have the following $m \times n$ matrix:

$$G = [\mathbf{g_1}^T \mathbf{g_2}^T \cdots \mathbf{g_n}^T], \tag{2}$$

where T denotes the transpose.

Let $\mathcal{C}$ be an $[n,k]$ linear code over $\mathbb{F}_p$. Then, the dual $\mathcal{C}^\perp$ of the code $\mathcal{C}$ is defined by $\mathcal{C}^\perp = \{\mathbf{w} \in \mathbb{F}_p^n : \mathbf{w} \cdot \mathbf{c} = 0 \text{ for all } \mathbf{c} \in \mathcal{C}\}$. If $\mathcal{C} \subseteq \mathcal{C}^\perp$, then $\mathcal{C}$ is called a *self-orthogonal* code. If $\mathcal{C}^\perp \subseteq \mathcal{C}$, then $\mathcal{C}$ is called a *dual-containing* code.

There is a simple characterization of those linear codes defined in Equation (1) in terms of their self-orthogonality as follows:

Lemma 1 ([23] (Corollary 16)). *Let $\mathcal{C}_D$ be the linear code in Equation (1). Then, $\mathcal{C}_D$ is self-orthogonal if and only if $GG^T = 0$, where the matrix G is given in Equation (2).*

2.2. Generating Functions and Hierarchical Posets with Two Levels

A set $\mathbb{P} = ([n], \preceq)$ is called a *partially ordered set* (abbreviated as a poset) if there is a partial order relation on $[n]$: for all $i, j, k \in [n]$, we have that (i) $i \preceq i$; (ii) $i \preceq j$ and $j \preceq i$ imply $i = j$; and (iii) $i \preceq j$ and $j \preceq k$ imply $i \preceq k$.

Let $\mathbb{P} = ([n], \preceq)$ be a poset. An *order ideal* I in $\mathbb{P}$ is exactly a nonempty subset and if $j \in I$ and $i \preceq j$ imply $i \in I$. For a given subset S of $\mathbb{P}$, $\langle S \rangle$ denotes the smallest order ideal of $\mathbb{P}$ containing S. For an order ideal I of $\mathbb{P}$, the set of order ideals of $\mathbb{P}$ which is contained in I is denoted by $I(\mathbb{P})$.

Let X be a collection of $2^{[n]}$. Chang and Hyun [9] defined the generating function

$$\mathcal{H}_X(x_1, x_2, \ldots, x_n) = \sum_{\mathbf{u} \in X} \prod_{i=1}^n x_i^{u_i} \in \mathbb{Z}[x_1, x_2, \ldots, x_n],$$

where $\mathbf{u} = (u_1, u_2, \ldots, u_n) \in \mathbb{F}_2^n$ and where $\mathbb{Z}$ is the ring of integers.

Example 1. *Let $X = \{(1,0,0), (1,1,0), (0,0,1)\}$ be a subset of $\mathbb{F}_2^3$. Then, $\mathcal{H}_X(x_1, x_2, x_3) = x_1 + x_1 x_2 + x_3$.*

Let m and n be positive integers with $m \leq n$. In [13], $\mathbb{H}(m,n) = ([n], \preceq)$ is a hierarchical poset with two levels if $[n]$ is the disjoint union of two incomparable subsets $U = \{1, \ldots, m\}$ and $V = \{m+1, \ldots, n\}$ and $i \prec j$ whenever $i \in U$ and $j \in V$. Its Hasse diagram is given in Figure 1. $\mathbb{H}(m,m)$ is considered an anti-chain.

Lemma 2 ([13]). *Every order ideal of $\mathbb{H}(m,n)$ can be expressed by $A \cup B$, where $A \subseteq [m]$ and $B \subseteq [n] \setminus [m]$ and where one of the following holds: (i) $B = \emptyset$ or (ii) $B \neq \emptyset$ and $A = [m]$.*

Lemma 3 ([13]). *Let $I = A \cup B$ be an order ideal of $\mathbb{P} = \mathbb{H}(m,n)$, where $A \subseteq [m]$ and $B \subseteq [n] \setminus [m]$.*
(1) *If $B = \emptyset$, then*

$$\mathcal{H}_{I(\mathbb{P})}(x_1, x_2 \ldots, x_n) = \sum_{\mathbf{u} \in I(\mathbb{P})} \prod_{i=1}^{n} x_i^{u_i} = \prod_{i \in A}(1 + x_i).$$

In particular, we have that $|I(\mathbb{P})| = 2^{|A|}$.
(2) *If $B \neq \emptyset$, then*

$$\mathcal{H}_{I(\mathbb{P})}(x_1, x_2 \ldots, x_n) = \prod_{i \in [m]}(1 + x_i) + \prod_{i \in [m]} x_i (\prod_{j \in B}(1 + x_j) - 1).$$

In particular, we have that $|I(\mathbb{P})| = 2^m + 2^{|B|} - 1$.

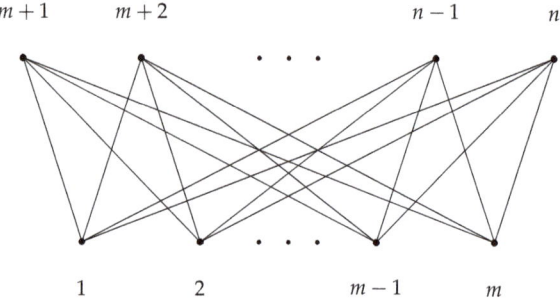

Figure 1. $\mathbb{H}(m,n)$.

2.3. Quantum Codes and CSS Construction

A q-ary quantum code Q with cardinality K and length n is exactly a K-dimensional subspace of the q^n-dimensional Hilbert space $(\mathbb{C}^q)^{\otimes n} \cong \mathbb{C}^{q^n}$. Let $k = \log_q(K)$. In the following, we always use the notation $[[n, k, d]]_q$ to denote a q-ary quantum code which has length n, cardinality q^k, and minimum distance d. For a given $[[n, k, d]]_q$ quantum code, it can detect any $d - 1$ quantum errors and can correct any $\lfloor \frac{d-1}{2} \rfloor$ quantum errors. In the research of quantum coding theory, one of the main subjects is to construct quantum codes with the best possible minimum distance.

In recent years, there has been active research done on construction of quantum codes using classical codes; for instance, refer to [24–40]. Many permutation-invariant quantum codes have been constructed from generating functions [5,6] and from the null-space of matrices [7].

An important result on constructing quantum error-correcting codes via classical linear codes over finite fields is presented by Robert Calderbank, Peter Shor, and Andrew Steane, which is well-known as the CSS construction. The construction can be stated as follows.

Lemma 4 ([3], CSS Construction). *Let C_1 and C_2 be $[n, k_1, d_1]$ and $[n, k_2, d_2]$ q-ary linear codes, respectively, with $C_2 \subseteq C_1$. Furthermore, let $d = \min\{d_1, d_2\}$. Then, there exists a quantum error-correcting code with parameters $[[n, k_1 + k_2 - n, d]]_q$. Moreover, if $C_1^{\perp} \subseteq C_1$, then there exists a quantum error-correcting code with parameters $[[n, 2k_1 - n, d_1]]_q$.*

3. Weight Distributions of Binary Linear Codes

In this section, we determine the weight distribution of the code in Equation (1), which is involved with hierarchical posets of two levels.

Assume that $\mathbb{P}$ is a hierarchical poset $\mathbb{H}(m,n)$ with two levels (which was introduced in Section 2) and $D = (I_1(\mathbb{P})) \setminus (I_2(\mathbb{P}))$, where I_1 and I_2 are two distinct order ideals of $\mathbb{P}$. Recall that D can be viewed as a subset of $\mathbb{F}_2^n$. We define a binary linear code associated with D as follows:

$$\mathcal{C}_D = \{c_{D,\mathbf{u}} = (\mathbf{u} \cdot \mathbf{x})_{\mathbf{x} \in D} : \mathbf{u} \in \mathbb{F}_2^n\}. \tag{3}$$

Then, the length of the code $\mathcal{C}_D$ is $|D|$ and its dimension is at most n. The Hamming weight of the codeword $c_{D,\mathbf{u}}$ of $\mathcal{C}_D$ is given by

$$\begin{aligned}
\mathrm{wt}(c_{D,\mathbf{u}}) &= |D| - \frac{1}{2} \sum_{y \in \mathbb{F}_2} \sum_{\mathbf{x} \in D} (-1)^{(\mathbf{u}\cdot\mathbf{x})y} = \frac{|D|}{2} - \frac{1}{2} \sum_{\mathbf{x} \in D} (-1)^{(\mathbf{u}\cdot\mathbf{x})} \\
&= \frac{|D|}{2} - \frac{1}{2} \sum_{\mathbf{x} \in (I_1(\mathbb{P})) \setminus (I_2(\mathbb{P}))} (-1)^{u_1 x_1} (-1)^{u_2 x_2} \cdots (-1)^{u_n x_n} \\
&= \frac{|D|}{2} - \frac{1}{2} \mathcal{H}_{I_1(\mathbb{P})}((-1)^{u_1}, \ldots, (-1)^{u_n}) + \frac{1}{2} \mathcal{H}_{I_2(\mathbb{P})}((-1)^{u_1}, \ldots, (-1)^{u_n}).
\end{aligned} \tag{4}$$

In general, it is hard to compute the value in Equation (4). However, when both I_1 and I_2 are generated by a single element, we obtain the following theorem.

Theorem 1. *Let $\mathbb{H}(m,n)$ be a hierarchical poset with two levels. Let $I_1 = A_1 \cup B_1$ and $I_2 = A_2 \cup B_2$ be two distinct order ideals of $\mathbb{H}(m,n)$, where $A_i \subseteq [m]$, $B_i \subseteq [n] \setminus [m]$, $i = 1, 2$, and $I_2 \subset I_1$. Let $D = (I_1(\mathbb{P})) \setminus (I_2(\mathbb{P}))$.*

(1) If $B_1 = \emptyset$, then the code $\mathcal{C}_D$ has parameters $[2^{|A_1|} - 2^{|A_2|}, |A_1|]$ and its weight distribution is given in Table 1.

Table 1. Weight distribution of the code in Theorem 1 (1).

Weight	Frequency
0	1
$2^{|A_1|-1}$	$2^{|A_1|-|A_2|} - 1$
$2^{|A_1|-1} - 2^{|A_2|-1}$	$2^{|A_1|} - 2^{|A_1|-|A_2|}$

(2) If $B_1 \neq \emptyset$ and $B_2 = \emptyset$, then we have the following two subcases:

(2a) If $|A_2| = m$, then the code $\mathcal{C}_D$ has parameters $[2^{|B_1|} - 1, 1 + |B_1|, 2^{|B_1|-1} - 1]$ and its weight distribution is given in Table 2.

Table 2. Weight distribution of the code in Theorem 1 (2a).

Weight	Frequency
0	1
$2^{|B_1|-1}$	$2^{|B_1|} - 1$
$2^{|B_1|} - 1$	1
$2^{|B_1|-1} - 1$	$2^{|B_1|} - 1$

(2b) If $|A_2| < m$, then the code $\mathcal{C}_D$ has parameters $[2^m + 2^{|B_1|} - 2^{|A_2|} - 1, m + |B_1|]$ and its weight distribution is given in Table 3.

Table 3. Weight distribution of the code in Theorem 1 (2b).

Weight	Frequency
0	1
$2^{|B_1|-1}$	$2^{|B_1|} - 1$
$2^{m-1} - 1 + 2^{|B_1|}$	$2^{m-1-|A_2|}$
$2^{m-1} - 1 + 2^{|B_1|} - 2^{|A_2|-1}$	$2^{m-1} - 2^{m-1-|A_2|}$
$2^{m-1} - 1 + 2^{|B_1|-1}$	$(2^{|B_1|} - 1)2^{m-|A_2|-1}$
$2^{m-1} - 1 + 2^{|B_1|-1} - 2^{|A_2|-1}$	$(2^{|B_1|} - 1)(2^{m-1} - 2^{m-1-|A_2|})$
2^{m-1}	$2^{m-|A_2|-1} - 1$
$2^{m-1} - 2^{|A_2|-1}$	$2^{m-1} - 2^{m-1-|A_2|}$
$2^{m-1} + 2^{|B_1|-1}$	$(2^{|B_1|} - 1)(2^{m-1-|A_2|} - 1)$
$2^{m-1} + 2^{|B_1|-1} - 2^{|A_2|-1}$	$(2^{|B_1|} - 1)(2^{m-1} - 2^{m-1-|A_2|})$

(3) If $B_1 \neq \emptyset$ and $B_2 \neq \emptyset$, then the code $\mathcal{C}_D$ has length $2^{|B_1|} - 2^{|B_2|}$ and its weight distribution is given in Table 4.

Table 4. Weight distribution of the code in Theorem 1 (3).

Weight	Frequency
0	1
$2^{|B_1|-1}$	$2^{|B_1|-|B_2|} - 1$
$2^{|B_1|} - 2^{|B_2|}$	1
$2^{|B_1|-1} - 2^{|B_2|}$	$2^{|B_1|-|B_2|} - 1$
$2^{|B_1|-1} - 2^{|B_2|-1}$	$2^{|B_1|+1} - 2^{|B_1|+1-|B_2|}$

Proof. Let $\mathbb{P} = \mathbb{H}(m, n)$. Recall that, for X, a subset of $\mathbb{F}_2^n$, there is a Boolean function in n-variable, denoted by $\chi(\mathbf{u}|X)$, and $\chi(\mathbf{u}|X) = 1$ if and only if $\mathbf{u} \cap X = \emptyset$. We also recall that, for $\mathbf{u} = (u_1, u_2, \ldots, u_n) \in \mathbb{F}_2^n$, we can write $\mathbf{u} = (v, w)$, where $\mathbf{v} = (u_1, \ldots, u_m)$ and $\mathbf{w} = (u_{m+1}, \ldots, u_n)$.

(1) Let $B = \emptyset$. By Lemma 2, the length of the code $\mathcal{C}_D$ is $2^{|A_1|} - 2^{|A_2|}$ and

$$\mathcal{H}_{I_1(\mathbb{P})}((-1)^{u_1}, (-1)^{u_2}, \ldots, (-1)^{u_n})$$
$$= \prod_{i \in A_1}(1 + (-1)^{u_i}) = \prod_{i \in A_1}(2 - 2u_i) = 2^{|A_1|}\prod_{i \in A_1}(1 - u_i) = 2^{|A_1|}\chi(v|A_1). \quad (5)$$

By Equation (4),
$$\text{wt}(c_{D,\mathbf{u}}) = 2^{|A_1|-1}(1 - \chi(\mathbf{v}|A_1)) - 2^{|A_2|-1}(1 - \chi(\mathbf{v}|A_2)).$$

(2) Let $B_1 \neq \emptyset$ and $B_2 = \emptyset$. By Lemma 2, the length of $\mathcal{C}_D$ is $2^m + 2^{|B_1|} - 2^{|A_2|} - 1$ and

$$\mathcal{H}_{I_1(\mathbb{P})}((-1)^{u_1}, \ldots, (-1)^{u_n})$$
$$= \prod_{i=1}^{m}(1 + (-1)^{u_i}) + (-1)^{u_1 + \cdots + u_m}(\prod_{j \in B_1}(1 + (-1)^{u_j}) - 1)$$
$$= 2^m \chi(\mathbf{v}|[m]) + (-1)^{\text{wt}(\mathbf{v})}(2^{|B_1|}\chi(\mathbf{w}|B_1) - 1). \quad (6)$$

By Equations (4)–(6), we have

$$\text{wt}(c_{D,\mathbf{u}}) = \frac{|D|}{2} - \frac{1}{2}\mathcal{H}_{I_1(\mathbb{P})}((-1)^{u_1}, \ldots, (-1)^{u_n}) + \frac{1}{2}\mathcal{H}_{I_2(\mathbb{P})}((-1)^{u_1}, \ldots, (-1)^{u_n})$$
$$= 2^{m-1}(1 - \chi(\mathbf{v}|[m])) + 2^{|B_1|-1}(1 - (-1)^{\text{wt}(\mathbf{v})}\chi(\mathbf{w}|B_1))$$
$$- 2^{|A_2|-1}(1 - \chi(\mathbf{v}|A_2)) - \frac{1}{2}(1 - (-1)^{\text{wt}(\mathbf{v})}).$$

(a) If $|A_2| = m$, then
$$\text{wt}(c_{D,\mathbf{u}}) = 2^{|B_1|-1}(1-(-1)^{\text{wt}(\mathbf{v})}\chi(\mathbf{w}|B_1)) - \frac{1}{2}(1-(-1)^{\text{wt}(\mathbf{v})}).$$

We divide the proof into three parts as follows:
(i) If $\text{wt}(v) \equiv 0 \pmod{2}$, then $\text{wt}(c_{D,\mathbf{u}}) = 2^{|B_1|-1}(1-\chi(\mathbf{w}|B_1))$.
(ii) If $\text{wt}(v) \equiv 1 \pmod{2}$, then $\text{wt}(c_{D,\mathbf{u}}) = 2^{|B_1|-1}(1+\chi(\mathbf{w}|B_1)) - 1$.
(b) If $|A_2| < m$, then we divide the proof into three parts as follows:
(i) If $v = 0$, then $\chi(\mathbf{v}|[m]) = \chi(\mathbf{v}|A_2) = 1$ and $\text{wt}(c_{D,\mathbf{u}}) = 2^{|B_1|-1}(1-\chi(\mathbf{w}|B_1))$.
(ii) If $v \neq 0$ and $\text{wt}(\mathbf{v})$ are odd, then $\chi(\mathbf{v}|[m]) = 0$ and
$$\text{wt}(c_{D,\mathbf{u}}) = 2^{m-1} - 1 + 2^{|B_1|-1}(1+\chi(\mathbf{w}|B_1)) - 2^{|A_2|-1}(1-\chi(\mathbf{v}|A_2)).$$

(iii) If $v \neq 0$ and $\text{wt}(\mathbf{v})$ are even, then $\chi(\mathbf{v}|[m]) = 0$ and
$$\text{wt}(c_{D,\mathbf{u}}) = 2^{m-1} + 2^{|B_1|-1}(1-\chi(\mathbf{w}|B_1)) - 2^{|A_2|-1}(1-\chi(\mathbf{v}|A_2)).$$

(3) Let $B_1 \neq \emptyset$ and $B_2 \neq \emptyset$. By Lemma 2, the length of $\mathcal{C}_D$ is $2^{|B_1|} - 2^{|B_2|}$.
By Equations (4) and (6), we have
$$\begin{aligned}\text{wt}(c_{D,\mathbf{u}}) &= \frac{|D|}{2} - \frac{1}{2}\mathcal{H}_{I_1(\mathbb{P})}((-1)^{u_1},\ldots,(-1)^{u_n}) + \frac{1}{2}\mathcal{H}_{I_2(\mathbb{P})}((-1)^{u_1},\ldots,(-1)^{u_n}) \\ &= 2^{|B_1|-1} - 2^{|B_2|-1} - \frac{1}{2}(-1)^{\text{wt}(\mathbf{v})}(2^{|B_1|}\chi(\mathbf{w}|B_1) - 2^{|B_2|}\chi(\mathbf{w}|B_2)).\end{aligned}$$

We divide the proof into two parts as follows:
(i) If $\text{wt}(v) \equiv 0 \pmod{2}$, then
$$\text{wt}(c_{D,\mathbf{u}}) = 2^{|B_1|-1}(1-\chi(\mathbf{w}|B_1)) - 2^{|B_2|-1}(1-\chi(\mathbf{w}|B_2)).$$

(ii) If $\text{wt}(v) \equiv 1 \pmod{2}$, then
$$\text{wt}(c_{D,\mathbf{u}}) = 2^{|B_1|-1}(1+\chi(\mathbf{w}|B_1)) - 2^{|B_2|-1}(1+\chi(\mathbf{w}|B_2)).$$

The frequency of each codeword can be computed by the vector u. This completes the proof. □

Remark 1. *Let us discuss the parameters of the code $\mathcal{C}_D$ in Theorem 1.*
(1) The parameters of the code $\mathcal{C}_D$ in Theorem 1 (1) are $[2^{|A_1|} - 2^{|A_2|}, |A_1|, 2^{|A_1|-1} - 2^{|A_2|-1}]$, and these are the same as that in [15].
(2) The parameters of the code $\mathcal{C}_D$ in Theorem 1 (3) are $[2^{|B_1|} - 2^{|B_2|}, k]$, where $k = |B_1| + 1$ or $|B_1|$. For instance, if $|B_1| = |B_2| + 1$, then $2^{|B_1|-1} - 2^{|B_2|} = 0$, and its dimension is $|B_1|$ in this case.

In the following corollary, we present some (almost) optimal binary linear codes which can be obtained from Theorem 1.

Corollary 1. *(1) The code in Theorem 1 (2a) has parameters $[2^{|B_1|} - 1, 1 + |B_1|, 2^{|B_1|-1} - 1]$ and meets the Griesmer bound with equality.*
(2) If $|B_1| = |B_2| + 1$, then the code in Theorem 1 (3) has parameters $[2^{|B_2|}, 2 + |B_2|, 2^{|B_2|}]$ and meets the Griesmer bound with equality; if $|B_2| = 1$ and $3 \leq |B_1|$, then the code has parameters $[2^{|B_1|} - 2, 1 + |B_1|, 2^{|B_1|-1} - 2]$ and it is almost optimal.

Proof. (1) By Table 2, the code has parameters $[2^{|B_1|} - 1, 1 + |B_1|, 2^{|B_1|-1} - 1]$. By the Griesmer bound,

$$\sum_{i=0}^{|B_1|} \left\lceil \frac{2^{|B_1|-1} - 1}{2^i} \right\rceil = (2^{|B_1|-1} - 1) + 2^{|B_1|-2} + \cdots + 2 + 1 + 1 = (2^{|B_1|} - 1) + 1 = 2^{|B_1|} - 1. \quad (7)$$

(2) Let $|B_1| = |B_2| + 1$. By Table 4, the code has parameters $[2^{|B_2|}, 2 + |B_2|, 2^{|B_2|}]$. By the Griesmer bound,

$$\sum_{i=0}^{|B_2|+1} \left\lceil \frac{2^{|B_2|}}{2^i} \right\rceil = 2^{|B_2|} + 2^{|B_2|-1} + \cdots + 2 + 1 + 1 = 2^{|B_2|}.$$

If $|B_2| = 1$ and $3 \leq |B_1|$, then the code has parameters $[2^{|B_1|} - 2, 1 + |B_1|, 2^{|B_1|-1} - 2]$. By Equation (7), the code is almost optimal. □

Next, we will determine the minimum distances of the dual codes of the codes obtained in Theorem 1. In particular, we agree with the reader that the minimum distance of $\{0\}$ is infinite.

Theorem 2. *Let $\mathbb{H}(m,n)$ be a hierarchical poset with two levels. Let $I_1 = A_1 \cup B_1$ and $I_2 = A_2 \cup B_2$ be two distinct order ideals of $\mathbb{H}(m,n)$, where $A_i \subseteq [m]$, $B_i \subseteq [n] \setminus [m]$, $i = 1, 2$, and $I_2 \subset I_1$. Let $D = (I_1(\mathbb{P})) \setminus (I_2(\mathbb{P}))$. Then, the minimum distance $d^\perp$ of $\mathcal{C}_D^\perp$ is given by*

$$d^\perp = \begin{cases} \infty & \text{if } B_1 = \emptyset \text{ and } 1 \leq |A_1| = |A_2| + 1 = 2 \\ & \text{or } 1 \leq |B_1| \leq 2 \text{ and } A_2 = [m] \\ & \text{or } |B_1| = 1 \text{ and } |A_2| = m - 1; \\ 4 & \text{if } B_1 = \emptyset \text{ and } |A_1| = |A_2| + 1 \geq 3 \\ & \text{or } |B_1| \geq 3, B_2 = \emptyset \text{ and } A_2 = [m] \\ & \text{or } |B_1| \geq 2, B_2 = \emptyset \text{ and } |A_2| = m - 1 \\ & \text{or } |B_1| \geq 3 \text{ and } B_2 \neq \emptyset; \\ 3 & \text{if } B_1 = \emptyset \text{ and } |A_1| > |A_2| + 1 \\ & \text{or } B_1 \neq \emptyset, B_2 = \emptyset \text{ and } |A_2| < m - 1. \end{cases}$$

Proof. Assume that $D = \{g_1, g_2, \ldots, g_l\} \subseteq \mathbb{F}_2^n$ with $l = |D|$. The generator matrix G' of the code $\mathcal{C}_D$ can be induced by the matrix G in Equation (2) by deleting all zero row vectors in G. Of course, G' is the parity-check matrix of $\mathcal{C}_D^\perp$. Since any two columns in G are distinct, the minimum distance of $\mathcal{C}_D^\perp$ should be greater than 2. By Theorem 1, we divide the proof into three cases.

(1) $B_1 = \emptyset$. Note that $A_2 \subseteq A_1 \subseteq [m]$. It is easy to check that, if $1 \leq |A_1| = |A_2| + 1 \leq 2$ and $\mathcal{C}_D^\perp = \emptyset$, by [15] (Theorem 1), the minimum distance of $\mathcal{C}_D^\perp$ is 4 when $|A_1| = |A_2| + 1 \geq 3$ and 3 when $|A_1| > |A_2| + 1$.

(2) $B_1 \neq \emptyset$ and $B_2 = \emptyset$. Then, we have $A_1 = [m]$, $A_2 \subseteq [m]$, and the following three subcases:

(2a) $A_2 = [m]$. Let $\mathbf{e}_k = (e_1, e_2, \ldots, e_n) \in \mathbb{F}_2^n$, where $e_k = 1$ and $e_l = 0$ if $l \neq k$. If $|B_1| \leq 2$, then $\mathcal{C}_D^\perp = \emptyset$ as $\mathbf{e}_1^T + \cdots + \mathbf{e}_m^T$ should appear in every column in G'. If $|B_1| \geq 3$, then for any three columns of G', they are linearly independent as $\mathbf{e}_1^T$ appears in every column of G'. Suppose that $i, j, k \in B_1$. Then, the following four vectors in G' are linear dependent:

$$\mathbf{e}_1^T + \cdots + \mathbf{e}_m^T + \mathbf{e}_i^T, \ \mathbf{e}_1^T + \cdots + \mathbf{e}_m^T + \mathbf{e}_j^T, \ \mathbf{e}_1^T + \cdots + \mathbf{e}_m^T + \mathbf{e}_k^T, \ \mathbf{e}_1^T + \cdots + \mathbf{e}_m^T + \mathbf{e}_i^T + \mathbf{e}_j^T + \mathbf{e}_k^T.$$

Therefore, the minimum distance of the dual code $\mathcal{C}_D^\perp$ is 4.

(2b) $|A_2| = m - 1$. If $|B_1| = 1$, then $\mathcal{C}_D^\perp = \emptyset$. If $|B_1| \geq 2$, then for any three columns of G', they are linearly independent as $\mathbf{e}_i^T$ appears in every column of G' where $i \in [m] \setminus A_2$. Suppose that $i, j \in B_1$. Then, the following four vectors in G' are linear dependent:

$$\mathbf{e}_1^T + \cdots + \mathbf{e}_m^T, \ \mathbf{e}_1^T + \cdots + \mathbf{e}_m^T + \mathbf{e}_i^T, \ \mathbf{e}_1^T + \cdots + \mathbf{e}_m^T + \mathbf{e}_j^T, \ \mathbf{e}_1^T + \cdots + \mathbf{e}_m^T + \mathbf{e}_i^T + \mathbf{e}_j^T.$$

Then, the minimum distance of $C_D^\perp$ is 4.

(2c) $|A_2| < m - 1$. Then, there are two distinct positive integers i and j in $[m]\setminus A_2$. Then, it is easy to check that $\mathbf{e}_i^T, \mathbf{e}_j^T$, and $\mathbf{e}_i^T + \mathbf{e}_j^T$ are three distinct linearly dependent columns of G'. Then, the minimum distance of $C_D^\perp$ is 3.

(3) $B_1 \neq \emptyset$ and $B_2 \neq \emptyset$. Then, we have $A_1 = A_2 = [m]$. If $|B_1| \leq 2$, then $C_D^\perp = \emptyset$ as $\mathbf{e}_1^T + \cdots + \mathbf{e}_m^T$ should appear in every column in G'. If $|B_1| \geq 3$, then for any three columns of G', they are linearly independent as $\mathbf{e}_1^T$ appears in every column of G'. Assume that $i, j, k \in B_1$ and $i \notin B_2$. Then, the following four vectors in G' are linear dependent:

$$\mathbf{e}_1^T + \cdots + \mathbf{e}_m^T + \mathbf{e}_i^T,\ \mathbf{e}_1^T + \cdots + \mathbf{e}_m^T + \mathbf{e}_i^T + \mathbf{e}_j^T,\ \mathbf{e}_1^T + \cdots + \mathbf{e}_m^T + \mathbf{e}_i^T + \mathbf{e}_k^T,\ \mathbf{e}_1^T + \cdots + \mathbf{e}_m^T + \mathbf{e}_i^T + \mathbf{e}_j^T + \mathbf{e}_k^T.$$

Then, the minimum distance of $C_D^\perp$ is 4.
This completes the proof. □

By Theorems 1 and 2, we have the following corollary.

Corollary 2. *Let $|A_2| = 0$ and $|A_1| > 1$ in Theorem 1 (1). Then, $C_D^\perp$ is a binary $[2^{|A_1|} - 1, 2^{|A_1|} - 1 - |A_1|, 3]$ Hamming code.*

4. Self-Orthogonal Binary Linear Codes and Quantum Codes

In this section, we will present some self-orthogonal binary linear codes based on the results in Section 3 and use these codes to construct quantum codes.

Theorem 3. *Let $\mathbb{H}(m, n)$ be a hierarchical poset with two levels. Let $I_1 = A_1 \cup B_1$ and $I_2 = A_2 \cup B_2$ be two distinct order ideals of $\mathbb{H}(m, n)$, where $A_i \subseteq [m]$, $B_i \subseteq [n] \setminus [m]$, $i = 1, 2$, and $I_2 \subset I_1$. Let $D = (I_1(\mathbb{P})) \setminus (I_2(\mathbb{P}))$. Then, the code C_D is self-orthogonal if and only if one of the following holds:*
  (1) $B_1 = \emptyset$, $A_2 = \emptyset$, and $3 \leq |A_1|$.
  (2) $B_1 = \emptyset$ and $3 \leq |A_2| < |A_1|$.
  (3) $B_1 \neq \emptyset$, $B_2 = \emptyset$, $3 \leq |B_1|$, $m = 1$, and $A_2 = \emptyset$.
  (4) $B_1 \neq \emptyset$ and $3 \leq |B_2|$.

Proof. Let $M = (m_{ij})_{m \times m} = GG^T$. By [23] (Lemma 18), suppose that $\mathbf{c}_i$ is the ith row vector of matrix G. Then, $m_{i,j} = \mathbf{c}_i \mathbf{c}_j^T$. Let $U_{i,j} = \{\mathbf{g} = (g_1, g_2, \ldots, g_m) \in D : g_i = g_j = 1\}$. Then, $m_{i,j} = |U_{i,j}|$ (mod 2). If $B_1 = \emptyset$, then the result holds by [15] (Theorem 3). Next, we always assume that $B_1 \neq \emptyset$. From Lemma 1, we have that C_D is self-orthogonal if and only if $GG^T = 0$. Next, we divide the proof into some cases:

(1) $B_2 = \emptyset$ and $A_2 = [m]$. Then, $U_{i,i} = 2^{|B_1|} - 1 \equiv 1 \pmod{2}$ for any $i \in [m]$ and, hence, C_D could not be self-orthogonal in this case.

(2) $B_2 = \emptyset$ and $|A_2| < m$. Suppose that $i \in [m]\setminus A_2$. Then, $U_{i,i} = 2^{|B_1|} - 1 + 2^{m-1}$. Hence, C_D cannot be self-orthogonal if $m \geq 2$. If $m = 1$, then

$$U_{i,j} = \begin{cases} 2^{|B_1|} & \text{if } i = j \in [m], \\ 2^{|B_1|-1} & \text{if } i \in [m], j \in B_1 \text{ or } j \in [m], i \in B_1, \text{ or } i = j \in B_1, \\ 2^{|B_1|-2} & \text{if } i \neq j, i, j \in B_1, \\ 0 & \text{otherwise.} \end{cases}$$

Hence, in this case, the code C_D is self-orthogonal if and only if $|B_1| \geq 3$ and $m = 1$.

(3) $B_2 \neq \emptyset$. If $|B_2| = 1$, then we have $U_{i,i} = 2^{|B_1|-1} - 1$ for $i \in B_2$. If $|B_2| = 2$, then we have $U_{i,j} = 2^{|B_1|-2} - 1$ for $i \neq j, i, j \in B_2$. Hence, $\mathcal{C}_D$ cannot be self-orthogonal if $|B_2| \leq 2$. Assume that $|B_2| \geq 3$. Then,

$$U_{i,i} = \begin{cases} 2^{|B_1|} - 2^{|B_2|} & \text{if } i \in [m], \\ 2^{|B_1|-1} - 2^{|B_2|-1} & \text{if } i \in B_2, \\ 2^{|B_1|-1} & \text{if } i \in B_1 \backslash B_2, \\ 0, & \text{otherwise} \end{cases}$$

and for $i \neq j$

$$U_{i,j} = \begin{cases} 2^{|B_1|} - 2^{|B_2|} & \text{if } i, j \in [m], \\ 2^{|B_1|-1} - 2^{|B_2|-1} & \text{if } i \in [m], j \in B_2 \text{ or } j \in [m], i \in B_2, \\ 2^{|B_1|-1} & \text{if } i \in [m], j \in B_1 \backslash B_2 \text{ or } j \in [m], i \in B_1 \backslash B_2, \\ 2^{|B_1|-2} & \text{if } i \in B_2, j \in B_1 \backslash B_2 \text{ or } j \in B_2, i \in B_1 \backslash B_2, \\ 2^{|B_1|-2} - 2^{|B_2|-2} & \text{if } i, j \in B_2, \\ 2^{|B_1|-2} & \text{if } i, j \in B_1 \backslash B_2 \\ 0 & \text{otherwise.} \end{cases}$$

Hence, $\mathcal{C}_D$ is self-orthogonal in this case. □

We present three examples of Theorem 3 as follows.

Example 2. *Let $\mathbb{H}(3,4)$ be a hierarchical poset with two levels. Let $I_1 = \{1,2,3\}$, $I_2 = \emptyset$, and*

$$D = (I_1(\mathbb{P})) \backslash (I_2(\mathbb{P})) = \{(1,0,0,0), (0,1,0,0), (0,0,1,0), (1,1,0,0), (1,0,1,0), (0,1,1,0), (1,1,1,0)\}.$$

It is easy to check that $GG^T = 0$. Then, $\mathcal{C}_D$ is a one-weight binary self-orthogonal $[7,3,4]$ code. The result is confirmed by Magma [41].

Example 3. *Let $\mathbb{H}(1,4)$ be a hierarchical poset with two levels. Let $I_1 = \{1,2,3,4\}$, $I_2 = \emptyset$, and*

$$D = (I_1(\mathbb{P})) \backslash (I_2(\mathbb{P}))$$
$$= \{(1,0,0,0), (1,1,0,0), (1,0,1,0), (1,0,0,1), (1,1,1,0), (1,1,0,1), (1,0,1,1), (1,1,1,1)\}.$$

It is easy to check that $GG^T = 0$. Then, $\mathcal{C}_D$ is a two-weight binary self-orthogonal $[8,4,4]$ code with weight enumerator $1 + 14z^4 + z^8$. The result is confirmed by Magma [41].

Example 4. *Let $\mathbb{H}(1,6)$ be a hierarchical poset with two levels. Let $I_1 = \{1,2,3,4,5,6\}$, $I_2 = \{1,2,3,4,5\}$, and*

$$D = (I_1(\mathbb{P})) \backslash (I_2(\mathbb{P}))$$
$$= \{(1,0,0,0,0,1), (1,1,0,0,0,1), (1,0,1,0,0,1), (1,0,0,1,0,1), (1,0,0,0,1,1), (1,1,1,0,0,1),$$
$$(1,1,0,1,0,1), (1,1,0,0,1,1), (1,0,1,1,0,1), (1,0,1,0,1,1), (1,0,0,1,1,1),$$
$$(1,0,1,1,1,1), (1,1,0,1,1,1), (1,1,1,0,1,1), (1,1,1,1,0,1), (1,1,1,1,1,1)\}.$$

It is easy to check that $GG^T = 0$. Then, $\mathcal{C}_D$ is a two-weight binary self-orthogonal $[16,5,8]$ code with weight enumerator $1 + 30z^8 + z^{16}$. The result is confirmed by Magma [41].

Note that, if a code is self-orthogonal, then its dual code will be a dual-containing code. Using Lemma 4 and Theorems 1, 2, and 3, we obtain the following theorem.

Theorem 4. *Let $\mathbb{H}(m,n)$ be a hierarchical poset with two levels. Let $I_1 = A_1 \cup B_1$ and $I_2 = A_2 \cup B_2$ be two distinct order ideals of $\mathbb{H}(m,n)$, where $A_i \subseteq [m]$, $B_i \subseteq [n] \setminus [m]$, $i = 1, 2$, and $I_2 \subset I_1$. Let $D = (I_1(\mathbb{P})) \setminus (I_2(\mathbb{P}))$.*

(1) If $B_1 = \varnothing$, $A_2 = \varnothing$, and $3 \leq |A_1|$, then there exists a quantum error-correcting code with parameters $[[2^{|A_1|} - 1, 2^{|A_1|} - 1 - 2|A_1|, 3]]_2$.

(2) If $B_1 = \varnothing$ and $3 \leq |A_2| < |A_1|$, then there exists a quantum error-correcting code with parameters $[[2^{|A_1|} - 2^{|A_2|}, 2^{|A_1|} - 2^{|A_2|} - 2|A_1|, \delta]]_2$, where

$$\delta = \begin{cases} 3 & \text{if } |A_1| > |A_2| + 1, \\ 4 & \text{if } |A_1| = |A_2| + 1. \end{cases}$$

(3) If $B_1 \neq \varnothing$, $B_2 = \varnothing$, $3 \leq |B_1|$, $m = 1$, and $A_2 = \varnothing$, then there exists a quantum error-correcting code with parameters $[[2^{|B_1|}, 2^{|B_1|} - 2 - 2|B_1|, 4]]_2$.

(4) If $B_1 \neq \varnothing$ and $3 \leq |B_2| < |B_1|$, then there exists a quantum error-correcting code with parameters $[[2^{|B_1|} - 2^{|B_2|}, 2^{|B_1|} - 2^{|B_2|} - 2\eta, 4]]_2$, where

$$\eta = \begin{cases} |B_1| & \text{if } |B_1| = |B_2| + 1, \\ 1 + |B_1| & \text{otherwise}. \end{cases}$$

Remark 2. *From Corollary 2, recall that there are binary Hamming codes with parameters $[2^{|A_1|} - 1, 2^{|A_1|} - 1 - |A_1|, 3]$, where $|A_1| > 1$. Using Theorem 4, we find an infinite family of quantum Hamming codes with parameters $[[2^{|A_1|} - 1, 2^{|A_1|} - 1 - 2|A_1|, 3]]_2$, where $|A_1| \geq 3$. In particular, the code with the smallest length in that family is $[[7,1,3]]_2$, called Steane code; this is a tool in quantum error correction. Consequently, it turns out that all binary quantum Hamming codes for which the length is greater than or equal to seven are special cases of the family above.*

Remark 3. *In [42], for a binary $[[n,k,d]]$ quantum code, there is a quantum Hamming bound:*

$$2^k \sum_{l=0}^{t} 3^l \binom{n}{l} \leq 2^n,$$

where $t = \lfloor \frac{d-1}{2} \rfloor$. A binary quantum code is called quantum perfect if its parameters attain the quantum Hamming bound.

We note that the minimum distance of the quantum codes in Theorem 4 is three or four; thus, we have $t = 1$ and the quantum Hamming bound is reduced to $1 + 3n \leq 2^{n-k}$. It is easy to verify that none of the quantum codes in Theorem 4 are quantum perfect. For example, in Theorem 4 (1), $[[2^{|A_1|} - 1, 2^{|A_1|} - 1 - 2|A_1|, 3]]_2$ quantum Hamming codes with $|A_1| \geq 3$ are quantum perfect if and only if $1 + 3(2^{|A_1|} - 1) = 4^{|A_1|}$, which is equivalent to $|A_1| = 0$ or $|A_1| = 1$. This implies that any of these quantum Hamming codes cannot be quantum perfect.

Remark 4. *In [17,18], the authors constructed many interesting binary quantum codes with minimum distance three or four. We compare our results with two papers [17,18] as follows. First of all, one of the major differences between theirs and ours is the code length. The lengths of our quantum codes are even or odd. On the other hand, the lengths of these binary quantum codes are all even. Moreover, comparing the parameters in the tables in [17,18] with the parameters of our quantum codes, we find that exactly one family of quantum codes are overlapped with theirs; these parameters are $[[2^l, 2^l - 2l - 2, 4]]_2$ with $l \geq 6$ in Theorem 4 (3). However, all other families of quantum codes are different from their parameters.*

Remark 5. *Tables 5 and 6 are obtained by using Theorem 4. We confirmed the optimality of the codes in the tables according to the database of Grassl [16], where he provides a list of binary quantum codes $[[n,k]]_2$ up to 256. We have constructed four families of binary quantum codes of infinite lengths in Theorem 4.*

Table 5. Binary quantum codes with minimum distance three from Theorem 4.

Parameters	Optimality	Remark
$[[7,1,3]]_2$	Optimal	Steane code
$[[15,7,3]]_2$	Optimal	Quantum Hamming code
$[[24,14,3]]_2$	Almost optimal	
$[[31,21,3]]_2$	Almost optimal	Quantum Hamming code
$[[48,36,3]]_2$	Almost optimal	
$[[63,51,3]]_2$	Almost optimal	Quantum Hamming code
$[[96,82,3]]_2$	Almost optimal	
$[[112,98,3]]_2$	Almost optimal	
$[[120,106,3]]_2$	Almost optimal	
$[[127,113,3]]_2$	Almost optimal	Quantum Hamming code
$[[224,208,3]]_2$	Almost optimal	
$[[240,224,3]]_2$	Almost optimal	
$[[248,232,3]]_2$	Almost optimal	
$[[255,239,3]]_2$	Almost optimal	Quantum Hamming code

Table 6. Binary quantum codes with minimum distance four from Theorem 4.

Parameters	Optimality	Reference
$[[8,0,4]]_2$	Optimal	[17]
$[[16,6,4]]_2$	Optimal	[17]
$[[24,14,4]]_2$	Optimal	Theorem 4
$[[32,20,4]]_2$	Optimal	[17]
$[[48,36,4]]_2$	Optimal	Theorem 4
$[[56,44,4]]_2$	Optimal	Theorem 4
$[[64,50,4]]_2$	Optimal	[17]
$[[96,82,4]]_2$	Optimal	Theorem 4
$[[112,98,4]]_2$	Optimal	Theorem 4
$[[120,106,4]]_2$	Optimal	Theorem 4
$[[128,112,4]]_2$	Optimal	[17]
$[[224,208,4]]_2$	Optimal	Theorem 4
$[[240,224,4]]_2$	Optimal	Theorem 4
$[[248,232,4]]_2$	Optimal	Theorem 4
$[[256,238,4]]_2$	Optimal	[17]

5. Concluding Remarks

In this paper, we constructed binary linear codes by using order ideals in hierarchical posets with two levels. We also explicitly determined the weight distributions of these codes, and we obtained some necessary and sufficient conditions for the binary codes constructed using posets to be self-orthogonal. Employing the CSS construction of quantum codes, we obtained four infinite families of binary quantum codes with minimum distance three or four. We also present Tables 5 and 6, which contain almost optimal or optimal binary quantum codes obtained from Theorem 4.

As a future work, we are interested in using other types of various posets for constructing more optimal binary linear codes, binary self-orthogonal codes, and optimal quantum codes.

Author Contributions: Conceptualization, Y.W.; formal analysis, Y.W.; investigation, Y.W. and Y.L.; supervision, Y.L.; writing—original draft, Y.W. All authors have read and agreed to the published version of the manuscript.

Funding: Y. Lee is supported by the National Research Foundation of Korea (NRF) grant funded by the Korea government (MEST)(NRF-2017R1A2B2004574) and by the Basic Science Research Program through the National Research Foundation of Korea (NRF) funded by the Ministry of Education (grant No. 2019R1A6A1A11051177).

Acknowledgments: We thank the reviewers of this paper for their helpful comments, which improved the clarity of this paper.

Conflicts of Interest: The authors declare no conflict of interest.

References

1. Ashikhmin, A.; Knill, E. Nonbinary quantum stabilizer codes. *IEEE Trans. Inf. Theory* **2001**, *47*, 3065–3072. [CrossRef]
2. Calderbank, A.K.; Rains, E.M.; Shor, P.W.; Sloane, N.J.A. Quantum error correction and orthogonal geometry. *Phys. Rev. Lett* **1997**, *78*, 405–408. [CrossRef]
3. Calderbank, A.R.; Rains, E.M.; Shor, P.W.; Sloane, N.J.A. Quantum error correction via codes over GF(4). *IEEE Trans. Inf. Theory* **1998**, *44*, 1369–1387. [CrossRef]
4. Shor, P.W.; Smith, G.; Smolin, J.A.; Zeng, B. High Performance Single-Error-Correcting Quantum Codes for Amplitude Damping. *IEEE Trans. Inf. Theory* **2011**, *57*, 7180–7188. [CrossRef]
5. Ouyang Y. Permutation-invariant quantum codes. *Phys. Rev. A* **2014**, *90*, 062317. [CrossRef]
6. Ouyang Y. Permutation-invariant qudit codes from polynomials. *Linear Algebra Appl.* **2017**, *532*, 43–59. [CrossRef]
7. Ouyang, Y.; Chao R. Permutation-invariant constant-excitation quantum codes for amplitude damping. *IEEE Trans. Inf. Theory* **2020**, *66*, 2921–2933 [CrossRef]
8. Ruskai, M.B. Pauli Exchange Errors in Quantum Computation. *Phys. Rev. Lett.* **2000**, *85*, 194–197. [CrossRef]
9. Chang, S.; Hyun, J.Y. Linear codes from simplicial complexes. *Des. Codes Cryptogr.* **2018**, *86*, 2167–2181. [CrossRef]
10. Hyun, J.Y.; Lee, J.; Lee, Y. Infinite families of optimal linear codes constructed from simplicial complexes. *IEEE Trans. Inf. Theory* **2020**. [CrossRef]
11. Wu, Y.; Hyun, J.Y. Few-weight codes over $\mathbb{F}_p + u\mathbb{F}_p$ associated with down sets and their distance optimal Gray image. *Discret. Appl. Math.* **2020**, *283*, 315–322. [CrossRef]
12. Wu, Y.; Zhu, X.; Yue, Q. Optimal few-weight codes from simplicial complexes. *IEEE Trans. Inf. Theory* **2020**, *66*, 3657–3663. [CrossRef]
13. Hyun, J.Y.; Kim, H.K.; Wu, Y.; Yue, Q. Optimal minimal linear codes from posets. *Des. Codes Cryptogr.* **2020**. [CrossRef]
14. Ashikhmin, A.; Barg, A. Minimal vectors in linear codes. *IEEE Trans. Inf. Theory* **1998**, *44*, 2010–2017. [CrossRef]
15. Wu, Y.; Lee, Y. Binary LCD and self-orthogonal codes via simplicial complexes. *IEEE Commun. Lett.* **2020**, *24*, 1159–1162. [CrossRef]
16. Grassl, M. Bounds on the Minimum Distance of Linear Codes. Available online: http://www.codetables.de (accessed on 15 May 2020).
17. Li, R.; Li, X. Binary construction of quantum codes of minimum distance three and four. *IEEE Trans. Inf. Theory* **2004**, *50*, 1331–1336. [CrossRef]
18. Li, R.; Li, X. Quantum codes constructed from binary cyclic codes. *Int. J. Quantum Inf.* **2004**, *2*, 265–272. [CrossRef]
19. Huffman, W.C.; Pless, V. *Fundamentals of Error-Correcting Codes*; Cambridge University Press: Cambridge, UK, 2003.
20. Griesmer, J.H. A bound for error correcting codes. *IBM J. Res. Dev.* **1960**, *4*, 532–542. [CrossRef]

21. Ding, C. Linear codes from some 2-designs. *IEEE Trans. Inf. Theory* **2015**, *61*, 3265–3275. [CrossRef]
22. Ding, C.; Niederreiter, H. Cyclotomic linear codes of order 3. *IEEE Trans. Inf. Theory* **2007**, *53*, 2274–2277. [CrossRef]
23. Zhou, Z.; Tang, C.; Li, X.; Ding, C. Binary LCD codes and self-orthogonal codes from a generic construction. *IEEE Trans. Inf. Theory* **2019**, *65*, 16–27. [CrossRef]
24. Chen, B.; Ling, S.; Zhang, G. Application of constacyclic codes to quantum MDS codes. *IEEE Trans. Inf. Theory* **2015**, *61*, 1474–1484. [CrossRef]
25. Hu, L.; Yue, Q.; Zhu, X. New quantum MDS codes from constacyclic codes. *Chin. Ann. Math* **2016**, *37B*, 891–898. [CrossRef]
26. Jin, L.; Kan, H.; Wen, J. Quantum MDS codes with relatively large minimum distance from Hermitian self-orthogonal codes. *Des. Codes Cryptogr.* **2017**, *84*, 463–471. [CrossRef]
27. Jin, L.; Xing, C. A construction of new quantum MDS codes. *IEEE Trans. Inf. Theory* **2014**, *60*, 2921–2925.
28. Kai, X.; Zhu, S. New quantum MDS codes from negacyclic codes. *IEEE Trans. Inf. Theory* **2013**, *59*, 1193–1197. [CrossRef]
29. Kai, X.; Zhu, S.; Li, P. Constacyclic codes and some new quantum MDS codes. *IEEE Trans. Inf. Theory* **2014**, *60*, 2080–2086. [CrossRef]
30. Ketkar, A.; Klappenecker, A.; Kumar, S.; Sarvepalli, P.K. Nonbinary stabilizer codes over finite fields. *IEEE Trans. Inf. Theory* **2006**, *52*, 4892–4914. [CrossRef]
31. Knill, E.; Laflamme, R. Theory of quantum error-correcting codes. *Phys. Rev. A* **1997**, *55*, 900–911. [CrossRef]
32. Li, R.; Wang, J.; Liu, Y.; Guo, G. New quantum constacyclic codes. *Quantum Inf. Process.* **2019**, *18*, 127. [CrossRef]
33. Li, S.; Xiong, M.; Ge, G. Pseudo-cyclic codes and the construction of quantum MDS codes. *IEEE Trans. Inf. Theory* **2016**, *62*, 1703–1710. [CrossRef]
34. Liu, Y.; Li, R.; Lv, L.; Ma, Y. A class of constacyclic BCH codes and new quantum codes. *Quantum Inf. Process.* **2017**, *16*, 66. [CrossRef]
35. Shi, X.; Yue, Q.; Zhu, X. Construction of some new quantum MDS codes. *Finite Fields Appl.* **2017**, *46*, 347–362. [CrossRef]
36. Steane, A.M. Multiple particle interference and quantum error correction. *Proc. Roy. Soc. Lond. A* **1996**, *452*, 2551–2577.
37. Steane, A.M. Enlargement of Calderbank-Shor-Steane quantum codes. *IEEE Trans. Inf. Theory* **1999**, *45*, 2492–2495. [CrossRef]
38. Xu, G.; Li, R.; Guo, L.; Ma, Y. New quantum codes constructed from quaternary BCH codes. *Quantum Inf. Process.* **2016**, *15*, 4099–4116. [CrossRef]
39. Zhang T.; Ge, G. Quantum MDS codes with large minimum distance. *Des. Codes Cryptogr.* **2016**, *83*, 503–517. [CrossRef]
40. Zhang T.; Ge, G. Quantum MDS codes derived from certain classes of polynomials. *IEEE Trans. Inf. Theory* **2016**, *62*, 6638–6643. [CrossRef]
41. Bosma, W.; Cannon, J.; Playoust, C. The Magma algebra system. I. The user language. *J. Symbolic Comput.* **1997**, *24*, 235–265. [CrossRef]
42. Gottesman, D. Class of quantum error-correcting codes saturating the quantum hamming bound. *Phys. Rev. A* **1996**, *54*, 1862–1868. [CrossRef]

© 2020 by the authors. Licensee MDPI, Basel, Switzerland. This article is an open access article distributed under the terms and conditions of the Creative Commons Attribution (CC BY) license (http://creativecommons.org/licenses/by/4.0/).

Article

A Multi-Criteria Computer Package-Based Energy Management System for a Grid-Connected AC Nanogrid

Carlos Roncero-Clemente [1], Eugenio Roanes-Lozano [2,*] and Fermín Barrero-González [1]

[1] Power Electrical and Electronic System Research Group (PE&ES), School of Industrial Engineering, University of Extremadura, 06006 Badajoz, Spain; carlosrc@unex.es (C.R.-C.); fbarrero@unex.es (F.B.-G.)

[2] Instituto de Matemática Interdisciplinar & Departamento de Didáctica de las Ciencias Experimentales, Sociales y Matemáticas, Facultad de Educación, Universidad Complutense de Madrid, c/ Rector Royo Villanova s/n, 28040 Madrid, Spain

* Correspondence: eroanes@mat.ucm.es; Tel.: +34-91-3946248

Citation: Roncero-Clemente, C.; Roanes-Lozano, E.; Barrero-González, F. A Multi-Criteria Computer Package-Based Energy Management System for a Grid-Connected AC Nanogrid. *Mathematics* **2021**, *9*, 487. https://doi.org/10.3390/math9050487

Academic Editor: Raúl M. Falcón

Received: 31 January 2021
Accepted: 22 February 2021
Published: 27 February 2021

Publisher's Note: MDPI stays neutral with regard to jurisdictional claims in published maps and institutional affiliations.

Copyright: © 2021 by the authors. Licensee MDPI, Basel, Switzerland. This article is an open access article distributed under the terms and conditions of the Creative Commons Attribution (CC BY) license (https://creativecommons.org/licenses/by/4.0/).

Abstract: The electric system scenario has been changing during the last years moving to a distributed system with a high penetration of renewables. Due to the unpredictable behavior of some renewables sources, the development of the energy management system is considered crucial to guarantee the reliability and stability of the system. At the same time, increasing the lifespan of the energy storage system is one of the most important points to take into account. In this sense, a software package implemented in the computer algebra system *Maple* is proposed in this work to control a grid-connected nanogrid with hybrid energy storage system (composed by batteries and supercapacitors). The energy management system considers several rules as the state of charge of the energy storage system, the photovoltaic power generation and the load profile, the nanogrid power trend and the energy prices. The improved performance of the nanogrid is proven by simulations in *MATLAB/Simulink*.

Keywords: energy management system; rule-based expert systems; microgrid; nanogrid; renewable energies

1. Introduction

The European Commission defines as main goals for 2030 a 40% reductions in greenhouse gas emissions compared to 1990 levels (although an increase up to 55% was recently established), a 32% share of green energies in the generation mix and an improvement of at least 32.5% in energy efficiency [1]). In this sense, a high penetration of renewable energies is currently being experienced.

Concurrently, microgrids (MG) are intended as the essential building blocks of smart grids, being the latter defined as "electricity network that can intelligently integrate the actions of all users connected to it (generators, consumers and those that do both) to efficiently deliver sustainable, economic and secure electricity supplies" [2]. At the same time, nanogrids (NGs) with various electric appliances were defined as kW scale smart grids that can combine different power sources with the help of information technology [3]. In the context of this paper, a NG is understood as a single-end user with embedded generation, storage and loads. Some examples of NG applications include households, buildings, businesses and campuses. This concept has been studied in several works in the last few years [4–7]. The NGs usually include emerging technologies as new power electronic converters acting as interfaces to distributed energy resources (DER), mainly based on renewable energy sources (RES) (e.g., solar and wind), which are able to operate in both grid-connected (GC) [4] and stand-alone (SA) [8,9] modes to supply the local consumers. The use of the energy storage system (ESS) is crucial in the NG operation to guarantee the continuity of supply. The optimal use of these resources allows the NG's users to obtain energy bills savings as the electricity is mainly supplied by the RES.

Furthermore, profits for owners of ESS and RES also rise because they can sell the energy to the utility grid during high-price periods [4,10] or they can even locally optimize their resources by using a peer-to-peer energy sharing approach [11].

The "brain" of the NG is the energy management system (EMS), which determines the power flows between the main grid, the loads existing in the NG, and the different DERs to achieve a finite set of goals, providing several benefits for the NG´s stakeholders. Some of these goals may include: a reduction in the NG operation costs, to maximize the overall efficiency, to minimize the peak demand and to minimize emissions or the fuel usage among others [12]. Communication between the EMS and other devices and sensors installed in the NG allows an optimal energy management by the EMS, collecting and computing some parameters, e.g., state of charge (SOC) of batteries, weather forecast, energy prices and consumption profiles [10]. Both DER and ESS are equipped with power electronic interfaces that are capable of tracking the set-points given by the EMS.

Once the NG topology has been designed and the main objectives to be met by the NG have been determined, the EMS can be implemented by different manners and techniques The techniques used for the EMS implementation in NG applications found in the literature can be based on: fuzzy logic control [10,13–16], linear programming [4,5], integer programming [17], dynamic programing [8], neural networks [10], a finite state machine [18], game theory approaches [7,19] and model predictive control [20]. The EMS for NG based on linear programming approaches defines a feasible region which is used to find the optimal solution considering a set of linear inequalities [4,5]. In order to reduce the computational time, the integer programming technique can be an alternative as expenses of relaxing the constraints, but the accuracy is sacrificed [17]. A neural network-based EMS has the advantage of being adaptive (with reinforcement learning) and being able to learn complex models. In fact, for our application field, the neural networks are commonly included in the forecast stage (e.g., solar irradiance) [10]. The implementation of a finite set of states to determine the operation mode of the NG by means of a finite state machine was studied in [18]. The main objectives were to provide ancillary services to the grid and to guarantee a coordination with the distribution system operation. From another side, some EMS for NG determines the operation mode by means of the Nash equilibrium point of the game [7,19]. This kind of method highlights because the motivation and incentives they generate among the users. Finally, model predictive control was used in a smart building EMS [20]. The basis of this technique is the analysis of the future trajectories of the plant states in a defined prediction horizon. Its main drawback is to require many plant parameters that can usually be unknown.

Fuzzy logic stands out among other control approaches for the design and implementation of EMS. Thus, this technique has been widely applied. In [13], fuzzy logic is applied to regulate the operation of the ESS of a direct current (DC) small microgrid and the energy trading. This fuzzy logic-based approach can also take into account the evolution of the energy prices, generation and demand [13]. As previously mentioned, if the MG/NG includes controllable loads (smart lighting, water pumps, etc.), the fuzzy logic control can perform some demand response strategies. Following this approach, an EMS for a residential grid-connected MG architecture based on wind and photovoltaic (PV) sources and ESS based on batteries is proposed in [14]. This study implements a 25-rules based fuzzy logic control to smooth the power exchanged with the utility, but meeting at any time the power consumption and some ESS constrains. An extension of previous works that considers the problems derived from the unpredictable nature of the energy consumption and production can be found in [15]. In that document, power demand and generation trends are included as extra inputs to the fuzzy logic controller (consisting of 50 control rules that define the operation of the EMS). The optimization of such an approach in order to reduce the system complexity is presented by the same authors in [16].

In this work, a software package in the computer algebra system *Maple* (Maple is a trademark of Waterloo Maple Inc.) is developed and implemented as EMS for a grid-connected alternating current (AC) NG with a hybrid ESS and a PV system. The package is based on a multi-criteria system approach, where several rules related to individual SOC, PV power, maximum charging/discharging ESS power, demanded power, NG power trend and energy prices are computed. The main goals of the proposed EMS are:

i. to smoothen the power exchanged with the utility;(be list format, and add the full bracket)
ii. to keep the SOC within secure thresholds;
iii. to apply energy curtailment to the PV power if required (when, for example, power injection into the utility network is not permitted by contract and there is a situation of high PV production, low local load and batteries fully charged);
iv. to guarantee a safety operation of the hybrid ESS in terms of power rating; and
v. to maximize the revenue coming from energy trading with the utility.

The contribution of this paper is as follows:

1. A new multi-criteria approach based on rules or knowledge is included in the EMS for controlling the operation of a NG.
2. The hybrid combination of batteries and supercapacitors at the residential level in the considered grid-connected NG is quite interesting for increasing the lifespan of such infrastructure.
3. The proposed package can be easily upgraded by including other rules or parameters in a very easy way. This fact is possible due to the powerful algebraic capabilities of *Maple*.

The rest of the paper is organized as follows. Section 2 describes the architecture and main variables of the NG under study as well as its modelling. Then, in Section 3; rules, constrains, thresholds and priorities are carefully described to develop the EMS. Sections 4–6 detail the step by step design of the multi-criteria computer package. Section 7 illustrates the NG performance through simulation results using *MATLAB/Simulink* (*MATLAB* and *Simulink* are registered trademarks of The MathWorks, Inc.) where the SOC improvements for both the battery and the supercapacitor are represented. Finally, Section 8 presents the main conclusions of this work.

2. Nanogrid (NG) under Study

The architecture of the residential NG under study is represented schematically in Figure 1. It is composed of a PV array with a peak power equal to 4 kW. The NG is capable to store electrical energy in the hybrid energy storage system (HESS) based on the association between a lead-acid battery pack and supercapacitors. The rated capacity of the battery pack and supercapacitors are 14.4 kWh and 15 F, respectively. Each of these equipment is connected to the DC voltage bus by means of a DC–DC power converter. A common DC–AC power converter interfaces the NG to the main grid, regulating the power flow between them. The static transfer switch (STS) connects the utility to the system at the PCC. Moreover, household loads belonging to the NG are also connected there.

2.1. NG Modelling

The PV and HESS are modelled to emulate the behavior of the DERs. The following subsections describe in detail the model implemented for the NG study by means of their mathematical expressions.

2.1.1. Photovoltaic (PV) Array Model

Manufacturers of PV modules provide the main parameters in their datasheet referred to reference values of irradiance (W) and temperature (T) at standard test conditions (STC), which corresponds to 1000 W/m^2 and 25 °C and a family of curves that illustrates how the panel curves are modified when those values change. An example of the named main parameters is available in Table 1, which shows the main specifications of module Shell SP150 referred to STC.

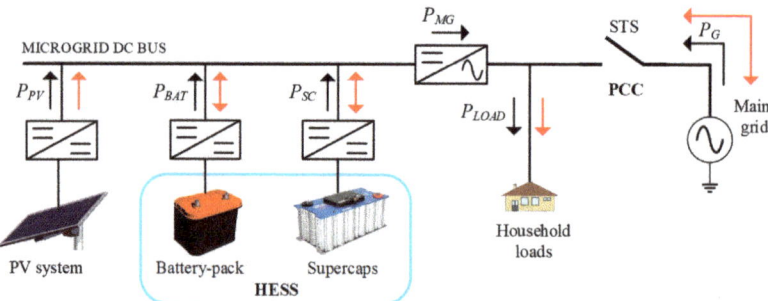

Figure 1. The residential nanogrid considered in the study.

Table 1. Electrical characteristics of Shell SP150-P module at standard test conditions (STC).

Parameter	Description	Value
P_{mpp} (W)	Power at maximum power point	150
V_{mpp} (V)	Voltage at maximum power point	34
V_{oc} (V)	Open circuit voltage	43.4
I_{sc} (A)	Short circuit current	4.8

Most of the models in the literature assume the PV cell to be an electrical equivalent circuit (Figure 2). Those models require some parameters such as shunt resistance (R_{sh}), series resistance (R_s), the diode factor and the effective cell area. Nevertheless, they are not provided by the manufacturers in the datasheet, so this makes them complex to use.

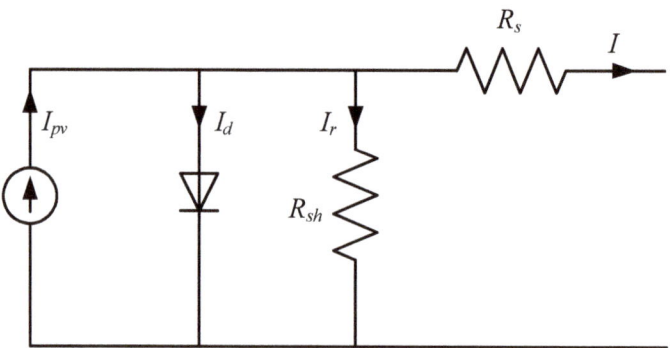

Figure 2. Equivalent circuit of a photovoltaic (PV) cell.

Due to the aforementioned reasons, the mathematical model proposed in [21] is used in the NG study. Firstly, the PV current and voltage (I–V) curve in the STC is fitted and then the influence of irradiance and temperature is taken into account. The equations that describe the model are expressed as follows (1)–(5):

$$I_{pv} = I_{SC,TW}\left(1 - Be^{(V_{pv} - V_{OC,TW})/\tau} - (1-B)e^{(V_{pv} - V_{OC,TW})/\tau/2}\right) \quad (1)$$

where I_{pv} and V_{pv} are the module current and voltage respectively. Short-circuit current at any irradiance and temperature conditions ($I_{SC,TW}$) is determined as (2):

$$I_{SC,TW} = I_{SC,STC}\frac{W}{W_{STC}}. \quad (2)$$

In (2), $I_{SC,STC}$ is the short-circuit current at STC, and W and W_{STC} are the current and the reference irradiance (1000 W/m^2) respectively. Open-circuit voltage at any irradiance and temperature conditions ($V_{OC,TW}$) are determined in (3):

$$V_{OC,TW} = V_{OC,STC} - k_T(T - T_{STC}) - k_W^{(W-W_{STC})/W} \qquad (3)$$

with $V_{OC,STC}$, T_{STC}, k_T and k_W as the open-circuit voltage at STC, the reference temperature (25 °C) and the temperature and irradiance coefficient respectively. Constants B and τ can be calculated by the expressions (4) and (5), being V_{MPP} and I_{MPP}, the voltage and current values at the maximum power point (MPP) respectively:

$$B = \frac{1 - \frac{I_{MPP}}{I_{SC}}}{e^{\frac{V_{MPP}-V_{OC}}{\tau}}} \qquad (4)$$

$$\tau = \frac{V_{MPP}}{I_{MPP}}(I_{SC} - I_{MPP}) \qquad (5)$$

To validate the accuracy of the model, these equations are implemented in *MATLAB/Simulink* using as input parameters those in Table 1. Figure 3a,c represents the curves provided by the manufacturer and Figure 3b,d the simulated ones, respectively.

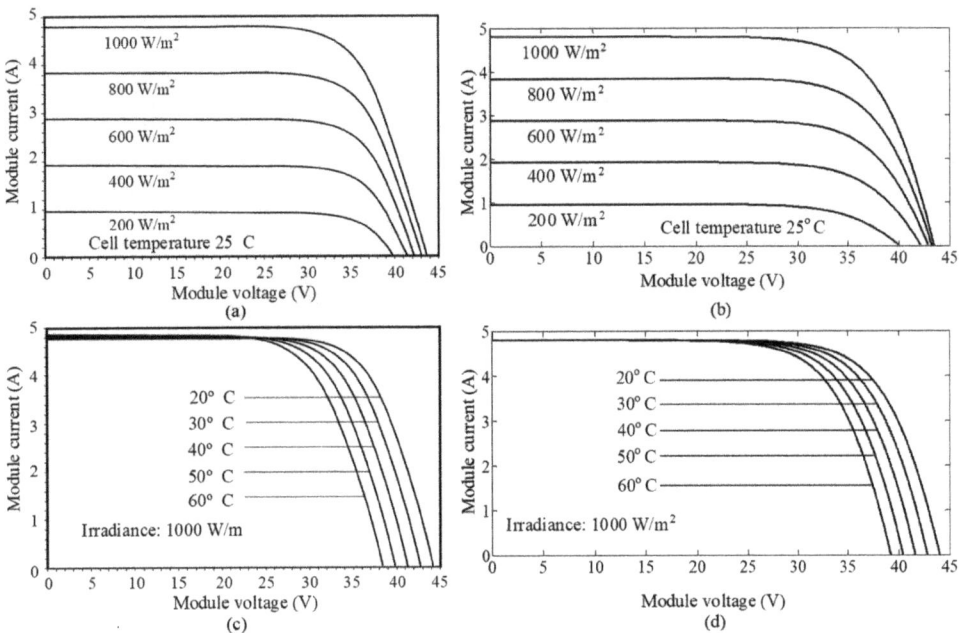

Figure 3. Current and voltage (I–V) photovoltaic (PV) curves. (**a**) I–V characteristics provided by the manufacturer for different irradiance values; (**b**) I–V characteristics simulated for different irradiance values; (**c**) I–V characteristics provided by the manufacturer for different temperatures and (**d**) I–V characteristics simulated for different temperatures.

2.1.2. Battery and Supercapacitor Models

One of the most common ESS model aims to estimate the battery open-circuit voltage ($V_{BAT,OC}$) as a function of the battery current (I_{BAT}). The estimated voltage can control a voltage source in series with a resistance that models the instantaneous voltage drop due to the internal ESS resistance. $V_{BAT,OC}$ is obtained from (6) [22]:

$$V_{BAT,OC} = V_{BAT0} - k\frac{Q}{Q - \int I_{BAT}dt} + Ae^{(-B\int I_{BAT}dt)} \quad (6)$$

where V_{BAT0} is the battery voltage, K is the polarization voltage, Q is the battery capacity, $\int I_{BAT}dt$ represents the actual battery charge, A is the exponential zone amplitude and B the exponential zone time constant inverse.

In a similar way, it is possible to develop a generic model based on the supercapacitor parameters. Supercapacitor voltage (V_{SC}) is estimated by the Stern Equation (7) [23]:

$$V_{SC} = \frac{N_S Q_T d}{N_p N_e \varepsilon \varepsilon_0 A_i} + \frac{2N_e N_s RT}{F}\sinh^{-1}\left(\frac{Q_T}{N_p N_e^2 A_i \sqrt{8RT\varepsilon\varepsilon_0 c}}\right) R_{SCu} i_{SCu}. \quad (7)$$

N_S, N_p and N_e represents the number of series and parallel supercapacitors, and the number of layers of electrodes respectively. Q_T, d, ε, ε_0, F, R and A_i correspond to the electric charge, molecular radius, permittivity of the material, permittivity of free space, Faraday constant, ideal gas constant and the area between electrodes and electrolyte. Finally, R_{SCu} and i_{SCu} stand for the total resistance and the supercapacitor current.

3. Residential Nanogrid Energy Management System

According to Figure 1, the power flow is considered positive in the direction of the corresponding black arrows. Red arrows represent the possibility of each element of the system to operate in unidirectional or bidirectional way. From the same figure, the main power flow relationships are derived as:

$$P_{NET} = P_{LOAD} - P_{PV} \quad (8)$$

$$P_{HESS} = P_{BAT} + P_{SC} \quad (9)$$

$$P_{NG} = P_{PV} + P_{BAT} + P_{SC} \quad (10)$$

where P_{NET} represents the net power. P_{PV} and P_{LOAD} corresponds to the PV power and the power demanded by the household loads respectively. At the same time, P_{HESS}, P_{BAT} and P_{SC} are the injected power by the HESS (total storage system, battery and supercapacitors). Finally, P_{NG} is the power generated by the residential NG under study. Furthermore, the power demanded from the utility P_{GRID} is positive when it injects power to the NG.

3.1. Hybrid Energy Storage System (HESS) Strategy and Constraints

Both battery and supercapacitor powers must be limited during their charging (P_{BAT-C} and P_{SC-C}) and discharging (P_{BAT-D} and P_{SC-D}) cycles to ensure their safety and life. In this sense, the following constrains have to be accomplished at any time ((11)–(14)):

$$P_{BAT-D} \leq P_{BAT-D}^{max} \quad (11)$$

$$P_{BAT-C} \leq P_{BAT-C}^{max} \quad (12)$$

$$P_{SC-D} \leq P_{SC-D}^{max} \quad (13)$$

$$P_{SC-C} \leq P_{SC-C}^{max}. \quad (14)$$

Just in case any of the previous variables overpass their maximum limits, the EMS will have to saturate the corresponding value, rearranging the energy surplus somehow. At the same time, the HESS has to operate within healthy SOC limits. Assuming that the initial SOC (SOC_0) is known, the current SOC for the battery and supercapacitors can be estimated. The selected method for estimating the current battery SOC is based on the Coulomb counting method, which integrates the battery current flow over time. This method presents a simple implementation and just one measurement is required. In our particular case, the current flowing from the battery to the DC bus is considered positive and the current battery SOC (SOC_{BAT}) is determined by Equation (15) [24]:

$$SOC_{BAT}(\%) = SOC_0(\%) - \frac{\int_0^t i_{BAT}(t)dt}{Q_{BAT}} \cdot 100 \qquad (15)$$

with $i_{BAT}(t)$ and Q_{BAT} as the battery current (A) and capacity (Ah), respectively. To determine the supercapacitor SOC (i.e., SOC_{SC}), the following expression is derived (16) [25]:

$$SOC_{SC}(\%) = \frac{1}{3}\left[4\left(\frac{V_{SC}}{V_{SC}^{NOM}}\right)^2 - 1\right] \cdot 100. \qquad (16)$$

In (16), V_{SC} and V_{SC}^{NOM} are the supercapacitor voltage and the supercapacitor nominal voltage. The HESS deals with several functionalities. For example, depending on the energy price, the HESS or the utility will release power when $P_{NET} > 0$ if possible. The battery and the supercapacitors can also fulfill energy shifting by storing energy in some strategical times. For these kinds of purposes, the SOC is considered as a crucial issue. The ideal situation for any practical NG operation would be to keep the SOC around 50%. To further distinguish a multi-criteria based decision making, five SOC intervals are proposed. The SOC is divided by 4 user-customizable levels, k_1, ..., k_4, which can be different for the battery and for the supercapacitors. Figure 4 represents such different levels and the action to be taken (if possible).

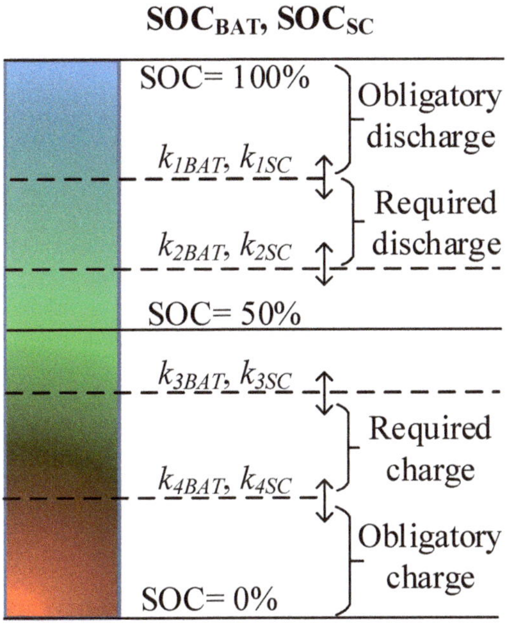

Figure 4. State of charge (SOC) intervals and corresponding energy management system (EMS) action.

As an example, if $k_{4BAT} < SOC_{BAT} < k_{3BAT}$ and $P_{NET} > 0$, probably (depending on other factors) the utility will provide power to guarantee the load supply and to charge the battery. Another situation could be that $0 < SOC_{SC} < k_{4SC}$ and $k_{2BAT} < SOC_{BAT} < k_{1BAT}$, and, depending on other factors to be detailed later, the battery will inject power to the supercapacitors.

In order to distribute the amount of P_{HESS} that will be delivered or stored by the battery or by the supercapacitor, the following reasons are considered. Batteries are usually devoted to providing the bulk of energy in the long term, presenting a slow dynamic. Meanwhile, supercapacitors are suitable for providing or absorbing the power generation or demand peaks because of its fast response. In this sense, many previous works like [25,26] aim to distinguish between the low-frequency component and the high-frequency component of the power to be delivered/absorbed by the HESS. For this purpose, a conventional low-pass filter (LPF) will be used to extract the low-frequency component, which is $LPF(P_{NET})$. Then, the power sharing will be as follows (17) and (18):

$$P_{BAT} = LPF(P_{NET}) - P_{GRID} \tag{17}$$

$$P_{SC} = P_{NET} - P_{BAT}. \tag{18}$$

3.2. NG Net Power Trend

A quite interesting parameter to develop operation rules in the EMS for controlling the NG is the consideration of both the generation and consumption trend within the NG. The NG net power trend (P_{NET}^T) can be understood as the predicted behavior of the net power. This parameter can help to improve the NG capability by storing or delivering power. In this sense, the NG can anticipate a future scenario with a more adequate HESS state. The P_{NET}^T will help to smooth the power exchanged with the main grid and to improve the SOC_{BAT}, besides contributing to increase the revenues for the NG users. It is important to note that this parameter will have only influence in the low-frequency component of P_{HESS}, that is, in the battery power. Calculation of P_{NET}^T is based on the derivative of P_{NET} (19):

$$P_{NET}^T = \frac{LPF(P_{NET}(t)) - LPF(P_{NET}(t-1))}{T_S} \tag{19}$$

where T_S is the sample rate (in the considered case of study is one hour).

A positive slope of P_{NET} means that P_{PV} is increased and/or P_{LOAD} is decreased. Nevertheless, a negative slope is related to an increase in P_{PV} generation and/or a reduction in P_{LOAD}. At the same time, P_{NET}^T values can be classified into several ranges: positive, slightly positive, zero, slightly negative or negative. Thresholds to determine this classification can be user-defined, depending on the power rating. In the NG under study, four thresholds are considered (τ_1, τ_2, τ_3 and τ_4) to define five ranges for P_{NET}^T, as shown in Table 2.

Table 2. Proposed ranges for P_{NET}^T.

Interval for P_{NET}^T	Consideration
$P_{NET}^T \geq \tau_1$	Power trend positive
$\tau_1 \geq P_{NET}^T \geq \tau_2$	Power trend slightly positive
$\tau_2 \geq P_{NET}^T \geq \tau_3$	Power trend null
$\tau_3 \geq P_{NET}^T \geq \tau_4$	Power trend slightly negative
$\tau_4 \geq P_{NET}^T$	Power trend negative

An example of a possible rule in our expert system based on the consideration of P_{NET}^T could be as follows. If $\tau_4 < P_{NET}^T < \tau_3$ (slightly negative) and $k_{2BAT} < SOC_{BAT} < k_{1BAT}$ (obligatory discharge), and, depending on other factors to be detailed later, the battery will supply the load power instead of the main grid.

3.3. PV Power Regulation

The main goal of a PV system is usually the extraction of the maximum possible power from the panels, i.e., operation at the MPP is required. This operation corresponds to the maximum environmental benefits and renewable resources exploitation but, in certain situation, it could be required to apply power generation curtailment, changing from MPP operation mode to reference power point (RPP) operation mode. In this work, the operation at RPP will be taken as a secondary option due to the aforementioned reasons. At the same time, RPP can help to maintain SOC_{BAT} and SOC_{SC} within healthy limits (for example, if P_{LOAD} is low and SOC_{BAT} is high) or for providing ancillary services to the main grid (voltage and frequency regulation). There are several approaches to implement a RPP algorithm in the PV DC/DC power converter. This algorithm calculates the proper duty cycle for the power electronics switches to make the PV array working at any reference working point. In this paper, an algorithm based on the perturb and observe (P&O) method with adaptive step to minimize the power fluctuation is implemented. Details of this method are available in [27].

Figure 5 represents a typical *P-V* curve where the maximum power point with coordinates (V_{MPP}, P_{MPP}) is marked. The EMS will generate a reference power for the PV system (P_{PV}^{REF}) depending on a specific situation. As can be seen, there are two feasible points that correspond with P_{PV}^{REF} (*x* and *y*). The one placed at the right of the MPP will be the desired one for a better operation as V_{PV} is higher (leading to a reduced duty cycle). For example, if during the NG operation P_{LOAD} is low and SOC_{BAT} is high, and at the same time the utility is not available, the EMS will determine the appropriate P_{PV}^{REF}.

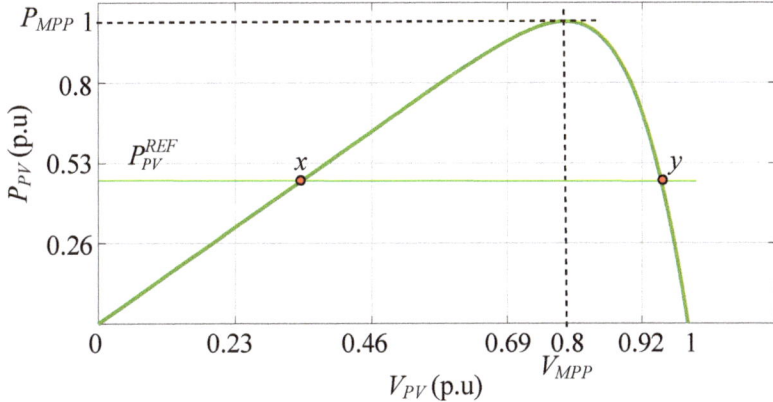

Figure 5. Traditional *P-V* curve.

3.4. Energy Price

The NG under study can produce renewable energy for its own usage and sell excess to the main grid. Besides the aim of obtaining a friendly bi-directional operation between the NG and the utility, maximization of revenues is interesting to incentive the NG user in this business model, establishing negotiations with the utility or any aggregator [19]. At the same time, the HESS can store the energy surplus to be delivered during high-price time periods. In the case supposed in this paper, the EMS considers the same energy price for selling the energy by the NG to the utility and vice versa. At the same time, high-price and low-price periods are distinguished.

3.5. Comtrol Rules

The proposed EMS strategy consists of a set of rules to control the energy flow between the different components of the NG. The main objectives are the stability and the economy of the system. From the stability point of view, the power generation must satisfy the load demand at any time, and the AC system voltage and frequency must remain within the allowed range. From the economic point of view, the cost must be reduced as much as possible under the premise of guaranteeing system stability. The instructions at time t + 1 are computed using multi-objective optimization rules at time t. Taking into account the consideration mentioned in the previous sub-sections, the detailed rules are summarized in Tables 3–5. The NG is working in grid-connected mode and the PV is operating at MPP. Remind that P_{NET}^T is not controllable as no demand response strategy is applied.

Table 3. EMS control rules for charging/discharging the batteries.

	St.1: $P_{NET}^T \geq \tau_1$		St.2: $\tau_1 \geq P_{NET}^T \geq \tau_2$		St.3: $\tau_2 \geq P_{NET}^T \geq \tau_3$		St.4: $\tau_3 \geq P_{NET}^T \geq \tau_4$		St.5: $\tau_4 \geq P_{NET}^T$	
St.1: $100\% \geq SOC_{BAT} \geq k_{1BAT}$ (strongly charged)	B2L	N2G	B2L	N2G B2G	B2L	N2G B2G	B2L	N2G B2G	B2L B2G	N2G B2G
St.2: $k_{1BAT} \geq SOC_{BAT} \geq k_{2BAT}$ (charged)	B2L	N2G	B2L B2G	N2G B2G	B2L B2G	N2G B2G	B2L B2G	N2G B2G	B2L B2G	N2G B2G
			B2L	N2G	B2L	N2G	B2L B2G	N2G B2G		
St.3: $k_{2BAT} \geq SOC_{BAT} \geq k_{3BAT}$ (intermediated)	G2L G2B	N2B	B2L	N2G B2G	B2L	N2G B2G	B2L B2G	N2G B2G	B2L	N2G B2G
			B2L G2L	N2B	G2L	N2G	B2L	N2G		
St.4: $k_{3BAT} \geq SOC_{BAT} \geq k_{4BAT}$ (discharged)	G2L G2B	N2B G2B	B2L	N2G	B2L	N2G N2B	B2L B2G	N2G B2G	G2L	N2G
			B2L G2L	N2B	B2L G2L	N2B	B2L	N2G		
St.5: $k_{4BAT} \geq SOC_{BAT} \geq 0\%$ (strongly discharged)	G2L G2B	N2B G2B	G2L G2B	N2B G2B	G2L G2B	N2B G2B	G2L G2B	N2B	G2L	N2B

Table 4. EMS control rules for supercapacitors.

	St.1 $100\% \geq SOC_{SC} \geq k_{1SC}$	St.2 $k_{1SC} \geq SOC_{SC} \geq k_{2SC}$	St.3 $k_{2SC} \geq SOC_{SC} \geq k_{3SC}$	St.4 $k_{3SC} \geq SOC_{SC} \geq k_{4SC}$	St.5 $k_{4SC} \geq SOC_{SC} \geq 0$
St.1 $100\% \geq SOC_{BAT} \geq k_{1BAT}$ (strongly charged)	- -	- -	- -	B2SC B2SC	B2SC B2SC
St.2: $k_{1BAT} \geq SOC_{BAT} \geq k_{2BAT}$ (charged)	- -	- -	- -	B2SC B2SC	B2SC B2SC
St.3: $k_{2BAT} \geq SOC_{BAT} \geq k_{3BAT}$ (intermediated)	- -	- -	- -	B2SC G2SC	B2SC G2SC
St.4: $k_{3BAT} \geq SOC_{BAT} \geq k_{4BAT}$ (discharged)	- -	- -	- -	G2SC G2SC	G2SC G2SC
St.5: $k_{4BAT} \geq SOC_{BAT} \geq 0\%$ (strongly discharged)	- -	- -	- -	G2SC G2SC	G2SC G2SC

Table 5. EMS control rules for the PV system.

	St.1: $P_{NET}^T \geq \tau_1$		St.2: $\tau_1 \geq P_{NET}^T \geq \tau_2$		St.3: $\tau_2 \geq P_{NET}^T \geq \tau_3$		St.4: $\tau_3 \geq P_{NET}^T \geq \tau_4$		St.5: $\tau_4 \geq P_{NET}^T$	
St.1 $100\% \geq SOC_{BAT} \geq k_{1BAT}$ (strongly charged)	MPPT	RPPT	MPPT	RPPT	RPPT	RPPT	RPPT	RPPT	RPPT	RPPT
St.2: $k_{1BAT} \geq SOC_{BAT} \geq k_{2BAT}$ (charged)	MPPT	RPPT	MPPT	RPPT	RPPT	RPPT	RPPT	RPPT	RPPT	RPPT
St.3: $k_{2BAT} \geq SOC_{BAT} \geq k_{3BAT}$ (intermediated)	MPPT	MPPT	MPPT	RPPT	RPPT	RPPT	RPPT	RPPT	RPPT	RPPT
St.4: $k_{3BAT} \geq SOC_{BAT} \geq k_{4BAT}$ (discharged)	MPPT	MPPT	MPPT	MPPT	MPPT	MPPT	MPPT	MPPT	MPPT	MPPT
St.5: $k_{4BAT} \geq SOC_{BAT} \geq 0\%$ (strongly discharged)	MPPT	MPPT	MPPT	MPPT	MPPT	MPPT	MPPT	MPPT	MPPT	MPPT

Table 3 shows the rules regarding charging/discharging the batteries and the injecting/extracting power into/from the utility grid, related to conditions about power production and load. The following acronyms are used for the power flows: B2L: Battery to load; B2G: Battery to Grid; G2B: Grid to Battery; N2G: Surplus to Grid; N2B: Surplus to Battery; G2L: Grid to Load. The inputs are SOC_{BAT} and P_{NET}^T. Each cell is divided into two or four sub-cells. The latter occupy the central part of the table. Within each cell, the sub-cells on the left represent the case of $P_{NET} > 0$ and those on the right $P_{NET} < 0$. On the other hand, also within each cell, the top ones correspond to the case of high energy prices and the bottom ones to low energy prices. When a sub-cell contains two lines, it indicates that two actions are executed simultaneously, both with equal power flow. For the cells outside the central box, the SOC is in the limit zone and P_{NET}^T presents a strong slope. In such a case, the priority will be to redirect the SOC to the central zone in order to assure the battery health. On the other hand, in the cells in the central box, attention will also be paid to the power purchase/sale price in order to get economic benefits. The reading of one of the cells is given below as an example (the one highlighted in yellow):

If ($k_{3BAT} \geq SOC_{BAT} \geq k_{4BAT}$-battery discharged) and ($\tau_1 \geq P_{NET}^T \geq \tau_2$-trends is slightly positive (*more power will be required for* P_{LOAD})) and ($P_{NET} > 0$-more power is required for P_{LOAD})) and (price is low) then the load will be supplied by the grid (50%, as the price is low) and by the battery (50%)(as we are not in the state of the battery "strongly discharged").

Table 4 shows the rules regarding the regulation of the SOC in the supercapacitors. The following acronyms are used for the power flows: B2SC: Battery to Supercapacitor; G2SC: Grid to Supercapacitor. Inside each main cell, division in left and right corresponds to high-price and low-price time respectively.

Table 5 shows the rules regarding the regulation the operation mode in the PV system: MPPT: Maximum Power Point Tracking; RPPT: Reference Power Point Tracking. Inside each main cell, the division into left and right corresponds to $P_{NET} > 0$ and $P_{NET} < 0$.

4. The Associated Rule-Based Expert System (RBES)

The NG described in this paper is a first step of a new development in the line of research of these authors. Therefore, the method and the representation of knowledge chosen is a frame designed to be reused in more complex (detailed) scenarios.

On the one hand, the experts summarize the electrical knowledge in tables, the conclusions of which have to be concatenated (in this first step that will take place only with Tables 3–5, but will be increased when further details are considered in future extensions of this work). The advantages of using rules when deductions have to be concatenated are well known.

4.1. Analysing the Structuring of the Information in the Tables

Let us use Table 3 to illustrate the procedure. This table is not homogeneous, as some cells have been merged.

Four variables are considered as input:

$$SOC_{BAT}, P^T_{NET}, P_{NET}, price$$

and 5 intervals are distinguished for the first and second variables and 2 possibilities for the third and fourth variables. In the expert system they will be abbreviated for the sake of simplicity:

- SOC_{BAT}: x_1, x_2, x_3, x_4, x_5
- P^T_{NET}: y_1, y_2, y_3, y_4, y_5
- P_{NET}: z_1, z_2
- Price: u_1, u_2

There are 6 possible conclusions (operations modes):

GRID2LOAD, GRID2BAT, NET2GRID, NET2BAT, BAT2LOAD, BAT2GRID.

In some cases (cells) there is one operation mode to be carried out, but in other cases there are two to be carried out.

In this case we would initially have a table with $5^2 \times 2^2$ cells = 100 cells. Nevertheless, the experts in electrical grids have grouped all cells outside the dark black rectangle in pairs (the third variable, z, is not considered for those cells), resulting in double height cells outside the dark black rectangle. One example is the upper left cell:

BAT2LOAD is recommended if we have x_1 and y_1 and u_1 (despite having z_1 or z_2)

(these groupings are from an engineering origin: in many cases it does not matter whether we have z_1 or z_2: the same operation mode(s) is(are) recommended).

The table with abbreviated names of variables can be found in Table 6.

4.2. Combinatorial Manual Grouping of the Information in the Tables

For instance, the cell in the upper left corner of the table can be merged with the one below it. The same can be said about the two cells to their right.

There are many other possible groupings. Using colors can simplify viewing possible groupings (a task to be performed by a second group of experts: mathematicians or computer scientists, that have to consider which cells can be easily grouped into a single logic rule or into a few logic rules).

For instance, as exactly one y_i must hold (because the intervals considered for P_{NET}^T are mutually exclusive), the information provided by all the cells containing GRID2BAT in the lower row of Table 6 (all columns but the last three ones) can be summarized as follows:

IF ×5 AND (NOT(y4 AND u2) OR NOT y5) THEN GRID2BAT

that is, "in the situation described by the last row (x5) and any of the possibilities for the columns yi (i∈{1,2,3,4,5}) except ((simultaneously y4 and u2) or y5) then GRID2BAT is operation mode is recommended". If we use the usual logic symbols: ∧ (conjunction), ∨ (disjunction), ¬ (negation) and → (implication), it can be written:

$$x5 \wedge (\neg(y4 \wedge u2) \vee \neg y5) \rightarrow GRID2BAT$$

Table 6. Table 3 with the notation of the rule-based expert system (RBES).

TABLE NUMBER 6		y1		y2		y3		y4		y5	
		u1	u2	u1	u2	u1	u2	u1	u2	u1	u2
x1	z1	BAT 2 LOAD	NET 2 GRID	BAT 2 LOAD	NET2GRID BAT2GRID	BAT2LOAD BAT2GRID	NET2GRID BAT2GRID	BAT2LOAD BAT2GRID	NET2GRID BAT2GRID	BAT2LOAD BAT2GRID	NET2GRID BAT2GRID
	z2										
x2	z1	BAT 2 LOAD	NET 2 GRID	BAT2LOAD BAT2GRID	NET2GRID BAT2GRID	BAT2LOAD BAT2GRID	NET2GRID BAT2GRID	BAT2LOAD BAT2GRID	NET2GRID BAT2GRID	BAT2LOAD BAT2GRID	NET2GRID BAT2GRID
	z2			BAT2LOAD	NET2GRID	BAT2LOAD	NET2GRID	BAT2LOAD BAT2GRID	NET2GRID BAT2GRID		
x3	z1	GRID2LOAD GRID2BAT	NET 2 BAT	BAT2LOAD BAT2LOAD GRID2LOAD	NET2GRID BAT2GRID NET2BAT	BAT2LOAD GRID2LOAD	NET2GRID BAT2GRID NET2GRID	BAT2LOAD BAT2GRID BAT2LOAD	NET2GRID BAT2GRID NET2GRID	BAT 2 LOAD	NET2GRID BAT2GRID
	z2										
x4	z1	GRID2LOAD GRID2BAT	NET2BAT GRID2BAT	BAT2LOAD BAT2LOAD GRID2LOAD	NET2GRID NET2BAT	BAT2LOAD BAT2LOAD GRID2LOAD	NET2GRID NET2BAT NET2BAT	BAT2LOAD BAT2GRID BAT2LOAD	NET2GRID BAT2GRID NET2GRID	GRID 2 LOAD	NET 2 GRID
	z2										
x5	z1	GRID2LOAD GRID2BAT	NET2BAT GRID2BAT	GRID2LOAD GRID2BAT	NET2BAT GRID2BAT	GRID2LOAD GRID2BAT	NET2BAT GRID2BAT	GRID2LOAD GRID2BAT	NET 2 BAT	GRID 2 LOAD	NET 2 BAT
	z2										

Nevertheless, that would imply to include an integrity constraint describing that exactly one y_i must hold. A preferable alternative equivalent way to express it (without the need to include integrity constraints) is:

$$x5 \wedge (y1 \vee y2 \vee y3 \vee (y4 \wedge u1)) \to GRID2BAT$$

that is, "in the situation described by the last row (x5) and the columns (y1 or y2 or y3 or (y4 and u1)) then *GRID2BAT* operation mode is recommended".

An advantage of the logic rule translation is that there are no problems if the groupings do not describe a partition of the set of cells but a covering, that is, if the subsets of cells are not disjointed two by two—that will only allow a conclusion (that is, the operation mode(s)) to be reached by forward firing more than one rule, which is not a problem.

For instance, an exact description of the information provided by the three cells containing *GRID2BAT* in the antepenultimate and penultimate rows and the first and second columns of the table is:

$$((x3 \vee x4) \wedge y1 \wedge u1) \vee (x4 \wedge y1 \wedge u2) \to GRID2BAT$$

which is equivalent to the two simpler rules:

$$(x3 \vee x4) \wedge y1 \wedge u1 \to GRID2BAT$$

$$x4 \wedge y1 \to GRID2BAT$$

The latter rules describing two intersecting (non-disjoint) subsets of cells (these will be the rules R2 and R3 of our RBES). Note that this is a technique typically used in Karnaugh maps.

5. About the Inference Engine Chosen

We have decided to use the algebraic inference engine described in detail in [28,29]. Among the many available existing approaches, we have chosen this one because of our experience with it and because of the possibility to straightforwardly move to a multivalued modal logic in future extensions, if necessary.

5.1. A Brief Overview of the Algebraic Model for Logic

Let us consider the Boolean logic case. If there are m propositional variables, $X_1, X_2, \ldots, X_m$, the algebraic model considers the polynomial variables $x_1, x_2, \ldots, x_m$ and the residue-class ring

$$Z_2[x_1, x_2, \ldots, x_m] / <x_1^2 - x_1, x_2^2 - x_2, \ldots, x_m^2 - x_m>$$

where $I = <x_1^2 - x_1, x_2^2 - x_2, \ldots, x_m^2 - x_m>$ denotes the ideal generated by $x_1^2 - x_1, x_2^2 - x_2, \ldots, x_m^2 - x_m$. If $X \wedge Y$, $X \vee Y$, X xor Y and $\neg X$ are translated by $x \cdot y$, $x + y - x \cdot y$, $x \cdot y$ and $1-x$, respectively, we have a ring isomorphism (or a Boolean algebra isomorphism, depending on the logic and algebraic operations considered).

The advantage of moving to the algebraic model is that we have an effective method for performing computations: *Gröbner bases* (and the derived *normal form* of a polynomial modulo an ideal) [30,31].

The main result is that Q is a tautological consequence of P ($P \to Q$) is equivalent in the algebraic model to *NormalForm*$(1 - q, <1 - p> + I) = 0$, where p and q are the translations of P and Q in the polynomial model, respectively (and let us recall that $1-p$ and $1-q$ are the translations of $\neg P$ and $\neg Q$ in the polynomial model, respectively).

In the n-valued modal logic case (n prime) the only differences are:
- Z_n is considered instead of Z_2 as the base field,
- the ideal $<x_1^2 - x_1, x_2^2 - x_2, \ldots, x_m^2 - x_m>$ is substituted by ideal $<x_1^n - x_1, x_2^n - x_2, \ldots, x_m^n - x_m>$

so the polynomial ring considered is $Z_n[x_1,x_2,\ldots,x_m]/<x_1{}^n - x_1 x_2{}^n - x_2, \ldots, x_m{}^n - x_m>$, and:
- the polynomial translations of the logic connectives do change.

5.2. A Brief Overview of the Algebraic Model for RBES (Boolean Case)

The facts, rules and integrity constraints are logic formulae stated as true. The rules and integrity constraints are fixed, meanwhile the set of facts stated as true change (although it must be a subset of the set of potential facts). The corresponding polynomial model presented in the previous subsection was $Z_2[x_1,x_2,\ldots,x_m]/<x_1{}^2 - x_1 x_2{}^2 - x_2, \ldots, x_m{}^2 - x_m> = Z_2[x_1,x_2,\ldots,x_m]/I$.

As the facts, rules and integrity constraints are stated as true, if
- J is the polynomial ideal generated by the polynomial translation of the negation of the rules and integrity constraints, and
- K is the polynomial ideal generated by the polynomial translation of the negation of the given facts,

Then its polynomial model is the residue-class ring:

$$(Z_2[x_1,x_2,\ldots,x_m]/I)/(J + K) = Z_2[x_1,x_2,\ldots,x_m]/(I + J + K).$$

5.3. The Maple Implementation of the Algebraic Model for RBES

The algebraic model for RBES can be easily implemented in any computer algebra system (CAS). For instance, in the CAS *Maple*, the implementation is straightforward. Firstly the packages Groebner and Ore_algebra (that allow to define the polynomial ring where the computations will take place) have to be loaded.

Afterwards the polynomial variables have to be declared. For instance, in the case of Table 6, we can store the x, z, y, u variables and the conclusions (operation modes) GRID2LOAD, GRID2BAT, etc. in a sequence (denoted, for instance, SV).

Then the polynomial ring where computations have to take place and the ordering to be applied and the order between variables have to be declared, and the polynomial ideal *I* has to be defined. At this point we are ready to define the polynomial translation of the logic connectives as *Maple* functions, which is straightforward and needs just 6 lines of code (the complete code required can be found in Appendix A in order the acquainted reader to be able to reproduce the computations).

For instance, the expression mentioned above:

$$(x3 \vee x4) \wedge y1 \wedge u1 \rightarrow GRID2BAT$$

is translated into Rule 2 of the RBES just by typing:

R2: = (x3 &OR x4) &AND y1 &AND u1 &IMP GRID2BAT:

which is very close to the usual notation in logic.

6. The Energy Management Nanogrid RBES Developed

The RBES developed will be described afterwards. It has been divided into 3 subsystems, each one dealing with the knowledge contained in one of the Tables 3–5.

6.1. Subsystem I

We have written 35 rules, similar to R2 in Section 5.3, that translate the knowledge contained in Table 6 (let as recall that this table is Table 3 with another notation). This translation can be made in several ways. The set (or list) of the negations of the chosen rules is a base of ideal J. Then we are ready to extract knowledge: if K is the ideal generated by the negation of the facts stated as true, the following two lines:

> B:=Basis([op(iI),op(J),op(K)], Orde);

> NormalForm(NEG(NET2BAT),B,Orde);

determine if *NET2BAT* can be deduced from the facts stated as true, by forward firing the 35 rules. The complete code of this subsystem can be found in Appendix B.

Nevertheless, it is usually more convenient to directly determine which of the possible operation modes (*GRID2LOAD, GRID2BAT, ... , BAT2GRID*) are recommended. A brief procedure, that we have denoted operation_mode, allows us to do this with a single order (see Appendix C for details).

Moreover, obtaining the operation modes is not restricted to a single cell. Other more complex tasks can be solved by the RBES (see Appendix C).

Finally, we could underline that it is possible to check that the rules developed correctly translate the knowledge summarized in Table 6 using a procedure developed ad hoc (see Appendix D).

6.2. Subsystem II

The variables considered in the five rows of Table 4 were denoted $x_1, ..., x_5$ in Table 6. The variables in the upper part of Table 4 (SOC_{SC}) are new, and are denoted $v_1, ..., v_5$, respectively. Each column is divided into two columns, corresponding variables of which (high-price, low-price), were denoted z_1 and z_2, respectively, in Table 6.

In this case we have written 4 rules that translate the knowledge contained in Table 4. For instance, the first rule, R101, is:

$$(x1 \lor x2) \land (v4 \lor v5) \rightarrow BAT2SC$$

The corresponding code and the way knowledge extraction is performed is similar to Subsystem I (see Appendix E).

6.3. Subsystem III

The variables considered in the five rows of Table 5 were denoted $x_1, ..., x_5$ in Table 6. Similarly, the variables in the upper part of Table 5 were denoted $y_1, ..., y_5$ in Table 6. Each column is divided into two columns, corresponding variables of which (P_{NET} positive or negative) will be denoted w_1, w_2, respectively.

In this case we have written 7 rules that translate the knowledge contained in Table 5. For instance, the first rule, R201, is:

$$(x1 \lor x2 \lor x3) \land (y1 \lor y2) \land w1 \rightarrow MPPT$$

The corresponding code and the way knowledge extraction is performed is similar to Subsystem I (see Appendix F).

7. Simulations

The associated RBES acting as EMS to the NG under study which was defined in Section 2 is tested through simulation using *MATLAB/Simulink*. Figure 6a shows an hourly PV generation and load consumption profiles for the NG under study. These curves are considered quite realistic for a 4 kW peak power PV generation system during a sunny day. P_{NET} is represented in Figure 6b. Positive and negative values of P_{NET} take place along the day. Thus, surplus or deficit must be compensated by the HESS or by the main grid. For simplicity, supposing that the main grid cannot participate ($P_{GRID} = 0$), P_{BAT} is represented in Figure 6c. It corresponds to the filtered value of P_{NET}. Meanwhile, the supercapacitors will compensate the peak power according to Equation (18) as depicted in Figure 6d. Subsequently, Figure 7a depicts P_{NET} and its slope is produced by two hourly consecutive samples. These slopes can be positive or negative. At the same time, P_{NET}^T is displayed in Figure 7b.

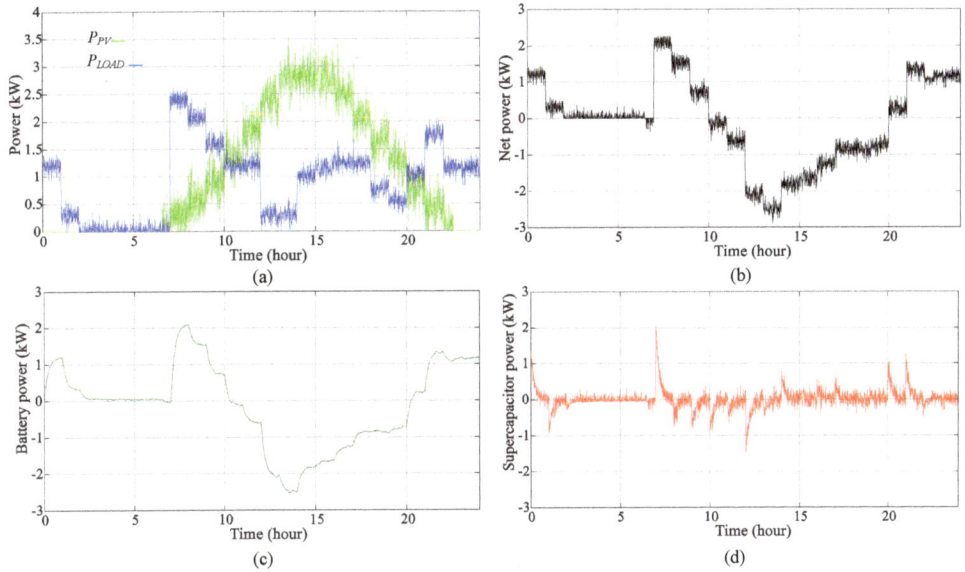

Figure 6. HESS power distribution. (a) P_{PV} and P_{LOAD}; (b) P_{NET}; (c) P_{BAT} and (d) P_{SC}.

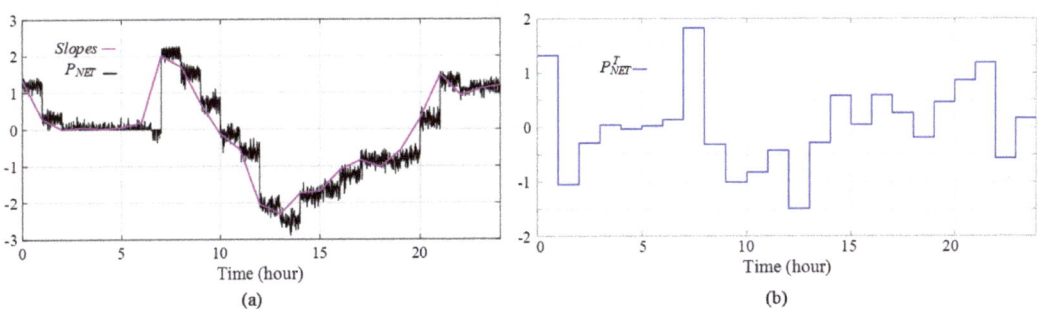

Figure 7. NG net power trend analysis. (a) P_{NET} and the slopes coming from two consecutive samples (hourly) and (b) P_{NET}^T.

From P_{NET}, just the sign (positive or negative) of this value is required as RBES input. The value of P_{NET}^T is given a consideration according to Table 2. For our case of study, thresholds equal to 1.5 kW, 0.5 kW, −0.5 kW and −1.5 kW are selected as constants τ_1, τ_2, τ_3 and τ_4 respectively. Current values of the SOC_{BAT} and SOC_{SC}, calculated with Equations (15) and (16), define specific intervals according to Figure 4. These intervals will also feed the RBES back (the facts stated as true at each moment). Regarding the SOC for both the battery and the supercapacitor, the following levels: 80%, 65%, 35% and 20%, were chosen for k_1, k_2, k_3 and k_4.

Considering as initial SOC_{BAT} equal to 50% and initial SOC_{SC} equal to 35%, the control of the NG with the proposed EMS and its associated RBES, clearly improves the performance of the HESS. Figure 8 represents the corresponding SOC before (SOC_{BAT} and SOC_{SC}) and after considering the proposed control (SOC'_{BAT} and SOC'_{SC}). Before the EMS activation, SOC_{BAT} reaches almost 100% (around 20:00 p.m.) and falls 10% (around 10 a.m.). The maximum SOC_{SC} corresponds to 14:30 p.m., with around 65%. On the other hand, at 7:30 a.m. the SOC_{SC} is around 5%. As we can see in Figure 8, after applying the proposed control, both SOC are maintained close to 50% during the day. Thus, both SOC are kept within secure thresholds, guaranteeing a safety operation of the HESS.

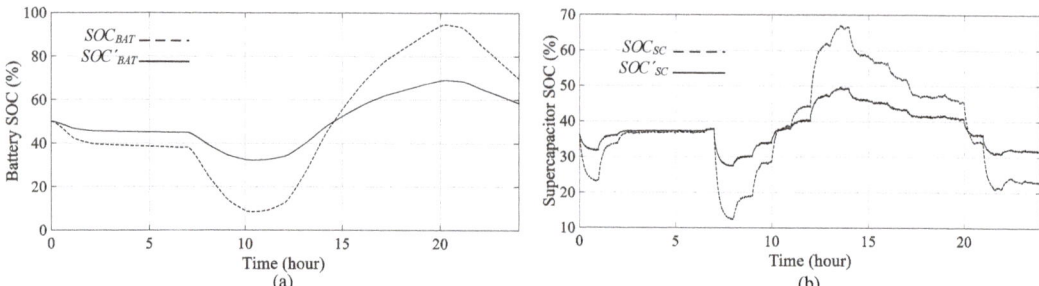

Figure 8. Improved performance of the NG thanks to the RBES acting as EMS. (**a**) SOC_{BAT} and SOC'_{BAT} and (**b**) SOC_{SC} and SOC'_{SC}.

Finally, battery and supercapacitor powers before and after (P'_{BAT} and P'_{SC} respectively) the EMS activation are represented in Figure 9a,b. Thanks to the EMS the system has a smoother response which also helps to improve the HESS lifespan.

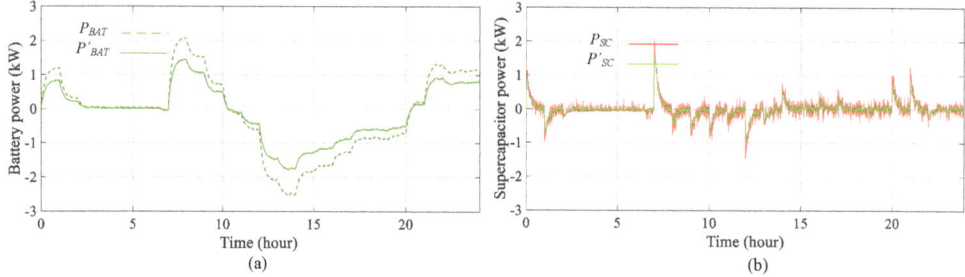

Figure 9. Smoother responses in the battery and supercapacitor powers thanks to the RBES acting as EMS. (**a**) P_{BAT} and P'_{BAT} and (**b**) P_{SC} and P'_{SC}.

8. Conclusions

This paper exposes the relevance of the EMS in the NG operation. A new approach to EMS for a NG was developed by designing a RBES step by step. The proposed approach has as its main advantage the reduction of the computational burden, while providing the possibility to straightforwardly move to a multivalued modal logic if the NG becomes more complex. At the same time, the possibility to concatenate the conclusions according to new variables or operation modes allows a modular design of the EMS. Further work will consider the presence of other energy sources in the NG, such as diesel generation, as well as the integration of some demand-side and peak load-shifting strategies. At the same time, environmental concerns are planned to be added in further extensions, as well as other energy required in the residential sector as thermal energy.

Regarding the chosen computational approach (a RBES), it has been shown how the knowledge included in table format can be conveniently condensed in the format of logic rules. The chosen inference engine (algebraic) is slower than other approaches already used by the authors, like answer set programming [32,33], but timings are very small, due to the size of problems treated (see Appendix B). The main advantage of the inference engine chosen is its simplicity (see Appendix A) and the fact that, during the development step, the underlying logic can be easily changed to a modal logic if desired (which is very convenient as this work is a first step in a new line of research by the authors).

Author Contributions: Conceptualization, C.R.-C. and E.R.-L.; methodology, C.R.-C. and E.R.-L.; validation, C.R.-C. and E.R.-L.; formal analysis, F.B.-G.; investigation, C.R.-C., E.R.-L. and F.B.-G.; writing—original draft preparation, C.R.-C. and E.R.-L.; writing—review and editing, E.R.-L. and F.B.-G.; supervision, C.R.-C., E.R.-L. and F.B.-G.; project administration, F.B.-G.; funding acquisition, C.R.-C., F.B.-G. and E.R.-L. All authors have read and agree to the published version of the manuscript.

Funding: This research was funded by the Junta de Extremadura within the programs "Ayudas Talento" (TA18003) and "Funding for Research Groups" (GR18087) and partially funded by the research project PGC2018-096509-B-100 (Government of Spain).

Institutional Review Board Statement: Not applicable.

Informed Consent Statement: Not applicable.

Data Availability Statement: Not applicable.

Acknowledgments: The authors would like to thank the anonymous reviewers for their most valuable comments and suggestions, that have greatly improved the final version of the article.

Conflicts of Interest: The authors declare no conflict of interest.

Appendix A

The Code of the Implementation Described in Section 5.3. The complete *Maple* code can be found afterwards. Note that the "&" symbols are necessary in *Maple* to declare infix operators.

```
> with(Groebner):
> with(Ore_algebra):
> SV:=x1,x2,x3,x4,x5,z1,z2,y1,y2,y3,y4,y5,u1,u2,GRID2LOAD,
>    GRID2BAT, NET2GRID, NET2BAT, BAT2LOAD, BAT2GRID:
> A:=poly_algebra(SV,characteristic=2):
> Orde:=MonomialOrder(A,'plex'(SV)):
> fu:=var->var^2-var:
> iI:=map(fu,[SV]):
> NEG :=(m::algebraic) -> NormalForm(1+'m',iI,Orde):
> '&AND' :=(m::algebraic,n::algebraic) ->
>         NormalForm(expand(m*n),iI,Orde):
> '&OR' :=(m::algebraic,n::algebraic) ->
>         NormalForm(expand(m+n+m*n),iI,Orde):
> '&IMP' :=(m::algebraic,n::algebraic) ->
>         NormalForm(expand(1+m+m*n),iI,Orde):
> '&XOR' :=(m::algebraic,n::algebraic) ->
>         (m &OR n) &AND NEG(m &AND n):
```

(observe that ideal I is denoted iI in the implementation above because I is a reserved word in Maple).

That is all the code required.

Appendix B. Subsystem I—Construction and Extracting Knowledge

The 35 rules that we have written to translate the knowledge contained in Table 6 are:

```
> R1 := x5 &AND (y1 &OR y2 &OR y3 &OR (y4 &AND u1)) &IMP GRID2BAT:
> R2 := (x3 &OR x4) &AND y1 &AND u1 &IMP GRID2BAT:
> R3 := x4 &AND y1 &IMP GRID2BAT:
> R4 := x5 &AND (y2 &OR y3 &OR y4) &AND u1 &IMP GRID2LOAD:
> R5 := (x3 &OR x4 &OR x5) &AND y1 &AND u1 &IMP GRID2LOAD:
> R6 := (x3 &OR x4) &AND (y2 &OR y3) &AND u1 &AND z2 &IMP GRID2LOAD:
> R7 := (x4 &OR x5) &AND y5 &AND u1 &IMP GRID2LOAD:
```

> R8 := x3 &AND y1 &AND u2 &IMP NET2BAT:
> R9 := x4 &AND y1 &AND u2 &IMP NET2BAT:
> R10:= x5 &AND (y1 &OR y2 &OR y3 &OR y4 &OR y5) &AND u2 &IMP NET2BAT:
> R11:= x3 &AND z2 &AND y2 &AND u2 &IMP NET2BAT:
> R12:= x4 &AND z1 &AND y3 &AND u2 &IMP NET2BAT:
> R13:= x4 &AND z2 &AND (y2 &OR y3) &AND u2 &IMP NET2BAT:
> R14:= (x1 &OR x2) &AND y1 &AND u1 &IMP BAT2LOAD:
> R15:= x1 &AND (y2 &OR y3 &OR y4 &OR y5) &AND u1 &IMP BAT2LOAD:
> R16:= (x2 &OR x3) &AND y5 &AND u1 &IMP BAT2LOAD:
> R17:= (x2 &OR x4) &AND (y2 &OR y3 &OR y4) &AND u1 &IMP BAT2LOAD:
> R18:= x3 &AND (y2 &OR y3 &OR y4) &AND z1 &AND u1 &IMP BAT2LOAD:
> R19:= x3 &AND (y2 &OR y4) &AND z2 &AND u1 &IMP BAT2LOAD:
> R20:= x1 &AND y2 &AND u2 &IMP BAT2GRID:
> R21:= x1 &AND (y3 &OR y4 &OR y5) &IMP BAT2GRID:
> R22:= x2 &AND z1 &AND (y2 &OR y3 &OR y4) &IMP BAT2GRID:
> R23:= x2 &AND z2 &AND y4 &IMP BAT2GRID:
> R24:= x3 &AND z1 &AND (y2 &OR y3 &OR y4) &AND u2 &IMP BAT2GRID:
> R25:= x3 &AND z1 &AND y4 &AND u1 &IMP BAT2GRID:
> R26:= x4 &AND z1 &AND y4 &IMP BAT2GRID:
> R27:= x2 &AND y5 &IMP BAT2GRID:
> R28:= x3 &AND y5 &AND u2 &IMP BAT2GRID:
> R29:= x1 &AND (y1 &OR y2 &OR y3 &OR y4 &OR y5) &AND u2 &IMP NET2GRID:
> R30:= x2 &AND y1 &AND u2 &IMP NET2GRID:
> R31:= (x2 &OR x3 &OR x4) &AND y5 &AND u2 &IMP NET2GRID:
> R32:= (x2 &OR x3 &OR x4) &AND (y2 &OR y3 &OR y4) &AND z1 &AND u2
        &IMP NET2GRID:
> R33:= x2 &AND (y2 &OR y3 &OR y4) &AND z2 &AND u2 &IMP NET2GRID:
> R34:= x3 &AND (y3 &OR y4) &AND z2 &AND u2 &IMP NET2GRID:
> R35:= x4 &AND y4 &AND z2 &AND u2 &IMP NET2GRID:

and the set (or list) of their negations is a base of ideal J:
J:=[NEG(R1),NEG(R2),NEG(R3),NEG(R4),NEG(R5),NEG(R6),NEG(R7),
    NEG(R8),NEG(R9),NEG(R10),NEG(R11),NEG(R12),NEG(R13),NEG(R14),
    NEG(R15),NEG(R16),NEG(R17),NEG(R18),NEG(R19),NEG(R20),
    NEG(R21),NEG(R22),NEG(R23),NEG(R24),NEG(R25),NEG(R26),
    NEG(R27),NEG(R28),NEG(R29),NEG(R30),NEG(R31),NEG(R32),
    NEG(R33),NEG(R34),NEG(R35)]:

Now we are ready to extract knowledge. For instance, let us state as facts x_2, z_2, y_2 and u_1:

K:=[NEG(x2),NEG(z2),NEG(y2),NEG(u1)]:

Which of *NET2BAT, BAT2GRID, BAT2LOAD, GRID2BAT, GRID2LOAD, NET2GRID* follow from these facts? (the ideal considered is iI+J+K and its basis, B, is computed firstly):

> B:=Basis([op(iI),op(J),op(K)], Orde);
> NormalForm(NEG(NET2BAT),B,Orde);
                NET2BAT + 1
> NormalForm(NEG(BAT2GRID),B,Orde);
                BAT2GRID + 1
> NormalForm(NEG(BAT2LOAD),B,Orde);
                0
> NormalForm(NEG(GRID2BAT),B,Orde);
                GRID2BAT + 1
> NormalForm(NEG(GRID2LOAD),B,Orde);
                GRID2LOAD + 1
> NormalForm(NEG(NET2GRID),B,Orde);
                NET2GRID + 1

(the 6 calculations above took 0.078 s on a standard computer with a 8 GB RAM). 0 is obtained only for *BAT2LOAD*, so that is the only operation mode recommended in this case.

Appendix C. Subsystem I—Simplifying Knowledge Extraction

Obtaining the operation modes can be simplified declaring them and using a simple procedure that performs the six questions and looks for the results equal to zero:

> Operation_Modes:=[NET2GRID,NET2BAT,BAT2LOAD,BAT2GRID,GRID2LOAD, GRID2BAT]:
> operation_mode:=proc(facts::list)
> local i,K,OM,B;
> OM:=[];
> K:=map(NEG,facts);
> B:=Basis([op(iI),op(J),op(K)], Orde);
> for i in Operation_Modes do
>   if NormalForm(NEG(i),B,Orde)=0 then OM:=[op(OM),i] end if;
> end do;
> OM;
> end proc:

For example:
> Facts:=[x1,u1,y1,z2]:
> operation_mode(Facts);

[BAT2LOAD]

> Facts:=[x4,z1,y3,u2]:
> operation_mode(Facts);

[NET2GRID, NET2BAT]

> Facts:=[x4,z1,y3,u2]:
> operation_mode(Facts);

[NET2GRID, NET2BAT]

As said above, other more complex tasks can be solved by the RBES. For instance: Can something be deduced from $x_1 \wedge u_1 \wedge (z_1 \vee z_2)$? Let us ask the system:

> Facts:=[x1,y1 &OR y2 &OR y3 &OR y4 &OR y5,u1,z1 &OR z2]:
> operation_mode(Facts);

[BAT2LOAD]

(if we have a look at the first row of the table, *BAT2LOAD* is obtained in the first three odd columns and *BAT2LOAD or BAT2GRID* is obtained in the rest of the odd columns).

Appendix D. Subsystem I—Checking the Correctness of the Rules

A simple procedure that generates the columns of Table 6 (with its peculiarities) can be easily implemented in Maple (in order to check the correctness of the rules):

> column:=proc(facts::list)
>   local i,j;
>   for i to 5 do
>   if {op(facts)} intersect {y2,y3,y4}<>{} and i in {2,3,4}
>   then
>   for j to 2 do
>   print(x||i,z||j,op(1,facts),op(2,facts),
>   operation_mode([op(facts),x||i,z||j]));
>   end do;
>   else
>   print(x||i,op(1,facts),op(2,facts),
>   operation_mode([op(facts),x||i]));
>   end if;
>   end do;

> end proc:

We can then ask, for example, for the first and fourth columns of Table 6 (note that the number of rows has been automatically adjusted):

> column([y1,u1]);

        x1, y1, u1, [BAT2LOAD]
        x2, y1, u1, [BAT2LOAD]
        x3, y1, u1, [GRID2LOAD, GRID2BAT]
        x4, y1, u1, [GRID2LOAD, GRID2BAT]
        x5, y1, u1, [GRID2LOAD, GRID2BAT]

> column([y2,u2]);

        x1, y2, u2, [NET2GRID, BAT2GRID]
        x2, z1, y2, u2, [NET2GRID, BAT2GRID]
        x2, z2, y2, u2, [NET2GRID]
        x3, z1, y2, u2, [NET2GRID, BAT2GRID]
        x3, z2, y2, u2, [NET2BAT]
        x4, z1, y2, u2, [NET2GRID]
        x4, z2, y2, u2, [NET2BAT]
        x5, y2, u2, [NET2BAT, GRID2BAT]

Appendix E. Subsystem II—Extracting Knowledge

The four rules describing the knowledge contained in Table 4 considered are:

> R101:= (x1 &OR x2) &AND (v4 &OR v5) &IMP BAT2SC:
> R102:= x3 &AND (v4 &OR v5) &AND z1 &IMP BAT2SC:
> R103:= x3 &AND (v4 &OR v5) &AND z2 &IMP GRID2SC:
> R104:= (x4 &OR x5) &AND (v4 &OR v5) &IMP GRID2SC:

and, in this case, the ideal J is:

> J:=[NEG(R101),NEG(R102),NEG(R103),NEG(R104)]:

We have, for example:

> Facts:=[x2,v4,z2]:
> operation_mode(Facts);

        [BAT2SC]

> Facts:=[x4,v4,z1 &OR z2]:
> operation_mode(Facts);

        [GRID2SC]

Appendix F. Subsystem III—Extracting Knowledge

The seven rules describing the knowledge contained in Table 5 are:

> R201:= (x1 &OR x2 &OR x3) &AND (y1 &OR y2) &AND w1 &IMP MPPT:
> R202:= x3 &AND (y1 &OR y2) &AND w1 &IMP MPPT:
> R203:= x3 &AND y1 &AND w2 &IMP MPPT:
> R204:= x4 &OR x5 &IMP MPPT:
> R205:= (x1 &OR x2) &AND y1 &AND w2 &IMP RPPT:
> R206:= (x1 &OR x2 &OR x3) &AND (y1 &OR y2) &AND w2 &IMP RPPT:
> R207:= (x1 &OR x2 &OR x3) &AND (y3 &OR y4 &OR y5) &IMP RPPT:

and, in this case, the ideal J is:

> J:=[NEG(R201),NEG(R202),NEG(R203),NEG(R204),NEG(R205),
   NEG(R206),NEG(R207)]:

For example:

> Facts:=[x3,y3,w1]:
> operation_mode(Facts);

        [RPPT]

> Facts:=[x4,y1 &OR y2 &OR y3 &OR y4 &OR y5, w1 &OR w2]:
> operation_mode(Facts);

        [MPPT]

Abbreviations

AC	Alternating Current
B2G, BAT2GRID	Battery to Grid
B2L, BAT2LOAD	Battery to Load
B2SC, BAT2SC	Battery to Supercapacitor
CAS	Computer Algebra System
DC	Direct Current
DER	Distributed Energy Resources
EMS	Energy Management System
ESS	Energy Storage System
G2B, GRID2BAT	Grid to Battery
G2L, GRID2LOAD	Grid to Load
G2SC, GRID2SC	Grid to Supercapacitor
GC	Grid-Connected
HESS	Hybrid Energy Storage System
LPF	Low-Pass Filter
MPP	Maximum Power Point
MG	Microgrid
MPPT	Maximum Power Point Tracking
N2B, NET2BAT	Surplus to Battery
N2G, NET2GRID	Surplus to Grid
NG	Nanogrid
P&O	Perturb and Observe
PV	Photovoltaic
PCC	Point of Common Coupling
RBES	Rule Based Expert System
RPP	Reference Power Point
RES	Renewable Energy Sources
RPPT	Reference Power Point Tracking
SA	Stand-Alone
STC	Standard Test Conditions
SOC	State of Charge
STS	Static Transfer Switch

References

1. European Commission. *2030 Climate & Energy Framework*; European Commission: Brussels, Belgium. Available online: https://ec.europa.eu/clima/policies/strategies/2030_en#tab-0-0 (accessed on 24 November 2020).
2. SETIS. Smart Electricity Grids. Available online: https://setis.ec.europa.eu/relatedjrc-activities/jrc-setis-reports/smart-electricity-grids (accessed on 3 April 2019).
3. Lee, S.; Jin, H.; Vecchietti, L.F.; Hong, J.; Har, D. Short-Term Predictive Power Management of PV-Powered Nanogrids. *IEEE Access* **2020**, *8*, 147839–147857. [CrossRef]
4. Sandgani, M.R.; Sirouspour, S. Energy Management in a Network of Grid-Connected Microgrids/Nanogrids Using Compromise Programming. *IEEE Trans. Smart Grid* **2018**, *9*, 2180–2191. [CrossRef]
5. Ban, M.; Shahidehpour, M.; Yu, J.; Li, Z. A Cyber-Physical Energy Management System for Optimal Sizing and Operation of Networked Nanogrids With Battery Swapping Stations. *IEEE Trans. Sustain. Energy* **2019**, *10*, 491–502. [CrossRef]
6. Luo, F.; Ranzi, G.; Wang, S.; Dong, Z.Y. Hierarchical Energy Management System for Home Microgrids. *IEEE Trans Smart Grid* **2019**, *10*, 5536–5546. [CrossRef]
7. Farzaneh, H.; Shokri, M.; Kebriaei, H.; Aminifar, F. Robust Energy Management of Residential Nanogrids via Decentralized Mean Field Control. *IEEE Trans. Sustain. Energy* **2020**, *11*, 1995–2002. [CrossRef]
8. Salazar, A.; Berzoy, A.; Song, W.; Velni, J.M. Energy Management of Islanded Nanogrids Through Nonlinear Optimization Using Stochastic Dynamic Programming. *IEEE Trans. Ind. Appl.* **2020**, *56*, 2129–2137. [CrossRef]
9. Lee, S.; Lee, J.; Jung, H.; Cho, J.; Hong, J.; Lee, S.; Har, D. Optimal power management for nanogrids based on technical information of electric appliances. *Energy Build.* **2019**, *191*, 174–186. [CrossRef]
10. Youssef, T.A.; Hariri, M.E.; Elsayed, A.T.; Mohammed, O.A. A DDS-Based Energy Management Framework for Small Microgrid Operation and Control. *IEEE Trans. Ind. Inform.* **2018**, *14*, 958–968. [CrossRef]
11. Roncero-Clemente, C.; Gonzalez-Romera, E.; Barrero-González, F.; Milanés-Montero, M.I.; Romero-Cadaval, E. Power-Flow-Based Secondary Control for Autonomous Droop-Controlled AC Nanogrids with Peer-to-Peer Energy Trading. *IEEE Access* **2021**, *9*, 22339–22350. [CrossRef]

12. Young, B.; Ertugrul, N.; Chew, H.G. Overview of optimal energy management for nanogrids (end-users with renewables and storage). In Proceedings of the 2016 Australasian Universities Power Engineering Conference (AUPEC), Brisbane, Australia, 25–28 September 2016; pp. 1–6. [CrossRef]
13. Bhosale, R.; Agarwal, V. Fuzzy Logic Control of the Ultracapacitor Interface for Enhanced Transient Response and Voltage Stability of a DC Microgrid. *IEEE Trans. Ind. Appl.* **2019**, *55*, 712–720. [CrossRef]
14. Barricarte, J.J.; Martín, I.S.; Sanchis, P.; Marroyo, L. Energy management strategies for grid integration of microgrids based on renewable energy sources. In Proceedings of the 10th International Conference on Sustainable Energy Technology, Istambul, Turkey, 4–7 September 2011; pp. 4–7.
15. Arcos-Aviles, D.; Espinosa, N.; Guinjoan, F.; Marroyo, L.; Sanchis, P. Improved fuzzy controller design for battery energy management in a grid connected microgrid. In Proceedings of the IECON 40th IEEE Annu. IEEE Industrial Electronics Society, Dallas, TX, USA, 29 October 2014; pp. 2128–2133.
16. Arcos-Aviles, D.; Pascual, J.; Marroyo, L.; Sanchis, P.; Guinjoan, F. Fuzzy Logic-Based Energy Management System Design for Residential Grid-Connected Microgrids. *IEEE Trans. Smart Grid* **2018**, *9*, 530–543. [CrossRef]
17. Ding, Y.; Wang, Z.; Liu, S.; Wang, X. Energy Management Strategy of PV Grid-Connected Household Nano-Grid System. In Proceedings of the 2019 IEEE Power & Energy Society General Meeting (PESGM), Atlanta, GA, USA, 4–8 August 2019; pp. 1–5. [CrossRef]
18. Ghiani, E.; Garau, M.; Celli, G.; Pilo, F.; Marongiu, G. Smart integration and aggregation of nanogrids: Benefits for users and DSO. In Proceedings of the 2017 IEEE Manchester PowerTech, Manchester, UK, 18–22 June 2017; pp. 1–6. [CrossRef]
19. Latifi, M.; Rastegarnia, A.; Khalili, A.; Bazzi, W.M.; Sanei, S. A Self-Governed Online Energy Management and Trading for Smart Micro/Nano-Grids. *IEEE Trans. Ind. Electron.* **2020**, *67*, 7484–7498. [CrossRef]
20. Caldognetto, T.; Mion, E.; Bruschetta, M.; Simmini, F.; Carli, R.; Tenti, P. A Model Predictive Approach for Energy Management in Smart Buildings. In Proceedings of the 2019 21st European Conference on Power Electronics and Applications (EPE '19 ECCE Europe), Genova, Italy, 3–5 September 2019; pp. P.1–P.10. [CrossRef]
21. Roncero-Clemente, C.; González-Romera, E.; Romero-Cadaval, E.; Milanés-Montero, M.I.; Miñambres-Marcos, V. PSCAD/EMTDC model for photovoltaic modules with MPPT based on manufacturer specifications. In Proceedings of the 2013 International Conference-Workshop Compatibility and Power Electronics, Ljubljana, Slovenia, 5–7 June 2013; pp. 69–74. [CrossRef]
22. Tremblay, O.; Dessaint, L.; Dekkiche, A. A Generic Battery Model for the Dynamic Simulation of Hybrid Electric Vehicles. In Proceedings of the 2007 IEEE Vehicle Power and Propulsion Conference, Arlington, TX, USA, 9–12 September 2007; pp. 284–289. [CrossRef]
23. Miniguano, H.; Barrado, A.; Fernández, C.; Zumel, P.; Lázaro, A. A General Parameter Identification Procedure Used for the Comparative Study of Supercapacitors Models. *Energies* **2019**, *12*, 1776. [CrossRef]
24. Kong, S.N.; Chin-Sien, M.; Yi-Ping, C.; Yao-Ching, H. Enhanced coulomb counting method for estimating state-of-charge and state-of-health of lithium-ion batteries. *Appl. Energy* **2009**, *86*, 1506–1511. [CrossRef]
25. Ruiz-Cortés, M.; Romero-Cadaval, E.; Roncero-Clemente, C.; Barrero-González, F.; González-Romera, E. Energy management strategy to coordinate batteries and ultracapacitors of a hybrid energy storage system in a residential prosumer installation. In Proceedings of the 2017 International Young Engineers Forum (YEF-ECE), Almada, Portugal, 5 May 2017; pp. 30–35. [CrossRef]
26. Ruiz-Cortés, M.; Romero-Cadaval, E.; Roncero-Clemente, C.; Barrero-González, F.; González-Romera, E. Comprehensive study of the benefits of integrating a sharing energy strategy between prosumers. In Proceedings of the IECON 2017—43rd Annual Conference of the IEEE Industrial Electronics Society, Beijing, China, 29 October–1 November 2017; pp. 3609–3614. [CrossRef]
27. Roncero-Clemente, C.; Vilhena, N.; Delgado-Gomes, V.; Romero-Cadaval, E.; Martins, J.F. Control and operation of a three-phase local energy router for prosumers in a smart community. *IET Renew. Power Gener.* **2020**, *14*, 560–570. [CrossRef]
28. Roanes-Lozano, E.; Laita, L.M.; Roanes-Macías, E. A Groebner Bases Based Many-Valued Modal Logic Implementation in Maple. In *AISC/Calculemus/MKM 2008, LNAI 5144*; Autexier, S., Campbell, J., Rubio, J., Sorge, V., Suzuki, M., Wiedijk, F., Eds.; Springer: Berlin/Heidelberg, Germany, 2008; pp. 170–183. [CrossRef]
29. Roanes-Lozano, E.; Laita, L.M.; Hernando, A.; Roanes-Macías, E. An algebraic approach to rule based expert systems. *Rev. R. Acad. Cien. Ser. A. Mat.* **2010**, *104*, 19–40. [CrossRef]
30. Buchberger, B. Bruno Buchberger's PhD Thesis 1965: An algorithm for finding the basis elements of the residue class ring of a zero dimensional polynomial ideal. *J. Symb. Comp.* **2006**, *41*, 3–4. [CrossRef]
31. Cox, D.; Little, J.; O'Shea, D. *Ideals, Varieties, and Algorithms*; Springer: Berlin/Heidelberg, Germany, 1992.
32. Smodels Web Page. Available online: http://www.tcs.hut.fi/Software/smodels/ (accessed on 14 February 2021).
33. Roanes-Lozano, E.; Alonso, J.A.; Hernando, A. An approach from answer set programming to decision making in a railway interlocking system. *RACSAM* **2014**, *108*, 973–987. [CrossRef]

Article

High-Speed Implementation of PRESENT on AVR Microcontroller

Hyeokdong Kwon [1], Young Beom Kim [2], Seog Chung Seo [2,3] and Hwajeong Seo [1,*]

[1] Division of IT Convergence Engineering, Hansung University, Seoul 136-792, Korea; hyeok@hansung.ac.kr
[2] Department of Financial Information Security, Kookmin University, Seoul 02707, Korea; darania@kookmin.ac.kr (Y.B.K.); scseo@kookmin.ac.kr (S.C.S.)
[3] Department of Information Security, Cryptology, and Mathematics, Kookmin University, Seoul 02707, Korea
* Correspondence: hwajeong@hansung.ac.kr; Tel.: +82-2-760-8033

Abstract: We propose the compact PRESENT on embedded processors. To obtain high-performance, PRESENT operations, including an add-round-key, a substitute layer and permutation layer operations are efficiently implemented on target embedded processors. Novel PRESENT implementations support the Electronic Code Book (ECB) and Counter (CTR). The implementation of CTR is improved by using the pre-computation for one substitute layer, two diffusion layer, and two add-round-key operations. Finally, compact PRESENT on target microcontrollers achieved 504.2, 488.2, 488.7, and 491.6 clock cycles per byte for PRESENT-ECB, 16-bit PRESENT-CTR (RAM-based implementation), 16-bit PRESENT-CTR (ROM-based implementation), and 32-bit PRESENT-CTR (ROM-based implementation) modes of operation, respectively. Compared with former implementation, the execution timing is improved by 62.6%, 63.8%, 63.7%, and 63.5% for PRESENT-ECB, 16-bit PRESENT-CTR (RAM based implementation), 16-bit PRESENT-CTR (ROM-based implementation), and 32-bit PRESENT-CTR (ROM-based implementation) modes of operation, respectively.

Keywords: PRESENT; counter mode of operation; AVR; software implementation

Citation: Kwon, H.; Kim, Y.B.; Seo, S.C.; Seo, H. High-Speed Implementation of PRESENT on AVR Microcontroller. *Mathematics* 2021, 9, 374. https://doi.org/doi:10.3390/math9040374

Academic Editor: Raúl M. Falcón

Received: 7 January 2021
Accepted: 4 February 2021
Published: 13 February 2021

Publisher's Note: MDPI stays neutral with regard to jurisdictional claims in published maps and institutional affiliations.

Copyright: © 2021 by the authors. Licensee MDPI, Basel, Switzerland. This article is an open access article distributed under the terms and conditions of the Creative Commons Attribution (CC BY) license (https://creativecommons.org/licenses/by/4.0/).

1. Introduction

Lightweight cryptography is getting more important than ever due to the emergence of the Internet of Things. The lightweight cryptography supports encryption in resource-constrained environments, such as sensor network, health care, and surveillance systems. Therefore, the implementation of lightweight cryptography aims at optimizing certain criteria, such as energy consumption, execution time, memory footprint, and chip size.

We propose a number of implementation techniques for well-known lightweight cryptography, namely PRESENT, and its Electronic Code Book (ECB) and Counter (CTR) on low-end embedded processors, where ECB encrypts the plaintext directly with the master key and CTR encrypts the counter value with the master key and then the result of encryption is XORed with the plaintext. In order to achieve optimal results on target microcontrollers, we used processor-specific optimizations for PRESENT block ciphers. Furthermore, the compact counter mode of PRESENT and its bit-slicing-based implementation are also presented. Novel implementation techniques for PRESENT block cipher can be extended to other lightweight cryptography algorithms and other platforms.

1.1. Contribution

1.1.1. Optimal Implementation of PRESENT Block Cipher on Embedded Processors

We implemented the PRESENT block cipher on low-end microcontrollers. The Alf and Vegard's RISC (AVR) processor is a resource-constrained device that is used extensively in low-end Internet of Things (IoT) applications, such as Arduino UNO and Arduino MEGA. The PRESENT-ECB implementation is optimized in terms of execution timing and other factors (e.g., code size and RAM). The word size of general purpose registers in the target

AVR microcontroller is 8-bit wise. All 16-bit wise PRESENT operations are optimized for 8-bit word and instruction set. Compared with the former implementation of PRESENT-ECB for a 128-bit security level on AVR microcontrollers, the proposed work improved the execution timing by 62.6% [1].

1.1.2. Pre-Computation for PRESENT with CTR

CTR is utilized in real applications and services, such as Transport Layer Security (TLS) and Virtual Private Network (VPN). CTR receives the input consisting of two parts, including constant nonce and variable counter. Since the nonce part is the constant variable, the constant nonce value is repeated several times throughout computations. For this reason, some computations of PRESENT block cipher can be optimized through pre-computation. By exploiting this feature, we further improved the execution timing of PRESENT-CTR. The method is a generic algorithm and can be implemented with other processors. Compared with the state-of-art implementation, the proposed works on embedded processors that have obtained performance enhancements by 63.8%, 63.7%, and 63.5% for 16-bit PRESENT-CTR (RAM), 16-bit PRESENT-CTR (ROM), and 32-bit PRESENT-CTR (ROM), respectively.

1.1.3. Open Source

The proposed PRESENT implementation is a public domain and full source codes are available at https://github.com/solowal/PRESENT_AVR (accessed on 7 January 2021). Source codes were written in (mixed) AVR assembly language (core algorithm) and C language (function call). Codes support four 128-bit PRESENT implementations, including PRESENT-ECB, PRESENT-CTR16 (RAM based implementation), PRESENT-CTR16 (ROM based implementation), and PRESENT-CTR32 (ROM based implementation). Projects were created and evaluated with `Atmel Studio 7.0` framework. Researchers can evaluate and re-create the result with the available source codes.

2. Related Works

2.1. PRESENT Block Cipher

PRESENT block cipher was introduced in CHES'07 [2]. PRESENT block cipher supports two parameters (i.e., PRESENT-64/80 and PRESENT-64/128). PRESENT block cipher requires 31 rounds and the Substitution-Permutation-Network (SPN) structure is adopted. PRESENT requires three computations including the substitution layer, permutation layer, and add-round-key.

The add-round-key operation performs exclusive-or computations with plaintext and round keys. Round keys ($roundkey = (roundkey_1, roundkey_2, ..., roundkey_{32})$) are generated from the key schedule. In particular, $roundkey_{32}$ is used for post-whitening. PRESENT block cipher uses a 4-bit substitution layer. The inner state of PRESENT block cipher ($S_{63}, ..., S_0$) can be seen as 16 4-bit words ($w_{15} ... w_0$), where one w word consists of four states (i.e., $w_x = \{S_{4\cdot x+3} \parallel S_{4\cdot x+2} \parallel S_{4\cdot x+1} \parallel S_{4\cdot x}\}$, $0 \leq x \leq 15$). The 4-bit substitution layer can be represented in Boolean operations for the bitslicing implementation. The PRESENT 4-bit S-box is designed for higher hardware efficiency and compact implementation. PRESENT block cipher uses a bit of permutation for the linear diffusion layer. The permutation layer performs bit permutation in the intermediate result. Each bit state (x) is permutated through $P(x)$.

2.2. Target Processor

The AVR microcontroller finds many interesting applications in embedded systems, such as sensor networks, surveillance systems, and health care. The number of available registers is only 32 8-bit long. Basic arithmetic instructions take a single clock cycle. The memory load/store instruction requires two clock cycles. The microcontroller supports an 8-bit instruction set, 128 KB of `FLASH` memory, 8 MHz of working frequency, two-stage pipeline design, and 4 KB of RAM (e.g., ATmega128). Among them, 6 registers (i.e.,

R26∼R31) are reserved for address pointers, and the remaining registers can be utilized for general purpose registers by a programmer. In particular, the R1 register is the ZERO register that should be cleared before function returns.

2.3. Former Implementations on Low-End Embedded Processors

Several works optimized the LEA on embedded processors [3–7]. They optimized execution timing and memory consumption. There are many implementations of lightweight cryptography such as CHAM, SPECK, and SIMON [5,7–17].

Many works are also devoted to improve the execution timing of AES on embedded processors [18–22]. In [23], the compact implementation of ARIA on low-end microcontrollers was proposed.

In CHES'17, optimized PRESENT implementation on embedded ARM CPUs was presented by using a novel decomposition of permutation layers (see Listing 1.2 of [24]), and bitsliced for the S-boxes [24]. A description of PRESENT is detailed in Algorithm 2 of [24]. Unlike a traditional PRESENT algorithm, it performs the permutation layer before the substitution layer. This order of computation is beneficial for bit-slicing-based substitution layer implementation.

In this paper, we presented the compact PRESENT implementation on AVR microcontrollers. We re-designed the PRESENT implementation for 8-bit architecture. Then, we also suggested the PRESENT-CTR. The CTR implementation technique optimizes 2 add-round-key, 2 permutation, and 1 substitution operations with a 1 look-up table operation.

3. Proposed Method

3.1. Optimization of PRESENT–ECB

For the efficient implementation of PRESENT block cipher, add-round-key, substituion, and permutation layers are optimized.

In Algorithm 1, add-round-key operation is described in a source code level. The computation is performed with XOR operations with round keys where XOR operation represents logical bitwise exclusive-or operation. The memory access for round keys is performed with the incremental memory pointer mode.

Algorithm 1: Add-round-key operation in assembly language.

Input: Intermediate data (reg0∼7), round key pointer (X).

Output: Output results (reg0∼7).

1: LD tmp, X+
2: EOR reg0, tmp
3: LD tmp, X+
4: EOR reg1, tmp
5: LD tmp, X+
6: EOR reg2, tmp
7: LD tmp, X+
8: EOR reg3, tmp
9: LD tmp, X+
10: EOR reg4, tmp
11: LD tmp, X+
12: EOR reg5, tmp
13: LD tmp, X+
14: EOR reg6, tmp
15: LD tmp, X+
16: EOR reg7, tmp

The efficient implementation of permutation ($P0$) is described in Algorithm 2. A 16-bit wise rotation operations are performed with LSR, ROR, LSL, and ROL instructions. Exclusive-or and logical and operations are performed with EOR and ANDI instructions. Similar to the $P0$ operation, the permutation ($P1$) is implemented, efficiently.

Algorithm 2: Permutation (P0) operation in assembly language.

Input: Intermediate data (reg0∼7).

Output: Result (reg0∼7).

//t=(X0⊕(ROR_u16(X1,1)))&0x5555

1: MOVW tmp0, reg4
2: LSR tmp1
3: ROR tmp0

4: EOR tmp0, reg6
5: EOR tmp1, reg7

6: ANDI tmp0, 0X55
7: ANDI tmp1, 0X55

//X0=X0⊕t; X1=X1⊕(ROL_u16(t,1));

8: EOR reg6, tmp0
9: EOR reg7, tmp1

10: LSL tmp0
11: ROL tmp1

12: EOR reg4, tmp0
13: EOR reg5, tmp1

//t=(X2⊕(ROR_u16(X3, 1)))&0x5555;

14: MOVW tmp0, reg0
15: LSR tmp1
16: ROR tmp0

17: EOR tmp0, reg2
18: EOR tmp1, reg3

19: ANDI tmp0, 0X55
20: ANDI tmp1, 0X55

//X2=X2⊕t; X3=X3⊕(ROL_u16(t, 1));

21: EOR reg2, tmp0
22: EOR reg3, tmp1

23: LSL tmp0
24: ROL tmp1

25: EOR reg0, tmp0
26: EOR reg1, tmp1

//t=(X0⊕(ROR_u16(X2, 2)))&0x3333;

27: MOVW tmp0, reg2
28: LSR tmp1
29: ROR tmp0
30: LSR tmp1
31: ROR tmp0

32: EOR tmp0, reg6
33: EOR tmp1, reg7

34: ANDI tmp0, 0X33
35: ANDI tmp1, 0X33

//X0=X0⊕t; X2=X2⊕(ROL_u16(t, 2));

36: EOR reg6, tmp0
37: EOR reg7, tmp1

38: LSL tmp0
39: ROL tmp1
40: LSL tmp0
41: ROL tmp1

42: EOR reg2, tmp0
43: EOR reg3, tmp1

//t=(X1⊕(ROR_u16(X3, 2)))&0x3333;

44: MOVW tmp0, reg0
45: LSR tmp1
46: ROR tmp0
47: LSR tmp1
48: ROR tmp0

49: EOR tmp0, reg4
50: EOR tmp1, reg5

51: ANDI tmp0, 0X33
52: ANDI tmp1, 0X33

//X1=X1⊕t; X3=X3⊕(ROL_u16(t, 2));

53: EOR reg4, tmp0
54: EOR reg5, tmp1

55: LSL tmp0
56: ROL tmp1
57: LSL tmp0
58: ROL tmp1

59: EOR reg0, tmp0
60: EOR reg1, tmp1

The bitslicing substitution operation is performed with Boolean operations. Detailed descriptions are given in Algorithm 3. Boolean operations, such as logical XOR, AND, OR, and one's complement are performed with EOR, AND, OR, and COM instructions. To move two adjacent registers in a single instruction, MOVW instruction is utilized.

Algorithm 3: Substitution operation in assembly language.

Input: Intermediate data (reg0~7).

Output: Result (reg0~7).

//T1=x2⊕x1;
1: MOVW tmp0, reg2
2: EOR tmp0, reg4
3: EOR tmp1, reg5

//T2=x1&T1;
4: MOVW tmp2, reg4
5: AND tmp2, tmp0
6: AND tmp3, tmp1

//T3=x0⊕T2;
7: MOVW tmp4, reg6
8: EOR tmp4, tmp2
9: EOR tmp5, tmp3

//T5=x3⊕T3;
10: MOVW tmp7, reg0
11: EOR tmp7, tmp4
12: EOR tmp8, tmp5

//T2=T1&T3;
13: MOVW tmp2, tmp0
14: AND tmp2, tmp4
15: AND tmp3, tmp5

//T1=T1⊕T5;
16: EOR tmp0, tmp7
17: EOR tmp1, tmp8

//T2=T2⊕x1;
18: EOR tmp2, reg4
19: EOR tmp3, reg5

//T4=x3|T2;
20: MOVW tmp6, reg0
21: OR tmp6, tmp2
22: OR tmp6, tmp3

//x2=T1⊕T4;
23: MOVW reg2, tmp0
24: EOR reg2, tmp6
25: EOR reg3, tmp6

//x3=x3⊕0xFFFF;
26: COM reg0
27: COM reg1

//T2=T2⊕x3;
28: EOR tmp2, reg0
29: EOR tmp3, reg1

//x0=x2⊕T2;
30: MOVW reg6, reg2
31: EOR reg6, tmp2
32: EOR reg7, tmp3

//T2=T2|T1;
33: OR tmp2, tmp0
34: OR tmp3, tmp1

//x1=T3⊕T2;
35: MOVW reg4, tmp4
36: EOR reg4, tmp2
37: EOR reg5, tmp3

//x3=T5;
38: MOVW reg0, tmp7

3.2. Optimization of PRESENT–CTR

For high-end IoT devices, such as 32-bit ARM-based processors, the size of the counter is fixed at 32-bit [20,25]. However, in an 8-bit ATmega processor, the memory size is limited to at least 2KB depending on the ATmega model (e.g., ATtiny). For this reason, block cipher encryption is usually performed by 2^{16} times [26]. From the security perspective of CTR mode, the attacker can pre-compute and collect ciphertext information relied on the IV. When the initial CTR mode is operated, the counter of IV (Initial Vector) is initialized to zero. If there is an unpredictable n-bit input in the encryption process other than the master key, the effective key size for Time-Memory Trade Off (TMTO) attack and Key Collision (KC) attacks increases by n-bit [27]. For an 8-bit AVR microcontroller with a small memory footprint, it is suitable to use a 16-bit counter. For general cases, a 32-bit counter is also widely used in practice. In this section, we present both PRESENT-CTR mode implementations with 16-bit and 32-bit counter modes of operation on the ATmega128 microcontroller.

PRESENT-CTR with a 16-bit counter is described in Figure 1. We represent the bit in square form. Since PRESENT block cipher performs 64-bit block-wise encryption, 64 squares are utilized (i.e., 64-bit data). The most left square and the most right square represent the first and last bit, respectively. Colored squares represent a counter part. The remaining white squares represent nonce part. The computation is performed from top to bottom.

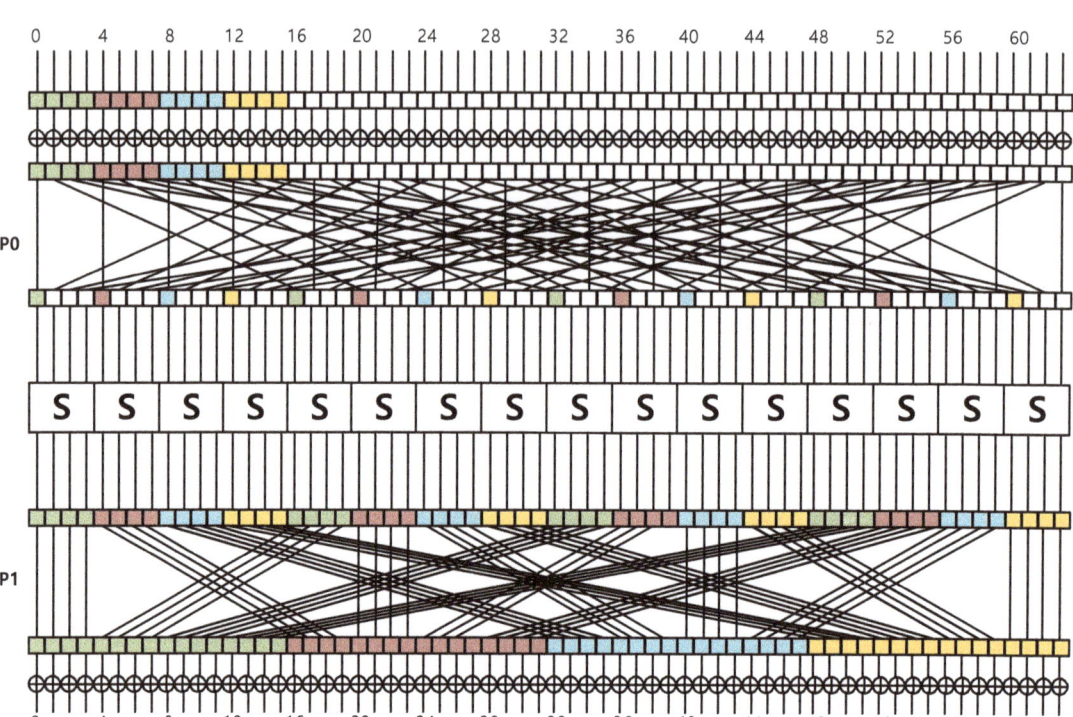

Figure 1. PRESENT-CTR with 16-bit counter.

1. First add-round-key. 64-bit plaintext is XORed with 64-bit round key. Since this is a bit-wise operation, each bits do not interfere with each other;
2. Permutation P0. The intermediate result is permuted. 16-bit counter values are distributed throughout the 64-bit intermediate result. Bits of the counter are arranged by 1 bit in the order of green, red, blue, and yellow according to a permutation rule;
3. Substitution. The 4-bit input values consist of 1-bit counter-part and 3-bit nonce part. The output of substitution can be pre-computed with the counter-part;
4. Permutation P1. The intermediate result is permuted again. After the permutation, the intermediate result is aligned by 16-bit wise;
5. Second add-round-key. The intermediate result is XORed with a second 64-bit round key.

The 4-bit data for each color of the initial 16-bit counter is distributed to the 16-bit data through permutation P0 and the bitslicing-substitution process. After the permutation P1 process is done, 16-bit data for each color is gathered regularly in the color (green, red, blue, and yellow) order of the initial counter. Through this, it is possible to predict 16-bit data through 4-bit of the initial counter. During the encryption process up to permutation P1, there is no interference between each color. For four 4-bit counter data, four 16-bit data can be pre-computed, independently. The required look-up table size is 128 bytes (4 colors × 2^4 counters × 16-bit size of data). A detailed description of look-up table generation is given in Algorithm 4. It generates 16 16-bit data with a counter divided into 4-bit data and repeats this process 4 times. The cost of generating a look-up table is less than performing PRESENT-ECB encryption by 4 times. We computed the pre-computation table in a parallel way, which generates four look-up tables at once. Four index parts (1~4-th bits, 5~8-th bits, 9~12-th bits, and 13~16-th bits) generate four pre-computed outputs (1~16-th bits, 17~32-th bits, 33~48-th bits, and 49~64-th bits). This ensures the generation of pre-computation is independent of each other. The computation of a look-up table on AVR requires only 4022 clock cycles. This is roughly one time of PRESENT-ECB encryption. The look-up table can be stored in RAM or ROM. If we allocate the look-up table to RAM, we can access to the data with the LD instruction in 2 clock cycles. Otherwise, we can store it to ROM and access to the data with the LPM instruction in 3 clock cycles. The encryption process of PRESENT-CTR mode can be optimized away from the operation up-to the second add-round-key operation by using the created look-up table. Overall, this approach replaces the two permutation layers, two add-round-key, and one substitution layer to one look-up table accesses.

Algorithm 4: Generation of look-up tables for proposed PRESENT-CTR16 encryption.

Input: 64-bit block of Initial Vector (16-bit counter and 48-bit nonce) B, roundkeys ($roundkey_1$, $roundkey_2$).

Output: Look-up tables for 16-bit counter ($LUT16_0$, $LUT16_1$, $LUT16_2$, $LUT16_3$).

1: $CTR \leftarrow 0$

2: $MASK \leftarrow \text{0xFFFFFFF0}$

3: **for** $i = 0$ **to** 3 **do**

4: $\quad C \leftarrow (B \& (MASK \lll 4i)) | (CTR \ll 4i)$

5: $\quad$ **for** $j = 0$ **to** 15 **do**

6: $\quad\quad C \leftarrow C \oplus roundkey_1$

7: $\quad\quad C \leftarrow P_0(C)$

8: $\quad\quad C \leftarrow S_{Bitslicing}(C)$

9: $\quad\quad C \leftarrow P_1(C)$

10: $\quad\quad C \leftarrow C \oplus P(roundkey_2)$

11: $\quad\quad LUT16_i(j) \leftarrow C$

12: $\quad$ **end for**

13: **end for**

14: **return** $LUT16_0, LUT16_1, LUT16_2, LUT16_3$

Algorithm 5 shows the proposed PRESENT-CTR16 implementation using a 16-bit counter. In steps 2–5, look-up table access with 16-bit counter is performed. Afterward, the remaining PRESENT computations are performed. Listing 1 shows the AVR assembly code for the 16-bit data look-up. In order to improve performance, 16-bit LUT is performed with two 8-bit memory accesses. The memory access for 16-bit data is 9 clock cycles. This process is repeated 4 times. PRESENT encryption is optimized at the cost of just 36 clock cycles.

Listing 1. Look up table access for 16-bit counter.

```
.macro LUT16 LUT0, LUT1, OFFSET, T0, T1
    LDI R31, hi8(LUT0)
    MOV R30, OFFSET
    LPM T0, Z
    LDI R31, hi8(LUT1)
    LPM T1, Z
.endm
```

Algorithm 5: Proposed PRESENT-CTR16 encryption.

Input: 64-bit plaintext B, a key K.

Output: 64-bit ciphertext C.

1: $roundkey = (roundkey_1, roundkey_2, ..., roundkey_{32}) \leftarrow keySchedule(K)$

2: $C_{0 \sim 15} \leftarrow LUT16_0(B_{0 \sim 3})$

3: $C_{16 \sim 31} \leftarrow LUT16_1(B_{4 \sim 7})$

4: $C_{32 \sim 47} \leftarrow LUT16_2(B_{8 \sim 11})$

5: $C_{48 \sim 63} \leftarrow LUT16_3(B_{12 \sim 15})$

6: $C \leftarrow S_{Bitslicing}(C)$

7: **for** $i = 2$ **to** 15 **do**

8: $\quad C \leftarrow C \oplus roundkey_{2i-1}$

9: $\quad C \leftarrow P_0(C)$

10: $\quad C \leftarrow S_{Bitslicing}(C)$

11: $\quad C \leftarrow P_1(C)$

12: $\quad C \leftarrow C \oplus P(roundkey_{2i})$

13: $\quad C \leftarrow S_{Bitslicing}(C)$

14: **end for**

15: $C \leftarrow C \oplus roundkey_{31}$

16: $C \leftarrow P(C)$

17: $C \leftarrow S_{Bitslicing}(C)$

18: $C \leftarrow C \oplus roundkey_{32}$

19: **return** C

PRESENT-CTR with 32-bit counter is described in Figure 2. The 1-th to 16-th counters are indicated by a colored square. The 17-th to 32-th counters are indicated by symbol squares. During the encryption process, the colored symbol square, which can be shown in Permutation P1, represents part of being affected by a color square and symbol square.

1. First add-round-key. Similarly to the 16-bit counter mode, the 64-bit plaintext is XORed with 64-bit round key. Since this is a bit-wise operation, bits do not interfere with each other;
2. Permutation P0. The intermediate result is permuted. 32-bit counter values are distributed throughout 64-bit intermediate results. The 16-bit to 32-bit of 32-bit counter are arranged one by one behind each color square;
3. Substitution. The 4-bit input values consist of a 2-bit counter part and 2-bit nonce part. The output of substitution can be pre-computed with the counter part;
4. Permutation P1. The intermediate result is permuted again. After the permutation, the intermediate result is aligned by 16-bit wise;
5. Second add-round-key. Similarly to the 16-bit counter mode of operation, the intermediate result is XORed with a second 64-bit round key.

Figure 2. PRESENT-CTR with 32-bit counter.

The 8-bit data for each 4-bit color and 4-bit symbol parts of the initial 32-bit counter is distributed to the 16-bit data through permutation P0 and bitslicing-substitution process.

Unlike the 16-bit counter case, the counter-part represented by the colored square and the counter-part represented by the symbol square interfere with each other during the bitslicing-substitution process. This can be seen in detail in Figure 2. When permutation (P1) is completed, the 16-bit data mixed by color and symbol is gathered in the color and symbolic order of the initial counter. This allows the pre-computation of 16-bit data through the 8-bit (4-bit color and 4-bit symbol) of the initial counter. At this time, the required lookup table size is 2048 bytes (= 4 color and symbol × 2^8 counter × 16-bit size of data). Unlike the 16-bit PRESENT-CTR implementation, 32-bit PRESENT-CTR implementation requires a huge look-up table (i.e., 2048). We placed a look-up table in ROM instead of RAM. The manufacture of AVR provides secure memory-based architecture (i.e., CryptoMemory; https:

//www.microchip.com/design-centers/security-ics/mature-products/cryptomemory accessed on 7 January 2021). For real world implementation, we can utilize this technology. A detailed description of look-up table generation is given in Algorithm 6.

Algorithm 6: Generation of look-up tables for proposed PRESENT-CTR32 encryption.

Input: 64-bit block of Initial Vector (32-bit nonce and 32-bit counter) B, roundkeys ($roundkey_1, roundkey_2$).

Output: Look-up tables for 32-bit counter ($LUT32_0, LUT32_1, LUT32_2, LUT32_3$).

1: $CTR \leftarrow 0$

2: $MASK \leftarrow \text{0xFFF0FFF0}$

3: **for** $i = 0$ **to** 3 **do**

4:     $C \leftarrow (B \& (MASK \lll 4i)) | (CTR_{0\sim 3} \lll 4i) | (CTR_{4\sim 7} \lll 4i + 16)$

5:     **for** $j = 0$ **to** 256 **do**

6:        $C \leftarrow C \oplus roundkey_1$

7:        $C \leftarrow P_0(C)$

8:        $C \leftarrow S_{Bitslicing}(C)$

9:        $C \leftarrow P_1(C)$

10:       $C \leftarrow C \oplus P(roundkey_2)$

11:       $LUT32_i(j) \leftarrow C$

12:     **end for**

13: **end for**

14: **return** $LUT32_0, LUT32_1, LUT32_2, LUT32_3$

Similarly to the 16-bit counter, the encryption process of PRESENT-CTR mode can be optimized from the operation up-to the second add-round-key by using the created look-up table. Overall, this approach replaces the two permutation layers, two add-round-key, and one substitution layer to one look-up table accesses.

Algorithm 7 shows the proposed PRESENT-CTR32 implementation using a 32-bit counter. In Steps 2~5, 16-bit data look-up with 8-bit (4-bit color and 4-bit symbol) counter is performed. Listing 2 shows the AVR assembly code for the 32-bit data look-up. The cost of looking-up 16-bit data is 10 clock cycles. This process is repeated 4 times. This is optimized at the cost of just 40 clock cycles.

Algorithm 7: Proposed PRESENT-CTR32 encryption.

Input: 64-bit plaintext B, a key K.

Output: 64-bit ciphertext C.

1: $roundkey = (roundkey_1, roundkey_2, ..., roundkey_{32}) \leftarrow keySchedule(K)$

2: $C_{0\sim15} \leftarrow LUT32_0(B_{0\sim3} \| B_{16\sim19})$

3: $C_{16\sim31} \leftarrow LUT32_1(B_{4\sim7} \| B_{20\sim23})$

4: $C_{32\sim47} \leftarrow LUT32_2(B_{8\sim11} \| B_{24\sim27})$

5: $C_{48\sim63} \leftarrow LUT32_3(B_{12\sim15} \| B_{28\sim31})$

6: $C \leftarrow S_{Bitslicing}(C)$

7: **for** $i = 2$ **to** 15 **do**

8:     $C \leftarrow C \oplus roundkey_{2i-1}$

9:     $C \leftarrow P_0(C)$

10:     $C \leftarrow S_{Bitslicing}(C)$

11:     $C \leftarrow P_1(C)$

12:     $C \leftarrow C \oplus P(roundkey_{2i})$

13:     $C \leftarrow S_{Bitslicing}(C)$

14: **end for**

15: $C \leftarrow C \oplus roundkey_{31}$

16: $C \leftarrow P(C)$

17: $C \leftarrow S_{Bitslicing}(C)$

18: $C \leftarrow C \oplus roundkey_{32}$

19: **return** C

Listing 2. Look up table access for 32-bit counter.

```
.macro LUT32 LUT0, LUT1, OFFSET1, OFFSET2, T0, T1
    LDI R31, hi8(LUT0)
    MOV R30, OFFSET1
    ADD R30, OFFSET2
    LPM T0, Z
    LDI R31, hi8(LUT1)
    LPM T1, Z
.endm
```

4. Evaluation

In CHES'17, bitslicing-based PRESENT implementation was proposed [24]. It has been theoretically and practically proven that the bitslicing technique shows the best results in 32-bit or higher processors. However, bitslicing-implementation in an 8-bit AVR environment has not been explored before. In embedded devices, bitslicing optimizes the memory access for the substitution layer but it requires Boolean operations. The AVR microcontroller has 8-bit wise 32 general-purpose registers and it should be carefully optimized to achieve high performance in bitslicing implementation. We evaluated PRESENT-ECB and PRESENT-CTR implementations and compared them with former works. ATmega128 is selected as a microcontroller, which is one of the most popular AVR microcontrollers in wireless sensor networks. In the case of CTR mode, 16-bit counter and 32-bit counter versions are evaluated. The software was evaluated with `Atmel Studio 7` and `-Os` option. Benchmarks are checked in clock cycles per byte which occurs when each mode of operation is called once.

Table 1 describe the comparison between this work and former implementations. PRESENT-ECB encryption by Dinu et al. (80-bit) and Engel et al. (128-bit) required 930.8 and 1349.0 clock Cycles Per Byte (CPB), respectively [1,28]. On the other hand, the proposed PRESENT-ECB implementation uses almost the same RAM as the existing implementation, but only requires 504.2 clock cycles per byte. For the code size, the proposed implementation utilized two permutation operations (P0, P1). The code size is bigger than former works. Since the proposed PRESENT-CTR implementation is optimized further by utilizing pre-computation, the proposed PRESENT-CTR mode achieved a higher performance than the existing PRESENT-ECB mode. The code size of the CTR mode of operation is bigger than the ECB mode of operation, but it achieved 488.2, 488.7, and 491.6 CPB, for 16-bit counter (RAM), 16-bit counter (ROM), and 32-bit counter (ROM). In Table 2, the comparison of execution timing depending on the message size is given. The RAM based 16-bit counter mode of operation requires look-up table generation online. For this reason, performance is lower than the ROM-based 16-bit counter mode of operation. However, the RAM-based implementation outperforms when the length is over 8192 bytes. PRESENT implementations are publicly available at: https://github.com/solowal/PRESENT_AVR (accessed on 7 January 2021), where anyone can access PRESENT implementations.

Table 1. Comparison of PRESENT on target embedded processors (Alf and Vegard's RISC (AVR)) in terms of timing (cycles per byte), RAM (bytes), and code size (bytes), [1]: Pre-computation in RAM, [2]: Pre-computation in ROM, †: 16-bit counter, ‡: 32-bit counter. ECB: Electronic Code Book.

Method	Security Level	Mode of Operation	Code Size	RAM	Timing
[28]	80	ECB	760	281	930.8
[1]	128	ECB	660	280	1349.0
This work		ECB	956	282	504.2
		CTR †,1	1150	420	488.2
		CTR †,2	1152	292	488.7
		CTR ‡,2	3072	292	491.6

Table 2. Comparison of PRESENT on target embedded processors (AVR) in terms of timing (10^6 clock cycles) depending on message size (bytes), [1]: Pre-computation in RAM, [2]: Pre-computation in ROM, †: 16-bit counter, ‡: 32-bit counter.

Method	Message Size (bytes)				
	4096	8192	16,384	32,768	65,536
CTR †,1	2.0038	4.0037	8.0035	16.0030	32.0019
CTR †,2	2.0010	4.0038	8.0076	16.0153	32.0307
CTR ‡,2	2.0136	4.0273	8.0547	16.1095	32.2191

In Table 3, a comparison with other lightweight block cipher implementations on target-embedded processors is given. On the 8-bit AVR environment, previous PRESENT implementation using 128-bit key shows a lower performance than other lightweight cryptographic algorithms [28], since substitution and permutation layers of the PRESENT algorithm incurs considerable overheads in an 8-bit AVR environment. We achieved the execution timing improvement of target block cipher implementation to 504 clock cycles per byte in an 8-bit AVR environment. Therefore, we believe that our optimization results are not only actually usable from real 8-bit AVR microcontrollers but can be applied to various cryptographic application algorithms.

Table 3. Comparison of other implementations on target embedded processors (AVR) in terms of timing (cycles per byte), RAM (bytes), and code size (bytes).

Algorithm	Plaintext	Security Level	Code Size	RAM	Timing
PIPO [29]			320	31	197
SIMON [17]			290	24	253
RECTANGLE [28]			466	204	403
RoadRunneR [30]	64	128	196	24	477
PRESENT [this work]			956	282	504
SKINNY [28]			502	187	877
PRIDE [28]			650	47	969
PRESENT [1]			660	280	1349
CRAFT [31]			894	243	1,504

5. Conclusions

We presented compact ECB and CTR for PRESENT on embedded processors. The ECB mode of operation was efficiently implemented in an optimization of diffusion layer, substitute layer, and add-round-key operations. The operation was accelerated with pre-computation in CTR. This new approach optimized away PRESENT operations by the substitution layer of second round. Finally, PRESENT block cipher on target microcontrollers consumed 504.2, 488.2, 488.7, and 491.6 CPB for ECB, 16-bit CTR (RAM-based implementation), 16-bit CTR (ROM-based implementation), and 32-bit CTR (ROM-based implementation) modes of operation, respectively.

Author Contributions: Investigation, H.K. and Y.B.K.; Software, H.K., Y.B.K., S.C.S., and H.S.; Writing-original draft, H.K. and Y.B.K.; Writing-review and editing, H.K., Y.B.K., S.C.S., and H.S. All authors have read and agreed to the published version of the manuscript.

Funding: This research of Hyeokdong Kwon and Hwajeong Seo was partly supported by the National Research Foundation of Korea(NRF) grant funded by the Korea government(MSIT) (No. NRF-2020R1F1A1048478) and this research of Hyeokdong Kwon and Hwajeong Seo was partly supported by Institute for Information & communications Technology Promotion(IITP) grant funded by the Korea government(MSIT) (No.2018-0-00264, Research on Blockchain Security Technology for IoT Services). This research of YoungBeom Kim and Seog Chung Seo was funded by National Research Foundation of Korea: 2019R1F1A1058494.

Conflicts of Interest: The authors declare no conflicct of interest.

References

1. Engels, S.; Kavun, E.B.; Paar, C.; Yalçin, T.; Mihajloska, H. A non-linear/linear instruction set extension for lightweight ciphers. In Proceedings of the 2013 IEEE 21st Symposium on Computer Arithmetic, Austin, TX, USA, 7–10 April 2013; IEEE: Piscataway, NJ, USA, 2013; pp. 67–75.
2. Bogdanov, A.; Knudsen, L.R.; Leander, G.; Paar, C.; Poschmann, A.; Robshaw, M.J.; Seurin, Y.; Vikkelsoe, C. PRESENT: An ultra-lightweight block cipher. In Proceedings of the International Workshop on Cryptographic Hardware and Embedded Systems, Vienna, Austria, 10–13 September 2007; Springer: Berlin/Heidelberg, Germany, 2007; pp. 450–466.
3. Hong, D.; Lee, J.K.; Kim, D.C.; Kwon, D.; Ryu, K.H.; Lee, D.G. LEA: A 128-bit block cipher for fast encryption on common processors. In Proceedings of the International Workshop on Information Security Applications, Jeju Island, Korea, 19–21 August 2013; Springer: Berlin/Heidelberg, Germany, 2013; pp. 3–27.
4. Seo, H.; Liu, Z.; Choi, J.; Park, T.; Kim, H. Compact implementations of LEA block cipher for low-end microprocessors. In Proceedings of the International Workshop on Information Security Applications, Jeju Island, Korea, 20–22 August 2015; Springer: Berlin/Heidelberg, Germany, 2015; pp. 28–40.
5. Seo, H.; Jeong, I.; Lee, J.; Kim, W.H. Compact implementations of ARX-based block ciphers on IoT processors. *ACM Trans. Embed. Comput. Syst. (TECS)* **2018**, *17*, 1–16. [CrossRef]
6. Seo, H.; An, K.; Kwon, H. Compact LEA and HIGHT implementations on 8-bit AVR and 16-bit MSP processors. In Proceedings of the International Workshop on Information Security Applications, Jeju Island, Korea, 23–25 August 2018; Springer: Berlin/Heidelberg, Germany, 2018; pp. 253–265.
7. Kim, Y.; Kwon, H.; An, S.; Seo, H.; Seo, S.C. Efficient Implementation of ARX-Based Block Ciphers on 8-Bit AVR Microcontrollers. *Mathematics* **2020**, *8*, 1837. [CrossRef]
8. Hong, D.; Sung, J.; Hong, S.; Lim, J.; Lee, S.; Koo, B.S.; Lee, C.; Chang, D.; Lee, J.; Jeong, K.; et al. HIGHT: A new block cipher suitable for low-resource device. In Proceedings of the International Workshop on Cryptographic Hardware and Embedded Systems, Yokohama, Japan, 10–13 October 2006; Springer: Berlin/Heidelberg, Germany, 2006; pp. 46–59.
9. Eisenbarth, T.; Gong, Z.; Güneysu, T.; Heyse, S.; Indesteege, S.; Kerckhof, S.; Koeune, F.; Nad, T.; Plos, T.; Regazzoni, F.; et al. Compact implementation and performance evaluation of block ciphers in ATtiny devices. In Proceedings of the International Conference on Cryptology in Africa, Ifrance, Morocco, 10–12 July 2012; Springer: Berlin/Heidelberg, Germany, 2012; pp. 172–187.
10. Kim, B.; Cho, J.; Choi, B.; Park, J.; Seo, H. Compact Implementations of HIGHT Block Cipher on IoT Platforms. *Secur. Commun. Netw.* **2019**, *2019*, 5323578. [CrossRef]
11. Koo, B.; Roh, D.; Kim, H.; Jung, Y.; Lee, D.G.; Kwon, D. CHAM: A family of lightweight block ciphers for resource-constrained devices. In Proceedings of the International Conference on Information Security and Cryptology, Xi'an, China, 3–5 November 2017; Springer: Berlin/Heidelberg, Germany, 2017; pp. 3–25.
12. Seo, H. Memory-efficient implementation of ultra-lightweight block cipher algorithm CHAM on low-end 8-bit AVR processors. *J. Korea Inst. Inf. Secur. Cryptol.* **2018**, *28*, 545–550.
13. Roh, D.; Koo, B.; Jung, Y.; Jeong, I.W.; Lee, D.G.; Kwon, D.; Kim, W.H. Revised Version of Block Cipher CHAM. In Proceedings of the International Conference on Information Security and Cryptology, Seoul, Korea, 4–6 December 2019; Springer: Berlin/Heidelberg, Germany, 2019; pp. 1–19.
14. Kwon, H.; Kim, H.; Choi, S.J.; Jang, K.; Park, J.; Kim, H.; Seo, H. Compact Implementation of CHAM Block Cipher on Low-End Microcontrollers. In Proceedings of the International Conference on Information Security Applications, Jeju Island, Korea, 26–28 August 2020; Springer: Berlin/Heidelberg, Germany, 2020; pp. 127–141.
15. Kwon, H.; An, S.; Kim, Y.; Kim, H.; Choi, S.J.; Jang, K.; Park, J.; Kim, H.; Seo, S.C.; Seo, H. Designing a CHAM Block Cipher on Low-End Microcontrollers for Internet of Things. *Electronics* **2020**, *9*, 1548. [CrossRef]
16. Beaulieu, R.; Shors, D.; Smith, J.; Treatman-Clark, S.; Weeks, B.; Wingers, L. The SIMON and SPECK Families of Lightweight Block Ciphers. *IACR Cryptol. EPrint Arch.* **2013**, *2013*, 404–449.
17. Beaulieu, R.; Shors, D.; Smith, J.; Treatman-Clark, S.; Weeks, B.; Wingers, L. The SIMON and SPECK block ciphers on AVR 8-bit microcontrollers. In Proceedings of the International Workshop on Lightweight Cryptography for Security and Privacy, Istanbul, Turkey, 1–2 September 2014; Springer: Berlin/Heidelberg, Germany, 2014; pp. 3–20.
18. Osvik, D.A.; Bos, J.W.; Stefan, D.; Canright, D. Fast software AES encryption. In Proceedings of the International Workshop on Fast Software Encryption, Seoul, Korea, 7–10 February 2010; Springer: Berlin/Heidelberg, Germany, 2010; pp. 75–93.
19. McGrew, D.; Viega, J. The Galois/counter mode of operation (GCM). *Submiss. NIST Modes Oper. Process* **2004**, *20*, 1–27.

20. Park, J.H.; Lee, D.H. FACE: Fast AES CTR mode Encryption Techniques based on the Reuse of Repetitive Data. *IACR Trans. Cryptogr. Hardw. Embed. Syst.* **2018**, 469–499.10.13154/tches.v2018.i3.469-499. [CrossRef]
21. Kim, K.; Choi, S.; Kwon, H.; Liu, Z.; Seo, H. FACE–LIGHT: Fast AES–CTR Mode Encryption for Low-End Microcontrollers. In Proceedings of the International Conference on Information Security and Cryptology, Seoul, Korea, 4–6 December 2019; Springer: Berlin/Heidelberg, Germany, 2019; pp. 102–114.
22. Kim, K.; Choi, S.; Kwon, H.; Kim, H.; Liu, Z.; Seo, H. PAGE–Practical AES-GCM Encryption for Low-End Microcontrollers. *Appl. Sci.* **2020**, *10*, 3131. [CrossRef]
23. Seo, H.; Kwon, H.; Kim, H.; Park, J. ACE: ARIA-CTR Encryption for Low-End Embedded Processors. *Sensors* **2020**, *20*, 3788. [CrossRef]
24. Reis, T.B.; Aranha, D.F.; López, J. PRESENT runs fast. In Proceedings of the International Conference on Cryptographic Hardware and Embedded Systems, Taipei, Taiwan, 25–28 September 2017; Springer: Berlin/Heidelberg, Germany, 2017; pp. 644–664.
25. Seo, H.; Lee, G.; Park, T.; Kim, H. Compact GCM implementations on 32-bit ARMv7-A processors. In Proceedings of the 2017 International Conference on Information and Communication Technology Convergence (ICTC), Jeju, Korea, 18–20 October 2017; IEEE: Piscataway, NJ, USA, 2017; pp. 704–707.
26. Kim, Y.; Seo, S.C. An Efficient Implementation of AES on 8-Bit AVR-Based Sensor Nodes. In Proceedings of the International Conference on Information Security Applications, Jeju Island, Korea, 26–28 August 2020; Springer: Berlin/Heidelberg, Germany, 2020; pp. 276–290.
27. McGrew, D.A. Counter mode security: Analysis and recommendations. *Cisco Syst. Novemb.* **2002**, *2*, 1–8..
28. Dinu, D.; Biryukov, A.; Großschädl, J.; Khovratovich, D.; Le Corre, Y.; Perrin, L. FELICS–fair evaluation of lightweight cryptographic systems. In Proceedings of the NIST Workshop on Lightweight Cryptography, Gaithersburg, MD, USA, 20–21 July 2015; Volume 128.
29. Kim, H.; Jeon, Y.; Kim, G.; Kim, J.; Sim, B.Y.; Han, D.G.; Seo, H.; Kim, S.; Hong, S.; Sung, J.; et al. A New Method for Designing Lightweight S-Boxes with High Differential and Linear Branch Numbers, and Its Application*. In Proceedings of the 23rd Annual International Conference on Information Security and Cryptology (ICISC 2020), Seoul, Korea, 2–4 December 2020; pp. 105–132.
30. Baysal, A.; Şahin, S. RoadRunneR: A small and fast bitslice block cipher for low cost 8-bit processors. In *Lightweight Cryptography for Security and Privacy*; Springer: Cham, Switzerland, 2015; pp. 58–76.
31. Beierle, C.; Leander, G.; Moradi, A.; Rasoolzadeh, S. CRAFT: Lightweight tweakable block cipher with efficient protection against DFA attacks. *IACR Trans. Symmetric Cryptol.* **2019**, *2019*, 5–45. [CrossRef]

Article

Efficient Implementation of ARX-Based Block Ciphers on 8-Bit AVR Microcontrollers

YoungBeom Kim [1], Hyeokdong Kwon [2], SangWoo An [3], Hwajeong Seo [2] and and Seog Chung Seo [1,*]

[1] Department of Information Security, Cryptology, and Mathematics, Kookmin University, Seoul 02707, Korea; darania@kookmin.ac.kr
[2] Division of IT Convergence Engineering, Hansung University, lSeoul 136792, Korea; hyeok@hansung.ac.kr (H.K.); hwajeong@hansung.ac.kr (H.S.)
[3] Department of Financial Information Security, Kookmin University, Seoul 02707, Korea; pinksnail06@kookmin.ac.kr
* Correspondence: scseo@kookmin.ac.kr; Tel.: +82-02-910-4742

Received: 24 August 2020; Accepted: 13 October 2020; Published: 19 October 2020

Abstract: As the development of Internet of Things (IoT), the data exchanged through the network has significantly increased. To secure the sensitive data with user's personal information, it is necessary to encrypt the transmitted data. Since resource-constrained wireless devices are typically used for IoT services, it is required to optimize the performance of cryptographic algorithms which are computation-intensive tasks. In this paper, we present efficient implementations of ARX-based Korean Block Ciphers (HIGHT and LEA) with CounTeR (CTR) mode of operation, and CTR_DRBG, one of the most widely used DRBGs (Deterministic Random Bit Generators), on 8-bit AVR Microcontrollers (MCUs). Since 8-bit AVR MCUs are widely used for various types of IoT devices, we select it as the target platform in this paper. We present an efficient implementation of HIGHT and LEA by making full use of the property of CTR mode, where the nonce value is fixed, and only the counter value changes during the encryption. On our implementation, the cost of additional function calls occurred by the generation of look-up table can be reduced. With respect to CTR_DRBG, we identified several parts that do not need to be computed. Thus, precomputing those parts in offline and using them online can result in performance improvements for CTR_DRBG. Furthermore, we applied several optimization techniques by making full use of target devices' characteristics with AVR assembly codes on 8-bit AVR MCUs. Our proposed table generation way can reduce the cost for building a precomputation table by around 6.7% and 9.1% in the case of LEA and HIGHT, respectively. Proposed implementations of LEA and HIGHT with CTR mode on 8-bit AVR MCUs provide 6.3% and 3.8% of improved performance, compared with the previous best results, respectively. Our implementations are the fastest compared to previous LEA and HIGHT implementations on 8-bit AVR MCUs. In addition, the proposed CTR_DRBG implementations on AVR provide better performance by 37.2% and 8.7% when the underlying block cipher is LEA and HIGHT, respectively.

Keywords: LEA block cipher; HIGHT block cipher; counter mode of operation; 8-bit AVR MCUs; CTR_DRBG; random bit; Internet of Things

1. Introduction

With the advent of Internet of Things (IoT), new types of services have become available. In these IoT services, a number of small and wireless devices around users collect the user data or surrounding information. Since the collected data are transmitted through wireless communication, the data can be easily revealed to attackers. For this reason, the sensitive data should be properly encrypted by a secure cryptographic algorithm before the transmission. Since it is required to transmit the data in an encrypted form rather than the original form, applying cryptographic algorithms is a fundamental building block for providing robust and secure communication in these IoT services. However, the implementing cryptographic algorithm on low-end IoT devices is not an easy task because typical client devices for these IoT services equip only limited resources, in terms of CPU, RAM, and ROM. For example, 8-bit AVR-based sensor nodes use in wireless sensor networks (WSNs), which is one of the representative IoT services, have only 4 KB of RAM, 128 KB of ROM, and 7.3728 MHz of computing frequency.

Recently, several lightweight block ciphers have been developed for efficient performance on IoT devices. Lightweight block ciphers ensure low-cost and simple computations. The computational structure is based on ARX (Addition, Rotation, and XOR) architecture. In South Korea, two ARX-based lightweight block ciphers, HIGHT [1] and LEA [2], have been developed and have been widely used. When data are larger than basic processing blocks (64-bit in HIGHT and 128-bit in LEA), the mode of operation needs to be applied. There are several modes of operations and CTR mode is the most popular among them. Until now, these ARX-based lightweight block ciphers have been optimized on resource-constrained 8-bit AVR Microcontrollers [1,3–5], which are widely used as sensor nodes in wireless sensor networks that are representative IoT services.

In addition to applying block ciphers to data to be transmitted, it is also important to securely generate secret keys used in block ciphers. If a weak key is used in a block cipher, the ciphertext can be revealed to attackers even if the underlying block cipher is secure. DRBGs (Deterministic Random Bit Generators) are widely used to generate secret information including keys. Among standardized DRBGs [6], CTR_DRBG provides strong resistance against backward security and forward security. Since CTR_DRBG makes use of CBC-MAC and CTR mode of operation in its derivation function and output generation function, it takes a larger execution time than executing block cipher algorithms. Thus, optimizing the performance of CTR_DRBG on the resource-constrained AVR-based devices is important for constructing secure and robust communications in IoT services [7].

In this paper, using a look-up table, we present optimized implementation of ARX-based lightweight block ciphers (HIGHT and LEA) on CTR mode and optimized CTR_DRBG implementation in an 8-bit AVR Microcontroller.

The contribution of this paper is as follows:

1. **Fast implementation for CTR mode of operation for LEA and HIGHT on 8-bit AVR MCUs**
   As nonce is repeatedly used in CTR mode, the result has an identical value when the nonce part is encrypted. Therefore, look-up tables can be generated using the results of encryption data of nonce. In this paper, we present efficient methods that generate look-up tables. Using the optimal implementation, we proposed, in a fixed key scenario, the performance of encryption can be improved by skipping the calculation procedure while loading only the calculation result from the look-up table. For better performance, optimizations of rotation operation and memory access are utilized. Finally, the implementation of LEA-CTR and HIGHT-CTR outperforms previous works by 6.3% and 3.8% than previous works, respectively. Our implementations of LEA and HIGHT are the fastest implementation compared to the previous implementation on 8-bit AVR MCUs. Furthermore, unlike the typical look-up table generation using a separated way, our implementation generates the look-up table, simultaneously, while executing the encryption process. Therefore, in our implementation, the cost of additional function calls that occurred from the generation of look-up table can be reduced. By using this, we obtained performance improvement of 6.7% and 9.1% compared to the previous separated encryption process which generates the look-up table, respectively.

2. **Optimized CTR_DRBG implementations on 8-bit AVR MCUs for fast random bit generation**
   The implementation of CTR_DRBG is optimized with the look-up table. In CBC-MAC of the Derivation Function, the look-up table is created for the encryption result of data depending on the initial block bit. The optimization of the Update Function is achieved with the look-up

table by taking advantage of the condition that the initial Operational Status is zero. In addition, the look-up table does not require an update, but also requires a low cost of 96 bytes, making it effectively applicable to 8-bit AVR Microcontrollers. Moreover, we presented methods to optimize Korean block cipher in the Extract Function on 8-bit AVR Microcontrollers. The Extract Function is optimized by utilizing the table for the CTR mode that uses fixed keys to reduce the execution timing. Our works of Derivation Function and Update Function outperform previous works by 13.3% and 72.4%, respectively. By applying CTR optimization methods, implementations of Extract Function using LEA and HIGHT outperform the standard implementation of Extract Function by 36.4% and 3.5%, respectively. By combining the proposed Derivation Function, Update Function, and Extract Function, overall, our CTR_DRBG implementation provides 37.2% and 8.7% of performance improvement compared with the native CTR_DRBG implementation using the works from [3–5] as an underlying block cipher of Extract Function.

3. **Proposing optimization methods that can be applied to various platforms**

In this paper, we propose general optimization methods for ARX-based block ciphers using the CTR mode. These methods have the advantage to be extended to other Addition-Rotation-XOR (ARX) based ciphers such as CHAM, Simon, and Speck [8,9]. While the significance of DBRG is increasing with the advent of the IoT era, there have been a few academic papers on optimization for CTR_DRBG that are popular to use. In this paper, we present CTR_DRBG optimization methods on 8-bit AVR Microcontrollers, the most limited IoT device. Our work is meaningful as it is the first attempt to optimize CTR_DRBG. Furthermore, our proposed Korean block cipher optimization methods and CTR_DRBG optimization methods are not only applicable to 8-bit AVR Microcontroller, but also to other low-end-processors and high-end-processors such as 16-bit MSP430, 32-bit ARM, and the CPU environment.

The rest of this paper is organized as follows. In Section 2, target platform, target ARX ciphers (LEA and HIGHT), target mode of operation, CTR_DRBG, and previous implementations are given. In Section 3, related work of Korean block ciphers (LEA and HIGHT) and CTR_DRBG is presented. In Section 4, optimized implementation of counter mode of operation is presented. In Section 5, optimized implementation of CTR_DRBG is presented. In Section 6, the performance is evaluated. Finally, Section 7 concludes the paper.

2. Background

2.1. 8-Bit AVR Microcontroller

AVR Microcontroller is based on Harvard architecture. All AVR commands require less than four clock cycles to execute. Table 1 shows operand and clock cycles of commands used in this paper. Currently, there are various types of AVR Microcontrollers, and they have various peripherals and memory sizes. This structure ensures that instructions always can be executed in a single cycle. There are 32 general-purpose registers with a single clock cycle. Of the 32 registers, six registers used for 16-bit indirect address register pointer for addressing, which these registers called X, Y, and Z registers [10]. These address pointers can also be used as a pointer for Flash Program memory. Our target device, in this paper, is ATmega128, which is used worldwide in the IoT era [11]. ATmega128 has a 128 KB of programmable flash memory, 4 KB SRAM, and 4 KB EEPROM.

Table 1. 8-bit AVR Assembly Instruction, *cc* means clock cycle [10,12].

Asm	Operands	Description	Operation	cc
ADD	Rd, Rr	Add without Carry	Rd ← Rd+Rr	1
ADC	Rd, Rr	Add with Carry	Rd ← Rd+Rr+C	1
EOR	Rd, Rr	Exclusive OR	Rd ← Rd⊕Rr	1
LSL	Rd	Logical Shift Left	C|Rd ← Rd≪1	1
LSR	Rd	Logical Shift Right	Rd|C ← 1≫Rd	1
ROL	Rd	Rotate Left Through Carry	C|Rd ← Rd≪1||C	1
ROR	Rd	Rotate Right Through Carry	Rd|C ← C||1≫Rd	1
BST	Rd, b	Bit store from Bit in Reg to T Flag	T ← Rd(b)	1
BLD	Rd, b	Bit load from T Flag to a Bit in Reg	Rd(b) ← T	1
MOV	Rd, Rr	Copy Register	Rd ← Rr	1
MOVW	Rd, Rr	Copy Register Word	Rd+1:Rd ← Rr+1:Rr	1
LDI	Rd, K	Load Immediate	Rd ← K	1
LD	Rd, X	Load Indirect from	Rd ← (X)	2
LPM	Rd, Z	Load Program Memory	Rd ← (Z)	3
ST	Z, Rr	Store Indirect	(Z) ← Rr	2

2.2. Target Block Ciphers

2.2.1. LEA Block Cipher

In WISA'13, lightweight block cipher LEA was presented [2]. With the development of IoT, it was developed to provide confidentiality in various embedded devices, cloud service, mobile environments, and so on. LEA is an algorithm that encrypts 128-bit data blocks. It can use 128, 192, and 256-bit secret keys, and its uses are classified according to required safety standards. LEA-128/128, LEA-128/192, and LEA-128/256 require 24, 28, and 32 rounds, respectively. While ensuring safety, it is possible to implement lightweight by eliminating the use of S-box. More information on parameters are shown in Table 2.

Table 2. Parameters of LEA block cipher, where n, k, rk, and r represent block size (bit), key size (bit), round key size (bit), and the number of rounds, respectively [2].

Cipher	n	k	rk	r
LEA-128/128	128	128	192	24
LEA-128/192	128	192	192	28
LEA-128/256	128	256	192	32

LEA block cipher performs encryption for 3 32-bit words in one round that represented in Figure 1. In the figure, the $X_i[0]$ word of round i directly becomes the input value to $X_{i+1}[3]$ word of round $i+1$. All words are moved to the left every end of rounds.

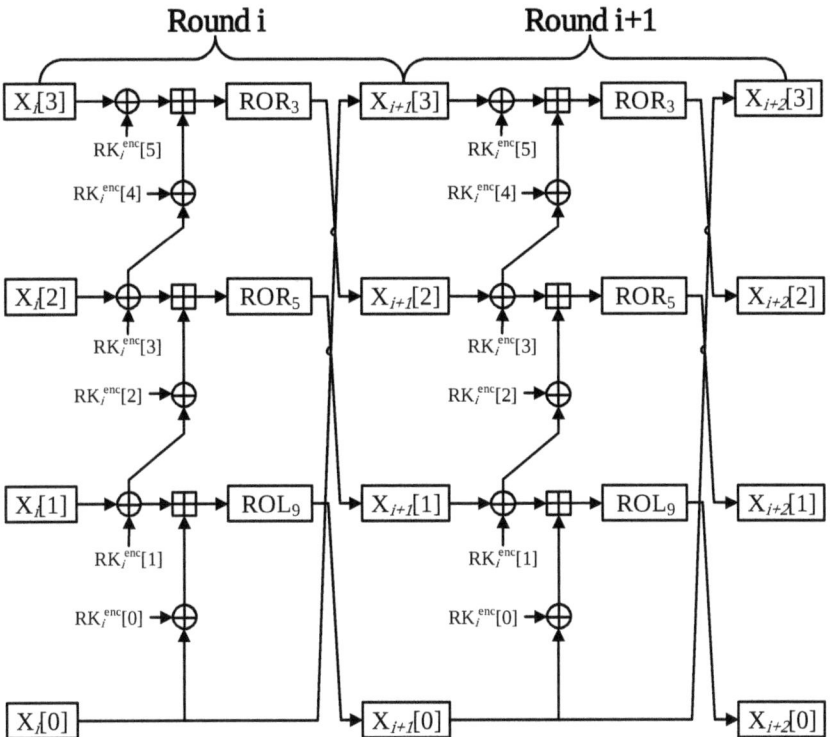

Figure 1. Encryption process of LEA block cipher [2].

2.2.2. HIGHT Block Cipher

HIGHT is a transformed Feistel ARX structure that encrypts 64-bit plaintext with a 128-bit secret key. The encryption process comprises of initial conversion, round functions, and final conversion. The key scheduling generates a round key of 136 bytes to be used for encryption with a 128-bit secret key. HIGHT performs encryption using 8-bit wise addition, rotate–shift, and XOR operation. Both encryption and decryption consist of 32 rounds. The structure of Round function in HIGHT block cipher is shown in Figure 2. During every single round, eight 8-bit words are encrypted. In each round in HIGHT, the four words are through by the F_0 or F_1 function. F_0 and F_1 functions perform left shift operation that is expressed in the following equations:

$$F_0(X) = X \lll 1 \oplus X \lll 2 \oplus X \lll 7$$

$$F_1(X) = X \lll 3 \oplus X \lll 4 \oplus X \lll 6$$

In each round, HIGHT uses a 64-bit round key. Since the number of round of HIGHT is 32, 2048-bit memory space is needed for storing roundkeys of each round. HIGHT parameters are represented in Table 3.

Table 3. Parameters of HIGHT block cipher, where n, k, rk, and r represent block size (bit), key size (bit), round key size (bit), and the number of rounds, respectively [1].

Cipher	n	k	rk	r
HIGHT-64/128	64	128	64	32

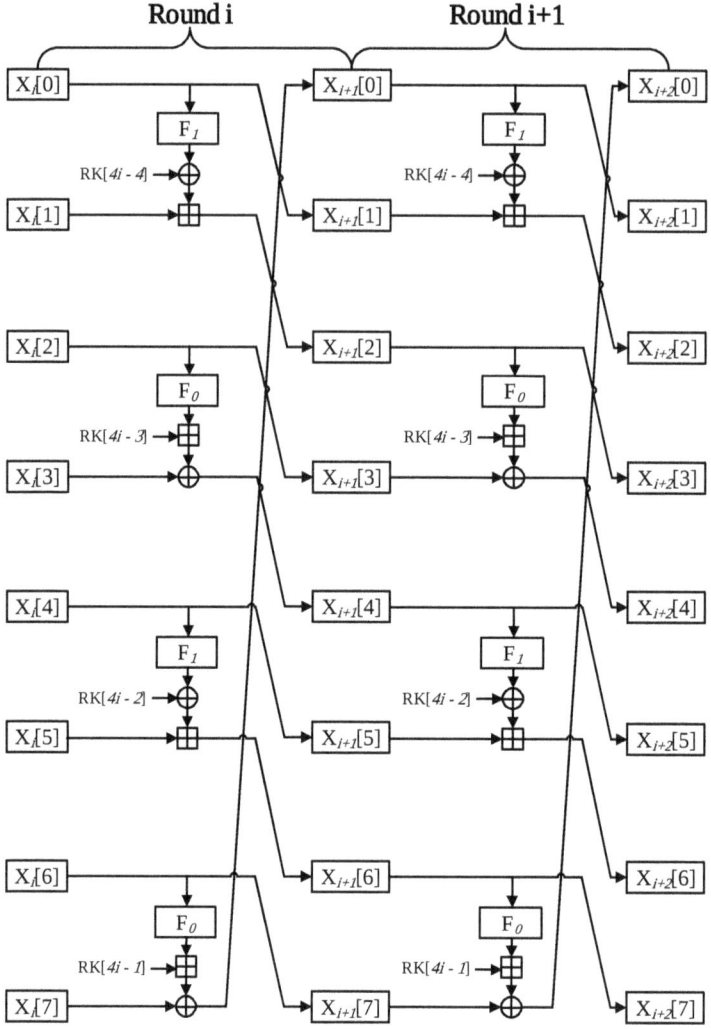

Figure 2. Round function scheme for the HIGHT block cipher [1].

2.3. CTR_DRBG

With the development of IoT, it is important to securely generate security keys when communicating with each other in WSNs (Wireless Sensor Network). For generating a security key safely, a true random bit generator should be used; however, in reality, the creation of a true random bit is almost impossible. Therefore, in the field, we use pseudo-random bits that are difficult to distinguish from true random bits. As pseudo-random bit generators, DRBGs (Deterministic Random Bit Generators) are used to securely generate random bit information, including secret keys, initial vectors, nonces, and so on [6,7]. There are CTR_DRBG based on a block cipher algorithm, HASH_DRBG using HASH Function, and HMAC_DRBG using HMAC among various types of pseudo-random number generators. HASH Function used in HASH_DRBG and HMAC_DRBG is mainly the SHA-2 Family. However, it is difficult to maintain the internal status of SHA-2 Family in the general-purpose register on 8-bit AVR MCUs. Note that internal states of SHA-256 and SHA-512 are 512-bit and 1024-bit, respectively [13,14]. However, with respect to the lightweight cryptography, blocks of LEA and HIGHT are 128-bit and 64-bit, respectively. Therefore, these blocks (states of LEA and HIGHT) can be stored in a general-purpose register.

Table 4 defines notations used in this paper and Table 5 shows parameters based on the block ciphers used in CTR_DRBG. Seed Bit is the addition of Key bit and Block Bit, and N is the representation of Seed Bit in bytes. Len_seed is the value of Seed Bit divided by Block Bit.

Figure 3 shows the detailed operational process of CTR_DRBG. Instantiate Function generates seed with Derivation Function. In addition, Instantiate Function updates Internal State, using the seed and Update Function. Reseed Function consists of Derivation Function and Update Function, and Generate Function consists of Reseed Function, Extract Function, and Update Function. Note that Update Function is called Instantiate Function, Generate Function, and Reseed Function. Generate Function outputs the random bits based on the internal state by using Extract Function. Before Extract Function is executed, if it supports Prediction Resistance or if Reseed Counter is greater than Reseed Interval, Generate Function calls Reseed Function to update Operational Status. In the opposite case, Generate Function calls an Extract Function to generate a random number, and calls the Update Function to update the Operational Status. When additional requests occur for random bit generations, a series of functions except for Instantiate Function are repeated.

Table 4. Notations for CTR_DRBG [6,7].

Notation	Descriptions
Personalization String	Information for differentiating the instances being created, non-confidential input (optional).
Nonce	Input information used to generate a seed during instance Function.
Internal State	Information used during CTR_DRBG. It consists of Operational Status and Control Information.
Operational Status	Information directly used for random number output. Consisting of C and V, C is the key used for block cipher, and V is the plain text used for block cipher.
Control Information	Information consists of security strength, Prediction Resistance flag and Derivation Function flag.
Prediction Resistance	Characteristics of the exposure of internal status information of CTR_DRBG without affecting future output.
Instantiate Function	Function to create and initialize CTR_DRBG instances as needed.
Derivation Function	Function called from an Instantiate Function to generate a seed using entropy input, Nonce and Personalization String.
Update Function	Function to update Internal State, using the CTR mode encryption
Reseed Function	Function to update Internal State using entropy and additional input. This function is affected by Reseed Counter.
Generate Function	Function to generate an output(random number) using Internal State and update Internal State.
Extract Function	Function to generate random number sequence, using the CTR mode encryption.

Figure 4 shows the structure of Derivation Function of CTR_DRBG. Derivation Function makes use of CBC-MAC in order to produce an output of seed length by inputting variable data S. Derivation Function is called in Instantiate Function and Reseed Function. Step 1 is a CBC-MAC encryption process by using counter value C. Step 2 is the process of CBC mode which encrypts V with Key generated from Step 1. First, it formats input S for CBC-MAC using Input Data consisting of Entropy, Nonce, and Personalization String. C, L, and N are 32-bit data. The initial C is zero, and padded to zero after C by the length of Block Bit minus 32-bit. L and N are byte lengths of Input Data and seed. Derivation Function makes S using C, L, N and Input Data. At this sequence of generating S, the length of S is padded to 0 so that it is a multiple of Block Bit. Then, Derivation Function increases C of S by 1 and repeats CBC-MAC as many times as Len_seed. Using the results of CBC-MAC as key and V, Derivation Function performs CBC mode encryption as many times as Len_seed to generate seed.

Table 5. Constant parameters of CTR_DRBG depending on block cipher [6,7].

Parameters	HIGHT-64/128	LEA-128/128	LEA-128/192	LEA-128/256
Key Bit	128	128	192	256
Block Bit	64	128	128	128
Seed Bit	192	256	320	384
N	0×18	0×20	0×30	0×40
Len_seed	3	2	3	3

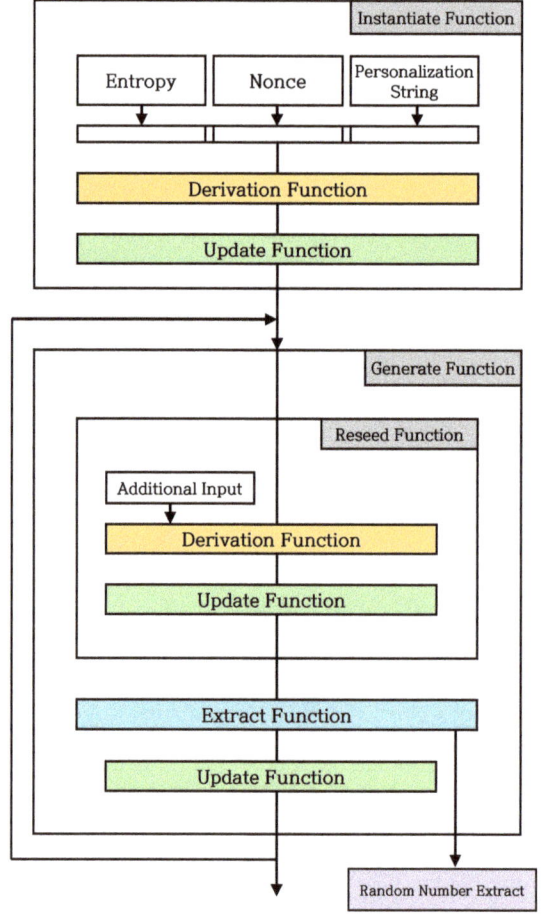

Figure 3. Detailed procedures of CTR_DRBG [6,7].

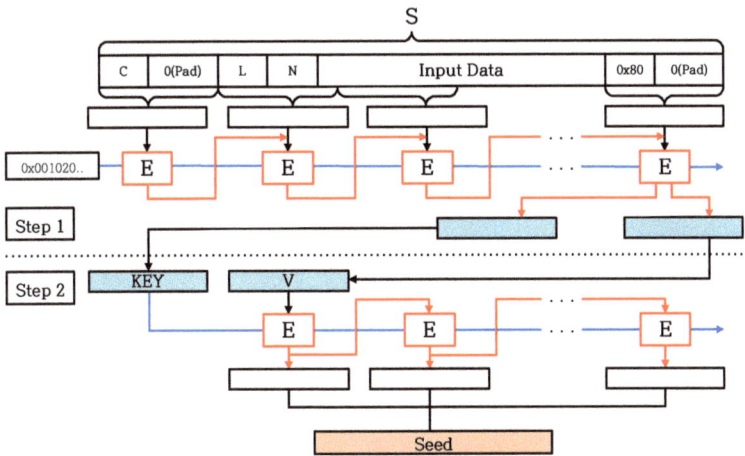

Figure 4. Overview of Derivation Function [6,7].

Figure 5 shows the structure of the Update Function in CTR_DRBG. Update Function updates C and V of Operational Status using CTR mode and Input data. Update Function performs with CTR mode encryption as many times as Len_seed. Update Function executes XOR operation on Input data and results generated in CTR mode encryption. Note that Update Function is called by Instantiate Function, Generate Function, and Reseed Function.

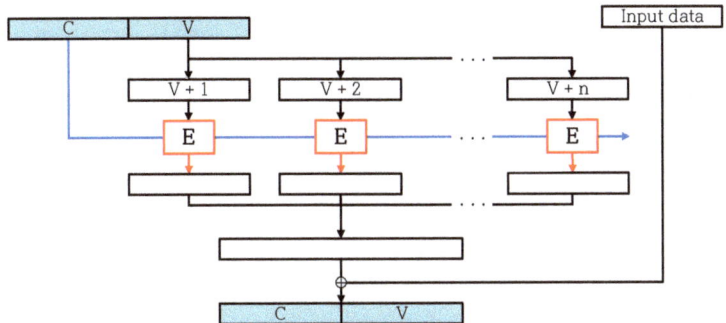

Figure 5. Overview of Update Function [6,7].

Generate Function consists of Reseed Function, Extract Function, and Update Function. As shown in Figure 3, Generate Function generates a random number using Extract Function. Figure 6 shows the structure of Extract Function called in Generate Function. Extract Function is a function that uses the same CTR mode as Update Function. Therefore, using Operational Status C as the key and V as the counter, Extract Function generates a random number by using CTR mode.

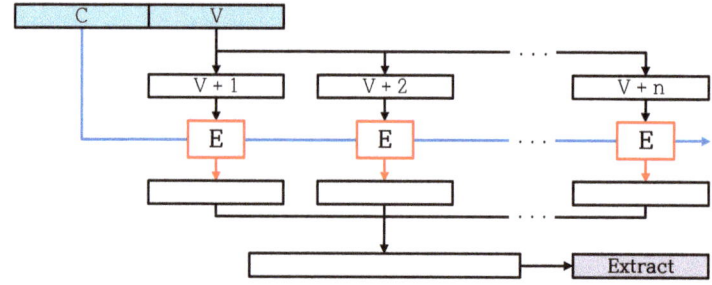

Figure 6. Overview of Extract Function [6,7].

3. Related Works

3.1. Block Cipher Implementations on AVR

Various studies have been conducted to improve performance for block ciphers in 8-bit AVR Microcontrollers. In 8-bit AVR MCUs, which are low-end-processors, the study of optimization has been mainly done using minimize memory access and pre-computation tables.

There are two main categories of block ciphers: Addition, Rotation, and eXclusive-or (ARX) based block ciphers and Substitution Permutation Network (SPN) based block ciphers.

Efficient implementations of ARX-based ciphers have been studied in various ways in an 8-bit AVR MCUs environment [1–5,8,15–21].

In WISA'13, the Institute of Electronics and Telecommunications Research Institute (ETRI) presented a light-weight LEA block cipher. In 8-bit AVR MCUs, the first LEA's implementation needed 3040 clock cycles for encryption [2].

In [19], the hardware design and implementation of LEA was proposed. Based on the key size, Ref. [19] introduced suitable hardware designs. For the area-optimized version, resource-shared structure for LEA was proposed.

In WISA'15, an efficient LEA implementation technique of dividing a 32-bit word operation using 4-byte units was proposed [3]. The method proposed in [3] minimizes memory access. A technique for efficiently operating rotate–shift used in 8-bit AVR MCUs was proposed. The proposed technique implicitly performs a byte-wise rotate–shift [3]. In addition, the source code was reduced by maximizing the use of the instruction set, and internal states of LEA were efficiently placed in general-purpose registers [3].

In [4], efficient implementation of LEA and method of rotate–shift-right were proposed, fully utilizing the AVR assembly instruction set and general-purpose registers in 8-bit AVR MCUs. For the optimized LEA implementation, Ref. [4] presented a compact ARX task on a target 8-bit AVR Microcontroller. Using both BST and BLD instructions in the AVR instruction, Ref. [4] improved the right rotation by 1 bit. By using the BST instruction in a 1-bit shift-right, the first bit of the register is reflected in the status flag. After that, rotate–shift-right is performed, using LSR and ROR instruction. Finally, Ref. [4] applied the status flag to the 8th bit in the register by using BLD instruction. By using this, when implementing LEA in 8-bit AVR MCUs, less than seven clock cycles are incurred for all rotate–shift operations. In addition, Ref. [4] efficiently places the LEA's internal state in a general-purpose register. Using MOVW instruction, clock cycles of execution time were reduced.

In [15], efficient LEA implementation was proposed in ARM Cortex-M3 processors. The general purpose registers are fully utilized to retain the required variables for the key scheduling and encryption operations and the rotation operation is optimized away by using the barrel-shifter technique. Since the on-the-fly method does not store the round keys, the RAM requirements are minimized.

In [5], efficient techniques using general-purpose registers were presented. The general-purpose registers in 8-bit AVR MCUs are compactly used for storing results during the key scheduling of LEA.

The HIGHT's implementation was first presented in [16]. Execution time of HIGHT for encryption and decryption in 8-bit AVR MCUs is 2438 and 2520 clock cycles, respectively [16].

In [21], efficient implementation using parallel architecture to enhance throughput was proposed. It shares key scheduling block for encryption and decryption to reduce hardware complexity.

In [20], hardware implementation for a significant reduction in the number of memory resources was proposed. Its implementation is useful for wireless applications such as a radio frequency identification system (RFID).

In [4], efficient rotation operations were introduced, and they achieved high performance. Like the LEA implementation proposed in [4], an efficient rotate–shift was used. Its implementation won the second round of Fair Evaluation of Lightweight Cryptographic Systems (FELCS).

In [17], fast HIGHT implementation was proposed. For optimizing delta update, F0 function, and F1 function, Ref. [17] uses the Look-Up Table (LUT). In addition, [17] proposed the memory-efficient way for F0 and F1 function, using bit-wise operations.

In 2015, SIMON and SPECK were presented by The US National Security Agency (NSA) [18]. Both SIMON and SPECK have advantages for efficient implementation in hardware and software environments. These two block ciphers support various block sizes and various key sizes. Therefore, in various IoT devices, SIMON and SPECK can be widely used. For 8-bit AVR MCUs, efficient implementation was presented in [8] using RAM-minimizing.

In an 8-bit AVR MCUs environment, block ciphers based on SPN also have also been actively studied. Since Advanced Encryption Standard (AES) is an international standard, AES implementations have widely studied.

In 2010, Ref. [22] presented efficient techniques for AES implementation, using a Z address pointer to perform SubBytes operation. In [22], MixColumns were implemented by a branch instruction set. Previous AES implementation in 8-bit AVR MCUs mainly focused on ECB Mode; however, in the field, AES-CTR Mode is more widely used (e.g., TLS/SSL) [23].

In ICISC'19, Fast AES-CTR Mode Encryption LIGHT (FACE-LIGHT) was presented by [24]. FACE-LIGHT is a variant of FACE implementation suggested by [25] in 8-bit AVR MCUs. FACE-LIGHT uses LUT for caching repeated data in IV. By using LUT, some operations can be omitted in 0,1, and 2 Round.

In WISA'20, efficient AES implementation was presented by [11]. The column-wise implementation was proposed. Proposed techniques have advantages for constant-time implementation and low cost for generating LUT. In addition, using 0 round optimization, Ref. [11] presented the optimized AES-CTR mode encryption for Wireless Sensor Network (WSN).

3.2. DRBG Implementations on AVR

To the best of our knowledge, the implementation of DRBG has not been presented in academic papers. The commercial product provides the AES-DRBG, but the performance is much slower than our work (http://cryptovia.com/cryptographic-libraries-for-avr-cpu/). Furthermore, the detailed information is not available. For this reason, our work is the-state-of-art work.

4. Optimized Implementations of LEA-CTR and HIGHT-CTR

The optimized implementation of a counter mode of operation for block cipher utilizes unique features of fixed nonce and variable counter values. The counter value indicates the block number, while the nonce is a fixed random value. Every block has the same nonce value. The calculation based on the nonce block is always a constant value. For this reason, the part can be pre-computed. The CTR implementation is categorized into two different scenarios, including fixed-key and variable-key. In this paper, we optimize both cases for various applications.

In the fixed-key scenario, the key value is fixed. For this reason, the precomputation result is always same and the precomputation table does not require update. In the implementation, the LDI instruction was used instead of the LD instruction to load the precomputation value from table. The LDI instruction operates at one cycle faster than the LD instruction.

On the other hand, the LDI instruction cannot be used for the variable-key scenario because the LDI instruction can only load the fixed value. Furthermore, the pre-computed table should be updated efficiently whenever the key is updated. This implementation shows the lower performance than that of fixed-key implementation. However, the variable-key implementation is able to perform the encryption with updated keys, which is more suitable for practical usages than fixed-key.

4.1. Optimized Implementation of LEA-CTR

The LEA algorithm was suggested [2]. However, we use [4] implementation. [4] has optimized key scheduling; in particular, LEA-128/128 can reuse some round keys.

- **Round 0** In one round of LEA, the operations are performed in three parts. In Round 0, only $X_0[0]$ word has a counterpart of IV. Consequently, two words can be implemented through the precomputation method.
- **Round 1** However, due to the Round 0, the $X_1[1]$ word is also beginning to be affected by the counter value. For this reason, it might be thought that the precomputation part is only available at $X_1[2]$ word. The part where $X_1[3]$ word is used as the input value of $X_1[0]$ in Round 1 can be expressed by the following equation:

$$\text{ROL}_3((X_1[3] \oplus RK_1^{enc}[2]) \boxplus (X_1[0] \oplus RK_1^{enc}[3]))$$

At this equation, it can be seen that the blue parts $X_1[3]$ word and round key are fixed values. Consequently, XOR instruction between $X_1[3]$ word and round key part can be skipped.
- **Round 2** In Round 2, only the $X_2[3]$ word is not affected by counter value. Therefore, precomputation is not applicable as a whole. However, like the previous round, in order to use $X_2[3]$ word as an input value for $X_3[0]$ word, the operation part that performs XOR instruction with a round key can be a precomputation implement. The optimized LEA-128/128 CTR mode of operation is described in Figure 7.
- **Generation of look-up table** When generating a look-up table, it has the advantage that the table can be generated during the encryption process. CACHE can be saved in the look-up table through the result of the operation in executing each round. When creating the look-up table, only the address translation cost based on ST instruction is incurred.

Optimization for LEA-128/192 and LEA-128/256

Our optimization strategy for LEA-128/128 can be directly applied to both LEA-128/192 and LEA-128/256 because their computational structures are identical except for the number of rounds. In addition, we combine each four rounds into one for better performance in our LEA implementations.

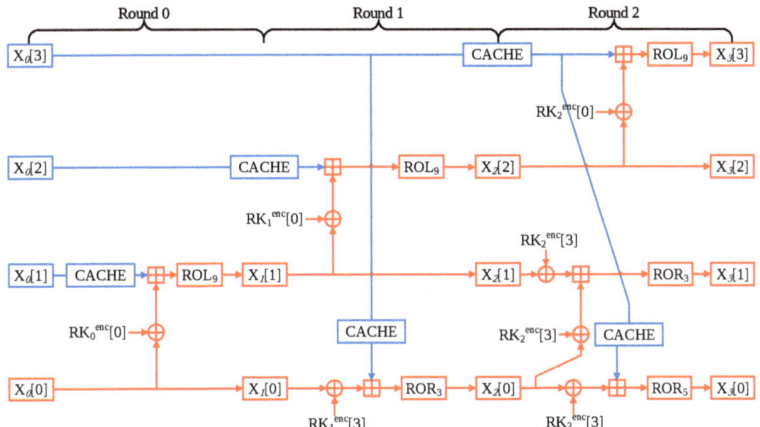

Figure 7. Optimized three rounds of LEA-128/128 block ciphers.

4.2. Optimized Implementation of HIGHT-CTR

The HIGHT-64/128 split input value into eight 8-bit words. The CTR mode of operation using 32-bit counter, so four words are affected by counter of IV in the initial round. Figure 8 shows this.

- **Round 0** The HIGHT performs four operations in a single round. In Round 0, the operation is performed using the following word pairs; $X_0[0]$ with $X_0[1]$, $X_0[2]$ with $X_0[3]$, $X_0[4]$ with $X_0[5]$, and $X_0[6]$ with $X_0[7]$. First of all, words of $X_0[0]$, $X_0[1]$, $X_0[2]$, $X_0[3]$ have counter values, which is variable. Thus, two of the four operations must be implemented. However, the other operations part uses only fixed values, which are nonce, and round keys, so precomputation is available for these parts.
- **Round 1** Unlike the previous round, the pair of words participating in the operation is slightly different. In this time, the $X_1[4]$ word is affected by the counter value; then, precomputation is not possible. $X_1[5]$ and $X_1[6]$ words still have nonce value, so this part is precomputation implementation available. In addition, lastly, $X_1[0]$ word operates with a $X_1[7]$ word that has nonce value. The whole operations cannot be skipped, but the result of $X_1[7]$ operation through the F1 function is can be omitted because $X_1[7]$ has nonce value, and the F1 function only conducts left shift operation.
- **Round 2** Round 2 has a similar structure to Round 0. However, in this time, $X_2[4]$ words are affected by counter value, so the precomputation part is reduced by one place and then the Round 0.
- **Round 3** Likewise this time, the Round 3 scheme is like Round 1. The difference is that the $X_4[6]$ word is affected by the counter value. For this reason, precomputation implementation is possible in only one part.
- **Generation of look-up table** In the same method as the proposed look-up table of LEA, the proposed method for HIGHT implementation has the advantage of generating a look-up table during the encryption process. CACHE data are saved during the CTR mode encryption. When creating the look-up table, only the address translation cost based on ST instruction is incurred.

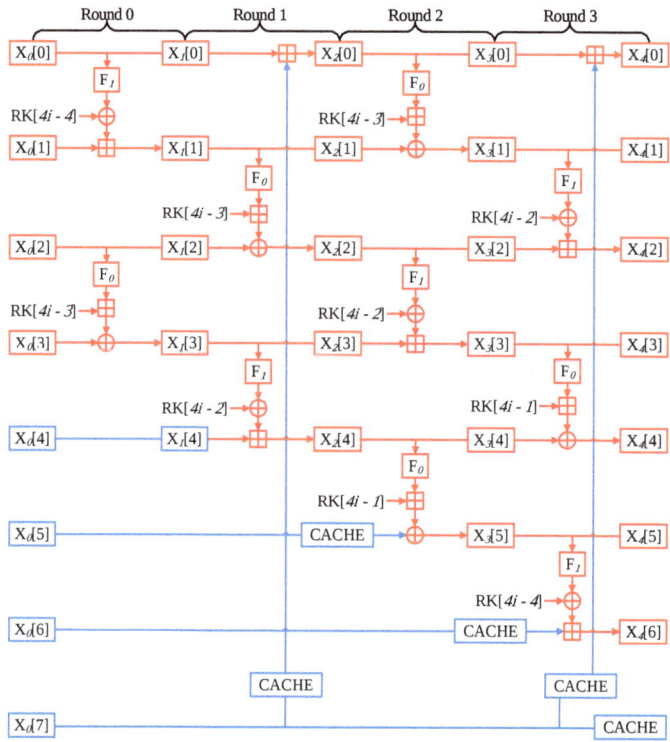

Figure 8. Optimized four rounds of HIGHT-64/128 block cipher.

4.3. Optimized Implementation of Rotation Operation

The 8-bit AVR microcontroller supports rotation instructions of 8-bit operands by one bit to left (ROL) and right (ROR). Since one general-purpose register in an 8-bit AVR microcontroller is 8-bit in size, additional computation is required to apply the rotate operation to data above 8-bit. If the offset of rotation operation is a multiple of 8-bit, the rotation operation can be optimized away by indexing the register directly. The optimized 16/32-bit word rotation operations are given in Table 6.

Table 6. Optimized 16/32-bit word rotation operations on 8-bit AVR Microcontroller.

16-bit ROL_1	16-bit ROL_8	32-bit ROL_1	32-bit ROL_8
		LSL R0	MOV TEMP, R3
LSL LOW	MOV TEMP, LOW	ROL R1	MOV R3, R2
ROL HIGH	MOV LOW, HIGH	ROL R2	MOV R2, R1
ADC LOW, ZERO	MOV HIGH, TEMP	ROL R3	MOV R1, R0
		ADC R0, ZERO	MOV R0, TEMP
3 cycles	3 cycles	5 cycles	5 cycles

5. Optimization for CTR_DRBG on 8-Bit AVR Microcontroller

In this section, we present optimization methods for an Instantiate Function of CTR_DRBG. The proposed method optimizes the constant data in Derivation Function and Update Functions called from Instantiate Function. This can be applied to any block ciphers used in CTR_DRBG. The proposed optimization approach with the constant data for Derivation Function and Update Function used in Instantiate Function is to generate a look-up table for the constant data.

In short, our strategy to speed-up an Instantiate Function is to generate the look-up table for the result of encryption for size of block from msb of S, which is used in CBC-MAC of Derivation Function. In addition, we optimize Instantiate Function by generating the look-up table for the result of Update Function called from an Instantiate Function by using the fact that both C and V values of the initial Operational Status are zero.

Figure 9 shows our optimization method for Derivation Function in an Instantiate Function. As mentioned in Section 2.3, Step 1 of Derivation Function uses CBC-MAC. When CBC-MAC is called in Derivation Function, the data from msb to Block Bit of S is zero. CBC-MAC executes encryption with increasing C by the number of times Len_seed. Since, at this time, the key used in CBC-MAC is fixed (0x00010203..), the result for encryption of Block Bit including C can be stored in a look-up table. For LEA-128/128, as shown in the yellow and green parts in Figure 9, the Derivation Function can reduce two encryptions during CBC-MAC computation. For other cases (HIGHT-64/128, LEA-128/192, and LEA-128/256), as shown in the yellow, green, and blue parts, Derivation Function can reduce three encryptions in the CBC-MAC computation process. The optimized method of Derivation Function we propose is applicable regardless of the length of Input Data entered in S. In addition, for CTR_DRBG that supports Prediction Resistance, Reseed Function is called from the Generate Function; even at this time, our main idea for Derivation Function is applicable. The constant data on the look-up table is the fixed data and requires the cost of Block Byte $*$ Len_seed. Based on the target block ciphers used in this paper, the look-up table requires up to 48 bytes. Since the look-up table is used as being semi-permanent when it is created (look-up table is constant data), the generation time of look-up table is not considered. Therefore, the look-up table can be used in environments where CTR_DRBG is repeatedly called.

Figure 10 shows the proposed optimization method for the Update Function of Instantiate Function. When the Instantiate Function is called, the Derivation Function generates the seed. After generating the seed, Instantiate Function calls the Update Function to execute an initial updating process for Operational Status. The initial Operational Status has a value of zero (C = 0, V = 0). Since Operational Status is zero when Instantiate Function generates the seed and updates Internal State, we can store the results of Update Function in the look-up table. The orange part in Figure 10 is the omitted encryption part. That is, the Instantiate Function can perform XOR operation immediately using Seed (red part) and look-up table without executing the Update Function. The proposed method that can be applied regardless of the block cipher algorithm, such as the optimization method applied to the Derivation Function. In addition, the look-up table for Update Function is a constant data table that can be used regardless of the number of calls made to CTR_DRBG, just like the look-up table generated by Derivation Function. The look-up table for Update Function requires up-to 48 bytes, the same as the look-up table generated for the Derivation Function.

The propose method for the Instantiate Function are to omit the encryption process as much as possible by using the look-up table. The cost of the look-up table requires up to 96 bytes. We can replace up-to six encryption operations using just 96 bytes. In the case of ATmega128, the most popular MCU in an 8-bit AVR MCUs environment, as mentioned in Section 2, has 4 KB of SRAM. Therefore, a maximum 96 bytes of the look-up table for the Instantiate Function can be stored in SRAM of ATmega128 sufficiently. In addition, the optimization methods we propose for Instantiate Function have the advantage of being applicable to various platforms such as low-end platforms and high-end platforms without relying on specific platforms.

The Extract Function called in the Generate Function is a function of extracting random numbers using the CTR mode. Figure 11 shows the proposed optimization method for the Extract Function of the Generate Function. The Extract Function uses C and V in Operational Status as a key and a counter to perform CTR mode to extract random numbers. Using the optimized CTR mode proposed in Section 4, we apply the optimized CTR mode of Extract Function. In order to apply the optimized CTR mode using the look-up table proposed in Section 4 to the Extract Function, the look-up table must be generated first. When Counter is V+1, we apply the optimized CTR mode with precomputation; through this process, we generate a look-up table. Note that the optimized CTR mode with precomputation only applies when the counter is V+1. If the counter is V+2 or higher, the optimized CTR mode using a look-up table is applied for the encryption of all CTR modes during Extraction Function.

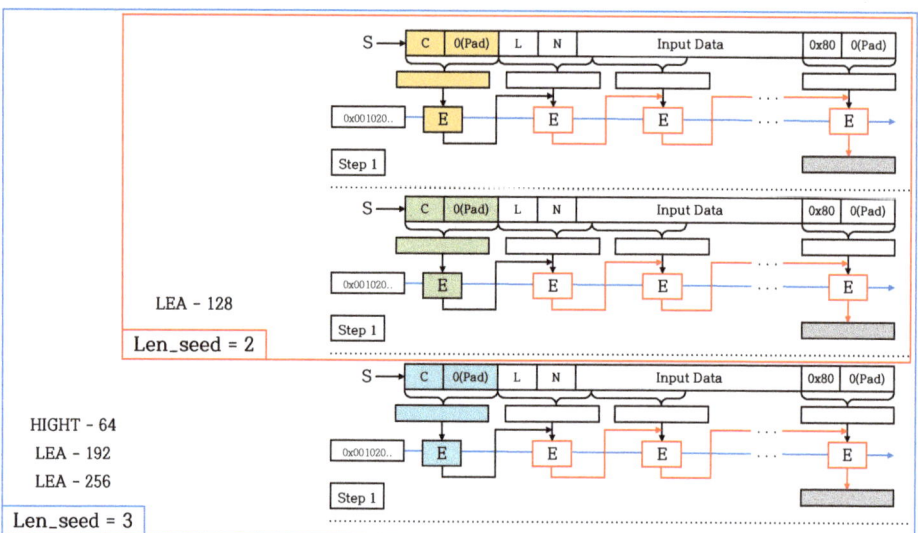

Figure 9. Optimized implementations for Derivation Function in the Instantiate Function.

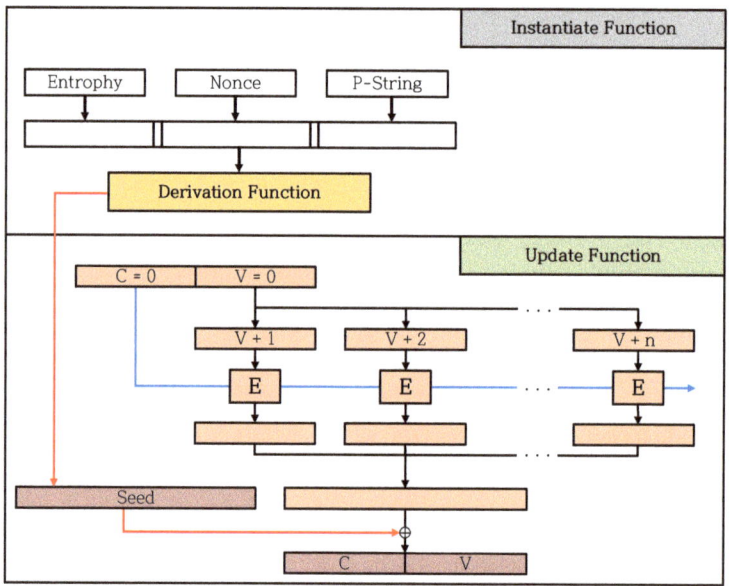

Figure 10. Optimized implementations for the Update Function in the Instantiate Function.

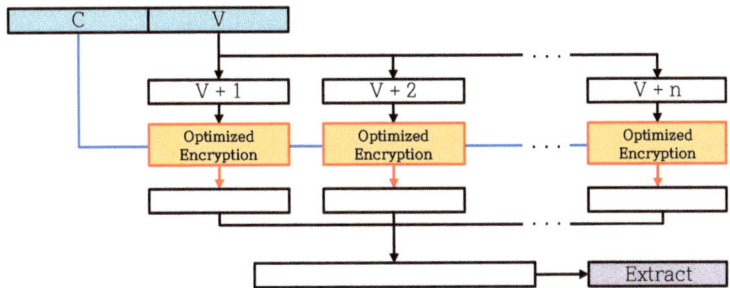

Figure 11. Optimized implementations for the Extract function of the Generate function.

6. Implementation Results

Proposed implementations of CTR mode and CTR_DRBG were evaluated on 8-bit AVR MCUs. The performance was measured in Clock cycles Per Byte (CPB). The measurement environment is Atmel Studio 7 and all code was compiled using an -O2 option.

The comparison criteria are as follows. For comparison, we define three versions of our implementations: the separation version (denoted as (c, s)), online version (denoted as (c, o)), and optimized encryption version (denoted as (c) in Figure 12). Both the separation version and the online version build the precomputation table by taking advantage of the property of CTR mode for fast encryption. Actually, they include the process for precomputation table generation and encryption. The difference between the separation version and the online version is that online version builds the precomputation table while executing encryption (Separation version builds the precomputation table separately from the encryption). Our optimized encryption version makes use of the precomputation table generated from either the separation version or the online version for fast encryption. Our three versions of LEA and HIGHT implementations will be compared with the previous best works from [3–5] and from [1,4], respectively.

6.1. LEA-CTR on 8-bit AVR Microcontrollers

The LEA implementation result is shown in Figure 12. Three LEA implementations exist on AVR environments [3–5]. The latest research is [5], but it contains only LEA-128 implementation. Therefore, in the case of LEA-128/192 and LEA-128/256, we compare our implementations to [3].

The separation version (denoted as (c, s) in the figure) of LEA-128 has worse performance by about 7.3% compared to [5]. In addition, LEA-128/192 and LEA-128/256 have slightly lower speeds than [3].

However, the precomputation in online version (denoted as (c, o) in the figure) of LEA-128 shows similar performance to [5]. The reason for the performance difference is that there is a part that calculates a cache table.

The reason for the performance difference compared to the separation version is that the online version combines the generation process of precomputation and the encryption process in order to reduce additional function calls.

The optimized LEA CTR mode implementations (denoted as (c) in the figure) clearly outperform the works from [3–5]. It shows around 4.8% performance improvement in case of LEA-128/128 compared with the work from [5]. In case of LEA-128/192, and LEA-128/256, our implementations provide around 6.3% and 6.3% improved performance compared to [3]. Our LEA implementations provide the fastest performance on 8-bit AVR platform compared with the previous results.

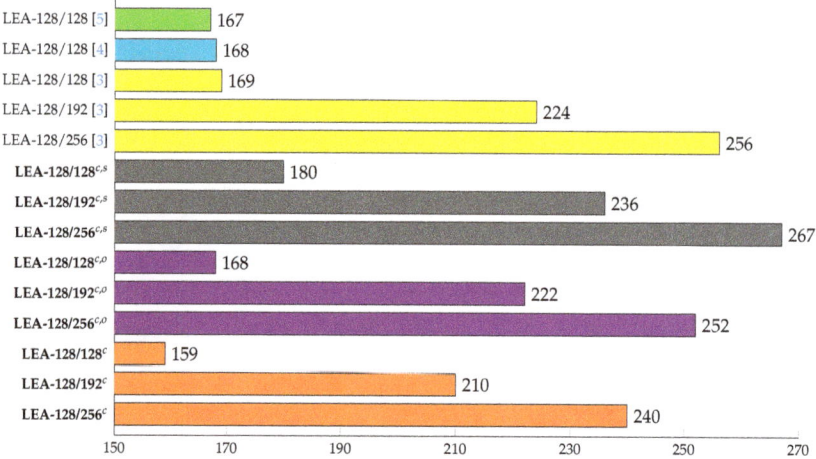

Figure 12. Comparison of execution time for LEA implementations on 8-Bit AVR Microcontrollers under the variable-key scenario in terms of clock cycles per byte, c: counter mode of operation (32-bit counter), s: building precomputation table separately from encryption process, o: building precomputation table in online while executing encryption process.

6.2. HIGHT-CTR on 8-Bit AVR Microcontrollers

The HIGHT is a 64-bit block cipher and until now there has only been one previous study for optimization on the AVR platform. Thus, we compare our implementation to the previous work [4], and the results are represented in Figure 13. Like performance analysis of LEA implementation described in the previous subsection, there are three HIGHT implementation versions such as the separation version, online version, and optimized CTR implementation, which are denoted as (c, s), (c, o), and (c), respectively, in Figure 13.

The separation version (denoted as c, s) has about 9.9% lower performance than [4]. However, the online version (denoted as c, o) provides a slightly better performance. The reason for this result is that the separation version performs encryption after calculating a precomputation table in independent functions. On the other hand, the online version keeps executing an encryption process, while generating the precomputation table. By using this, additional function calls overhead for generating a precomputation table can be reduced. Given these points, the online version has better performance compared with the separation version.

Finally, an optimized CTR mode of operation version (denoted as c) gets 3.8% better performance than [4]. This is because some of the calculation intervals are skipped through the use of precomputed values, and this is the fastest timing compared with the previous best results on the same platform.

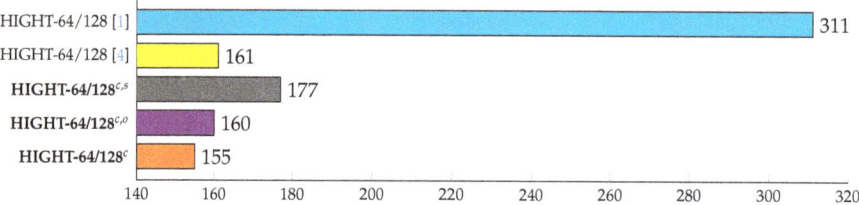

Figure 13. Comparison of execution time for HIGHT implementations on 8-Bit AVR Microcontrollers under the variable-key scenario in terms of clock cycles per byte, c: counter mode of operation (32-bit counter), s: building precomputation table separately from encryption process, o: building precomputation table online while executing the encryption process.

6.3. CTR_DRBG on 8-Bit AVR Microcontrollers

The proposed CTR_DRBG was implemented in Atmel Studio 7, as the same implementation environment as Section 6.1. In addition, the code was complied in an -O2 option. We implemented CTR_DRBG using the optimization method proposed in Section 4 and 5. Therefore, we measured the ratio of performance improvement by comparing our proposed implementation of CTR_DRBG (using optimized LEA-CTR, and optimized HIGHT-CTR) and CTR_DRBG with LEA [3,5], and HIGHT [4]. Since until now there have been no implementations of CTR_DRBG, we implement the naive version ourselves. As the underlying block cipher, we utilize the previous works of LEA implementation from [3,5], and of HIGHT from [4].

Table 7 shows the ratio of performance improvement to Derivation Function and Update Function, and shows the ratio of performance improvement in Extract Function depending on the length of the extracted random number. When measuring the ratio of performance improvement, an Input Data of Derivation Function was fixed at 64 bytes (which is reasonable because, on AVR platforms, the noise data are typically collected from hardware noise sources, which contain larger entropy than software noise sources). The encryption process as much as Len_seed is omitted in the Derivation Function proposed in Section 5. The block ciphers except HIGHT-64/128 show a performance improvement of more than 10% in Derivation Function as the Block size is 128-bit.

The actual computation of the method, proposed in Section 5, in the Update Function is only the XOR operation for the length of the seed. Since, in the Update Function as much encryption process as Len_seed has been omitted, the ratio of performance improvement is much larger than that of Derivation Function. We measure performance according to the length of the extracted random number in the Extract Function. In addition, we implemented the Extract Function using methods proposed in Sections 4 and 5. In other words, our implementation generates a look-up table when the Counter equals V+1, and uses a look-up table when the Counter more than V+2. Therefore, it can be seen that the longer the length of the extracted random number, the greater the ratio of the performance improvement of the Extract Function for each algorithm.

Figure 14 shows the ratio of performance improvement for CTR_DRBG with the target block ciphers according to the length of the extracted random number. The ratio of performance improvement is measured by comparing the previous best results shown in [3–5]. Table 8 shows the ratio of performance improvement, which shows the best performance among the ratios in Figure 14.

Table 7. Performance improvement of proposed Derivation function and Update function compared the naive implementation version on 8-bit AVR MCUs [3–5]. The result is based on the number of extracted random numbers, where B, *D.Fnc*, *U.Fnc*, and *E.Fnc* represent byte, Derivation Function, Update Function, and Extract Function, respectively.

Block Cipher		LEA-128/128	LEA-128/192	LEA-128/256	HIGHT-64/128
D.Fnc		10.1%	13.4%	14.1%	5.6%
U.Fnc		51.1%	69.4%	72.4%	40.6%
32B	E.Fnc	13.6%	22.0%	23.5%	1.4%
64B	E.Fnc	16.7%	25.1%	26.5%	1.9%
128B	E.Fnc	20.2%	28.7%	29.9%	2.4%
256B	E.Fnc	23.4%	31.9%	32.8%	3.0%
512B	E.Fnc	25.8%	34.3%	35.0%	3.3%
1024B	E.Fnc	27.3%	35.8%	36.4%	3.5%

The optimized implementations of CTR_DRBG used LEA-128/128, LEA-128/192, and LEA-128/256 increase the ratio of performance improvement as the length of the extracted random number increases. In Table 7, the ratio of performance improvement to Extract Function for LEA-128/128, LEA-128/192, and LEA-128/256 increases by a greater width than HIGHT-64/128 as the length of the extracted random number increases. Therefore, the ratio of performance improvement to Extract Function for LEA-128/128, LEA-128/192, and LEA-128/256 affects the performance improvement ratio of CTR_DRBG over the ratio of performance improvement for Derivation Function and Update Function. HIGHT-64/128 has a difference of approximately 2.1% in the ratio of performance improvement between 32 bytes and 1024 bytes extracted random number, and the overall ratio of performance improvement of CTR_DRBG does not increase. In other words, in the case which uses HIGHT-64/128, the ratio of performance improvement for Extract Function has less effect on the ratio of performance improvement in CTR_DRBG than the ratio of performance improvement for Derivation Function and Update Function.

Table 8. The best performance improvement ratio (%) of CTR_DRBG using our LEA and HIGHT implementation compared to CTR_DRBG using previous LEA and HIGHT implementation [3–5]. The result is based on the number of extracted random numbers, Byte represents the number of bytes with best performance of CTR_DRBG.

Block Cipher	LEA-128/128	LEA-128/192	LEA-128/256	HIGHT-64/128
Byte	1024	1024	1024	32
CTR_DRBG	26.7%	36.2%	37.2%	8.7%

The ratio of performance improvement of CTR_DRBG using HIGHT-64/128 drops as the length of the extracted random number increases. Table 7 shows that the performance increase in the Extract Function of HIGHT-64/128 results in a performance improvement of less than 3% as the length of the extracted random number increases. According to our observation, in the ratio of performance improvement to the extracted 32 byte random numbers and 1024 byte random numbers from the Extract Function, if the difference between the ratio of performance improvement when extracting random numbers is less than 8.3%, the ratio of performance improvement in CTR_DRBG does not increase depending on the length of the extracted random number. The longer the extracted random number is, the more encryption process is added. The longer the extracted random number, the more encryption process is added. Therefore, if the ratio of performance improvement of the Extract Function is significantly less than the ratio of performance improvement for Derivation Function and Update Function, the ratio of performance improvement for CTR_DRBG is lower. Our work of optimized CTR_DRBG in this paper shows up to 37.2% performance improvement when using proposed LEA implementation, and up to 8.7% performance improvement when using proposed HIGHT-64/128 implementation.

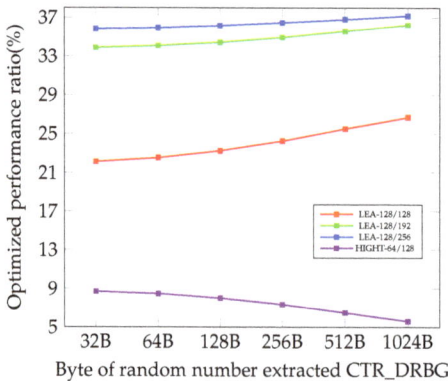

Figure 14. Performance improvement ratio (%) for CTR_DRBG using our LEA and HIGHT implementations on 8-bit AVR MCUs, compared to CTR_DRBG using previous LEA and HIGHT implementation [3–5]. The result is based on the number of extracted random numbers. B represents byte.

7. Conclusions

In this paper, we have presented optimized implementations of ARX-based Korean block ciphers (LEA and HIGHT) with CTR mode of operation, and CTR_DRBG using them on low-end 8-bit AVR microcontrollers. With respect to CTR mode optimization, the proposed implementation method for generating look-up tables has the advantage of reducing additional function calls compared to the existing naive methods. By using this technique, our proposed table generation method reduced the cost of building precomputation table by around 6.7% and 9.1% in the case of LEA and HIGHT, respectively. In addition, using the generated look-up table in a fixed key scenario, our CTR implementations based on LEA and HIGHT provide 6.3% and 3.8% improvements compared with the previous best results, respectively. Our CTR implementations are the fastest compared to existing LEA and HIGHT implementations. Regarding CTR_DRBG optimization, we proposed to precompute several parts of CTR_DRBG, which results in performance improvement. The proposed method is the first CTR_DRBG optimization technique, and can be applied regardless of any cipher used for CTR_DRBG. By using this, our CTR_DRBG's implementations using LEA and HIGHT on 8-bit AVR MCUs provide 37.2% and 8.7% of performance improvement compared with the previous naive implementation. We believe that our work can be widely used for building various types of secure IoT services. Furthermore, the optimization techniques from this work can be applied to the other platforms without difficulties.

Author Contributions: Writing—original draft, Y.K., H.K., and S.A.; Writing—review and editing, H.S. and S.C.S. All authors have read and agreed to the published version of the manuscript.

Funding: This work was supported by the National Research Foundation of Korea (NRF) grant funded by the Korea government (MSIT) (No. 2019R1F1A1058494).

Conflicts of Interest: The authors declare no conflict of interest.

References

1. Hong, D.; Sung, J.; Hong, S.; Lim, J.; Lee, S.; Koo, B.S.; Lee, C.; Chang, D.; Lee, J.; Jeong, K.; et al. HIGHT: A new block cipher suitable for low-resource device. In *International Workshop on Cryptographic Hardware and Embedded Systems*; Springer: Berlin/Heidelberg, Germany, 2006; pp. 46–59.
2. Hong, D.; Lee, J.K.; Kim, D.C.; Kwon, D.; Ryu, K.H.; Lee, D.G. LEA: A 128-bit block cipher for fast encryption on common processors. In *International Workshop on Information Security Applications*; Springer: Berlin/Heidelberg, Germany, 2013; pp. 3–27.
3. Seo, H.; Liu, Z.; Choi, J.; Park, T.; Kim, H. Compact implementations of LEA block cipher for low-end microprocessors. In *International Workshop on Information Security Applications*; Springer: Berlin/Heidelberg, Germany, 2015; pp. 28–40.
4. Seo, H.; Jeong, I.; Lee, J.; Kim, W.H. Compact implementations of ARX-based block ciphers on IoT processors. *ACM Trans. Embed. Comput. Syst. (TECS)* **2018**, *17*, 1–16. [CrossRef]
5. Seo, H.; An, K.; Kwon, H. Compact LEA and HIGHT implementations on 8-bit AVR and 16-bit MSP processors. In *International Workshop on Information Security Applications*; Springer: Berlin/Heidelberg, Germany, 2018; pp. 253–265.
6. Meltem, S.T.; Elaine, B.; John, K.; Kerry, M.; Mary, B.; Michael, B. *Recommendation for the Entropy Sources Used for Random Bit Generation*; NIST DRAFT Special Publication 800-90B; NIST: Gaithersburg, MD, USA, 2018; pp. 4–47.
7. Kim, Y.; Seo, S. Study on CTR_DRBG Optimization in 8-bit AVR Encironment. In Proceedings of the Conference on Information Security and Cryptography-Summer 2020 (CICS-S'20), Seoul, Korea, 15 July 2020.
8. Beaulieu, R.; Shors, D.; Smith, J.; Treatman-Clark, S.; Weeks, B.; Wingers, L. The SIMON and SPECK block ciphers on AVR 8-bit microcontrollers. In *International Workshop on Lightweight Cryptography for Security and Privacy*; Springer: Berlin/Heidelberg, Germany, 2014; pp. 3–20.
9. Koo, B.; Roh, D.; Kim, H.; Jung, Y.; Lee, D.G.; Kwon, D. CHAM: A Family of Lightweight Block Ciphers for Resource-Constrained Devices. In Proceedings of the International Conference on Information Security and Cryptology (ICISC'17), Seoul, Korea, 29 November–1 December 2017.

10. Atmel. AVR Instruction Set Manual. 2012. Available online: http://ww1.microch-\ip.com/downloads/en/devicedoc/atmel-0856-avr-instruction-set-manual.pdf (accessed on 10 October 2020).
11. Kim, Y.; Seo, S.C. An Efficient Implementation of AES on 8-bit AVR-based Sensor Nodes. In Proceedings of the 21th World Conference on Information Security Applications, Jeju island, Korea, 26–28 August 2020.
12. Kwon, H.; Kim, H.; Choi, S.J.; Jang, K.; Park, J.; Kim, H.; Seo, H. Compact Implementation of CHAM Block Cipher on Low-End Microcontrollers. In Proceedings of the The 21th World Conference on Information Security Applications, Jeju island, Korea, 26–28 August 2020.
13. Balasch, J.; Ege, B.; Eisenbarth, T.; Gérard, B.; Gong, Z.; Güneysu, T.; Heyse, S.; Kerckhof, S.; Koeune, F.; Plos, T.; et al. Compact Implementation and Performance Evaluation of Hash Functions in ATtiny Devices. *IACR Cryptol. ePrint Arch.* **2012**, *2012*, 507.
14. Cheng, H.; Dinu, D.; Großschädl, J. Efficient Implementation of the SHA-512 Hash Function for 8-Bit AVR Microcontrollers. In *Innovative Security Solutions for Information Technology and Communications*; Springer: Berlin/Heidelberg, Germany, 2018; Volume 11359, pp. 273–287.
15. Seo, H.J. High Speed Implementation of LEA on ARM Cortex M3 processor. *J. Korea Inst. Inf. Commun. Eng.* **2018**, *22*, 1133–1138.
16. Eisenbarth, T.; Gong, Z.; Güneysu, T.; Heyse, S.; Indesteege, S.; Kerckhof, S.; Koeune, F.; Nad, T.; Plos, T.; Regazzoni, F.; et al. Compact implementation and performance evaluation of block ciphers in ATtiny devices. In *International Conference on Cryptology in Africa*; Springer: Berlin/Heidelberg, Germany, 2012; pp. 172–187.
17. Kim, B.; Cho, H.; Choi, B.; Park, J.; Seo, H. Compact Implementations of HIGHT Block Cipher on IoT Platforms. *Secur. Commun. Netw.* **2019**, *2019*, 1–10. [CrossRef]
18. Beaulieu, R.; Treatman-Clark, S.; Shors, D.; Weeks, B.; Smith, J.; Wingers, L. The SIMON and SPECK lightweight block ciphers. In *Proceedings of the 52nd Annual Design Automation Conference*; IEEE: Piscataway, NJ, USA, 2015; pp. 1–6.
19. Lee, D.; Kim, D.; Kwon, D.; Kim, H. Efficient Hardware Implementation of the Lightweight Block Encryption Algorithm LEA. *Sensors* **2014**, *14*, 975–994, doi:10.3390/s140100975. [CrossRef] [PubMed]
20. Aguilar, J.; Sierra, S.; Jacinto, E. Implementation of 'HIGHT' encryption algorithm on microcontroller. In Proceedings of the 2015 CHILEAN Conference on Electrical, Electronics Engineering, Information and Communication Technologies (CHILECON), Santiago, Chile, 28–30 October 2015; pp. 937–942.
21. Lee, J.H.; Lim, D.G. Parallel Architecture for High-Speed Block Cipher, HIGHT. *Int. J. Secur. Its Appl.* **2014**, *8*, 59–66. [CrossRef]
22. Osvik, D.A.; Bos, J.W.; Stefan, D.; Canright, D. Fast software AES encryption. In *International Workshop on Fast Software Encryption*; Springer: Berlin/Heidelberg, Germany, 2010; pp. 75–93.
23. McGrew, D.; Viega, J. The Galois/counter mode of operation (GCM). *Submiss. Nist Modes Oper. Process.* **2004**, *20*, 1–13.
24. Kim, K.; Choi, S.; Kwon, H.; Liu, Z.; Seo, H. FACE–LIGHT: Fast AES–CTR Mode Encryption for Low-End Microcontrollers. In *International Conference on Information Security and Cryptology*; Springer: Berlin/Heidelberg, Germany, 2019; pp. 102–114.
25. Park, J.H.; Lee, D.H. FACE: Fast AES CTR mode Encryption Techniques based on the Reuse of Repetitive Data. *IACR Trans. Cryptogr. Hardw. Embed. Syst.* **2018**, *2018*, 469–499.

Publisher's Note: MDPI stays neutral with regard to jurisdictional claims in published maps and institutional affiliations.

© 2020 by the authors. Licensee MDPI, Basel, Switzerland. This article is an open access article distributed under the terms and conditions of the Creative Commons Attribution (CC BY) license (http://creativecommons.org/licenses/by/4.0/).

Article

Comparison of Entropy and Dictionary Based Text Compression in English, German, French, Italian, Czech, Hungarian, Finnish, and Croatian

Matea Ignatoski [1], Jonatan Lerga [1,2,*], Ljubiša Stanković [3] and Miloš Daković [3]

1. Department of Computer Engineering, Faculty of Engineering, University of Rijeka, Vukovarska 58, HR-51000 Rijeka, Croatia; mignatoski@riteh.hr
2. Center for Artificial Intelligence and Cybersecurity, University of Rijeka, R. Matejcic 2, HR-51000 Rijeka, Croatia
3. Faculty of Electrical Engineering, University of Montenegro, Džordža Vašingtona bb, 81000 Podgorica, Montenegro; ljubisa@ac.me (L.S.); milos@ac.me (M.D.)
* Correspondence: jlerga@riteh.hr; Tel.: +385-51-651-583

Received: 3 June 2020; Accepted: 17 June 2020; Published: 1 July 2020

Abstract: The rapid growth in the amount of data in the digital world leads to the need for data compression, and so forth, reducing the number of bits needed to represent a text file, an image, audio, or video content. Compressing data saves storage capacity and speeds up data transmission. In this paper, we focus on the text compression and provide a comparison of algorithms (in particular, entropy-based arithmetic and dictionary-based Lempel–Ziv–Welch (LZW) methods) for text compression in different languages (Croatian, Finnish, Hungarian, Czech, Italian, French, German, and English). The main goal is to answer a question: "How does the language of a text affect the compression ratio?" The results indicated that the compression ratio is affected by the size of the language alphabet, and size or type of the text. For example, The European Green Deal was compressed by 75.79%, 76.17%, 77.33%, 76.84%, 73.25%, 74.63%, 75.14%, and 74.51% using the LZW algorithm, and by 72.54%, 71.47%, 72.87%, 73.43%, 69.62%, 69.94%, 72.42% and 72% using the arithmetic algorithm for the English, German, French, Italian, Czech, Hungarian, Finnish, and Croatian versions, respectively.

Keywords: arithmetic; Lempel–Ziv–Welch (LZW); text compression; encoding; English; German; French; Italian; Czech; Hungarian; Finnish; Croatian

1. Introduction

We live in a digital age. One of the main characteristics of this age is the ability of individuals to exchange information freely. Daily, dozens of billions of digital messages are exchanged, photos are taken, articles are written, and so forth. These activities produce data that must be stored or transmitted. As data size increases, the cost of data storage and transmission time increases. To prevent these problems, we need to compress the data [1–4]. Data compression is the process of reducing the quantity of data used to represent a text file, an image, audio, or video content. There are two categories of data compression methods—lossy and lossless [5,6]. Lossy compression methods reduce the file size by removing some of the file's original data [7,8]. The resulting file cannot be completely reconstructed. Lossy compression methods are generally used for compressing file types where data loss is not noticeable, such as video, audio, and image files. On the other hand, lossless data compression methods also reduce file size, but they also preserve file content, so there is no data loss when data is uncompressed. Of course, text files must be compressed using lossless data compression methods [9–12].

In this paper, we focus on text file compression, and therefore we study lossless compression methods. There are a few commonly used lossless compression methods such as Shannon-Fano Coding, Huffman Coding, Lempel–Ziv–Welch (LZW) Algorithm, and Arithmetic Coding [13–17]. The optimal compression method depends on many factors, including the text length and amount of repeating characters. Previous work has focused on the analysis of the compression of texts in languages whose scripts are less represented in computing [18–21]. Kattan and Poli developed an algorithm that identifies best combination of compression algorithms for each text [22]. Grabowski and Swacha developed a dictionary based algorithm for language independent text compression [23]. Nunes et al. developed a grammar compression algorithm based on induced suffix sorting [24].

In this paper, the main question that will be answered is—"How does the language of a text affect the compression ratio?" We have collected and compared texts of various types such as stories, books, legal documents, business reports, short articles and user manuals. Some of the texts were collected only in English and Croatian, and others were collected in Croatian, Czech, Italian, French, German, English, Hungarian and Finnish. We limited research to languages based on Latin script due to the required number of bits to encode a single character. The algorithms we used for compression are Arithmetic Coding, as a representative of entropy encoding methods and LZW Algorithm, as a representative of dictionary-based encoding methods. LZW algorithm is used in Unix file compression utility *compress*.

The rest of the paper is organized as follows—we present a discussion of algorithms in Section 2 before presenting experimental results in Section 3, followed by a discussion Section 4. Finally, we draw our conclusions in Section 5.

2. Methods

2.1. Arithmetic Coding

Arithmetic coding is a lossless data compression method that encodes data composed of characters and converts it to a decimal number greater than or equal to zero and less than one. The compression performance depends on the probability distribution of each character in the text alphabet. The occurrence of infrequent characters significantly extends encoded data [4,25–27].

Entropy encoding is a type of lossless compression method which is based on coding frequently occurring characters with few bits and rarely occurring characters with more bits [28–30]. As in the most entropy encoding methods, the first step is creating a probability dictionary. This is done by counting the number of occurrences of each character and dividing it by the total number of characters in the text. The next step is assigning each character in the text alphabet a subinterval in the range $[0, 1)$ in proportion to its probability. When all characters have been assigned subintervals, the algorithm can start executing. In this step, a character that is not used in the text can be selected as the "end of text" character.

As can be seen from the given pseudocode in Algorithm 1 and in Figure 1, in the beginning, interval bounds are $[0, 1)$. The algorithm calculates new interval bounds for each character in the text. Once the algorithm reads the last character, which was determined previously, the algorithm stops. The encoded word can be any number from the resulting interval. It is recommended to take the final lower boundary of the resulting interval as the encoded word. Instead of using a distinctive character to determine the end of the text, the length of the text can be used to determine when the algorithm has to stop executing.

Algorithm 1: Arithmetic Coding Algorithm

$l \leftarrow 0;$
$h \leftarrow 1;$
$x_i \leftarrow first\ input\ character\ ;$
while x_i not endOfMessage **do**
$\quad | \quad l \leftarrow l + (h-l) * l_i\ ;$
$\quad | \quad h \leftarrow l + (h-l) * h_i\ ;$
$\quad | \quad x_i \leftarrow x_{i+1}\ ;$
end
$encodedMessage \leftarrow (l)_2$

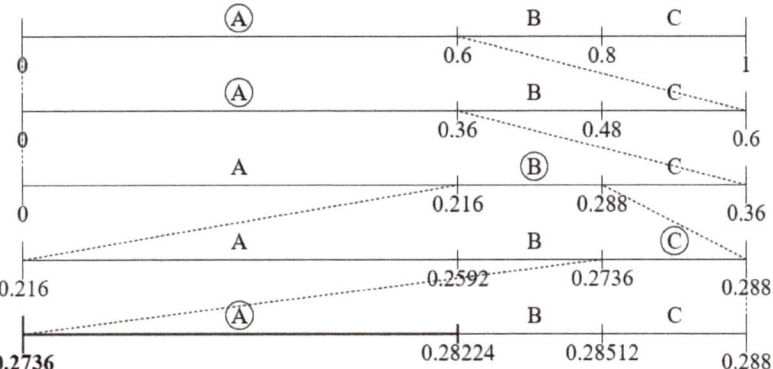

Figure 1. Arithmetic encoding the word AABCA.

Finally, the encoded text needs to be converted into binary code. The length of the binary code depends on the Shannon information value, which quantifies the amount of information in a message [31]. One can calculate the Shannon information using the following formula:

$$I(x_1 x_2 x_3 ... x_n) = -log_2(p(x_1) * p(x_2) * p(x_3) * ... * p(x_n)) = -\sum_{i=1}^{n} log_2(p(x_i)). \quad (1)$$

First, the probabilities of each character in the text need to be multiplied, and then the binary logarithm of a product is calculated. The length of the binary code is one integer larger than the result of the previous calculation. Once the text is converted to binary, it is ready to be transmitted or stored.

For decoding text (pseudocode of the arithmetic decoding algorithm is given in Algorithm 2), a subinterval dictionary made in the first step of the algorithm is used. Decoding begins with converting binary code to a decimal number. In the next step, the algorithm finds a subinterval where encoded text fits, and then it concatenates a subinterval key to the decoded message. The next step is to calculate a new value of the encoded text and repeat the subinterval search. There are two conditions on which the algorithm exits: either when it decodes an "end of text" distinctive character or after a preset number of repetitions. It depends which information the decoder has, "end of text" character or length of text.

Algorithm 2: Arithmetic Decoding Algorithm

$l \leftarrow (encodedMessage)_{10}$;
$decodedMessage \leftarrow$ "";
while x_i *not endOfMessage* **do**
　　$find\ x_i,\ l \in I(x_i)$;
　　$decodedMessage \leftarrow decodedMessage + x_i$;
　　$l \leftarrow \frac{l-l_i}{h_i-l_i}$;
end

2.2. Lempel–Ziv–Welch Algorithm

The Lempel–Ziv–Welch (LZW) Algorithm (pseudocode of which is given in Algorithm 3) is a dictionary-based lossless data compression method. Unlike Arithmetic Coding, for LZW compression, there is no need to know the probability distribution of each character in the text alphabet. This allows compression to be done while the message is being received. The main idea behind compression is to encode character strings that frequently appear in the text with their index in the dictionary. The first 256 words of the dictionary are assigned to extended ASCII table characters [13,32,33].

Algorithm 3: LZW Coding Algorithm

$w \leftarrow first\ input\ character$;
while x *not endOfMessage* **do**
　　$x \leftarrow next\ input\ character$;
　　if wx *not in dictionary* : **then**
　　　　$dictionary[w]\ append\ to\ encoded\ word$;
　　　　$add\ wx\ to\ dictionary$;
　　　　$w \leftarrow x$;
　　else
　　　　$w \leftarrow wx$
　　end
end

The pseudocode and Figure 2 present the steps of the algorithm. Two main values are stored in the algorithm, the word w, and current character x. In the beginning, the word w is the first text character. In each iteration, the algorithm reads a text character x and checks if there is a wx key in the dictionary. If wx is in the dictionary, w takes a value of wx, and the algorithm continues with the execution. In the other case, the corresponding value of w in the dictionary is added to the encoded word, whereafter the dictionary is upgraded with wx key and w takes a value of x. The algorithm stops when the end of file character is read.

s	a	m	o	u	p	r	a	v	n	o	p	r	a	v	n	i	w	x	Encoded message	Dictionary (index)
•																	s	a	115	sa (257)
	•																a	m	97	am (258)
		•															m	o	109	mo (259)
			•														o	u	111	ou (260)
				•													u	p	117	up (261)
					•												p	r	112	pr (262)
						•											r	a	114	ra (263)
							•										a	v	97	av (264)
								•									v	n	118	vn (265)
									•								n	o	110	no (266)
										•							o	p	111	op (267)
											•						p	r		
												•					pr	a	262	pra (268)
													•				a	v		
														•			av	n	264	avn (264)
															•		n	i	110	
																•	i	end	105	ni (265)
																	end		256	

Figure 2. Lempel–Ziv–Welch (LZW) encoding of the word SAMOUPRAVNOPRAVNI.

The LZW algorithm achieves the excellent compression ratio when compressing long text files that contain repeated strings [32].

The LZW Decoding Algorithm (pseudocode of which is given in Algorithm 4) creates the dictionary the same way as it is created for encoding. The first 256 words of the dictionary are assigned to extended ASCII table characters as well. The algorithm reads each code in the encoded word, writes its value from the dictionary to a decoded word, and upgrades a dictionary.

Algorithm 4: LZW Decoding Algorithm

$decodedMessage \leftarrow$ "";
foreach *code in encodedWord* **do**
    | $w \leftarrow dictionary[code]$;
    | $decodedMessage \leftarrow decodedMessage + w$;
    | $x \leftarrow first\ character\ in\ dictionary[nextCode]$;
    | *add to dictionary wx;*
end

---

3. Results

The representative test data are prose texts, two legal texts and two user manuals. Because some of the test alphabets consist of non-ASCII characters, each character is stored using 16 binary bits. The output of the LZW Coding Algorithm is a sequence of integers; each of them is stored using 16 binary bits as well. The size of data compressed using the Arithmetic Algorithm in binary bits is equal to Shannon's information Equation (1) of the original data. The compression results are shown in the Figures 3–5. Data compressed using the LZW Coding Algorithm varies from 20% to 45% of its original size. Text data compressed using Arithmetic Coding is ∼30% of its original size.

3.1. Literary Text Compression

We present results for three prose texts of different lengths—a short story The Little Match Girl by Hans Christian Andersen, novella The Decameron, Tenth Day, Fifth Tale by Giovanni Boccaccio and novella The Metamorphosis by Franz Kafka (shown in Figures 3–5, respectively).

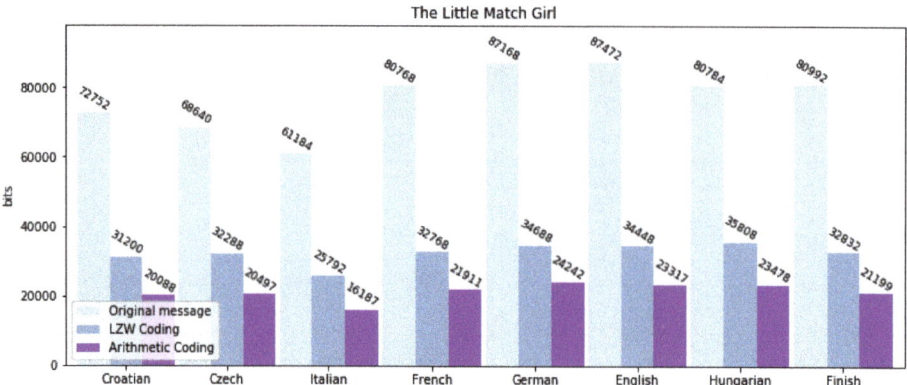

Figure 3. Encoding The Little Match Girl.

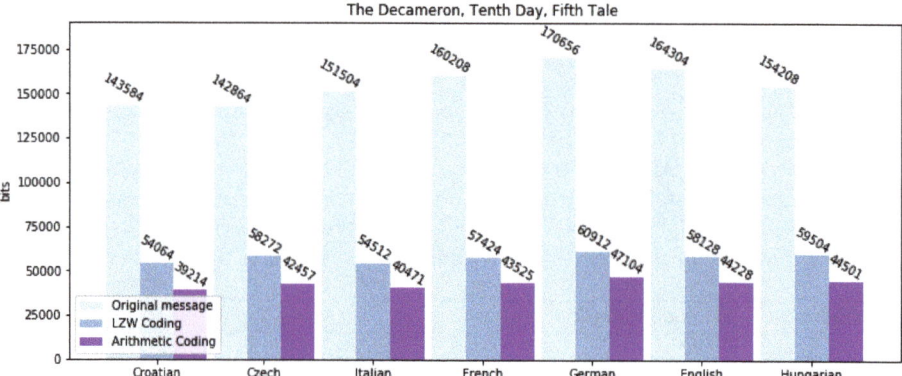

Figure 4. Encoding The Decameron Tale.

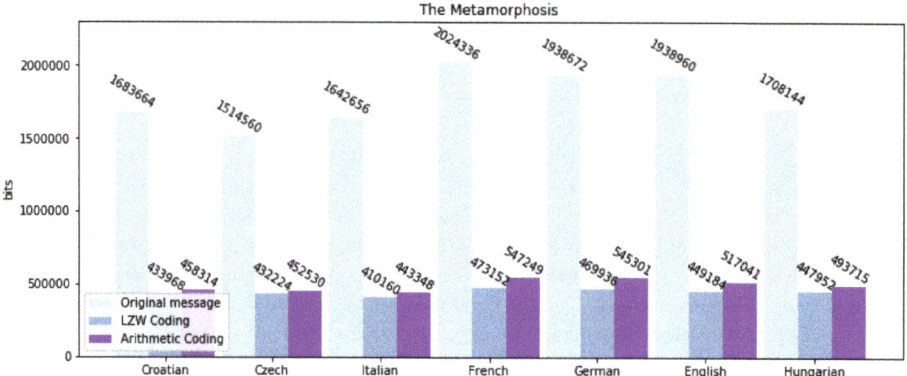

Figure 5. Encoding The Metamorphosis.

3.2. Legal Text Compression

As legal text compression, we present compression results for The European Green Deal and Charter of Fundamental Rights of the European Union given in Figures 6 and 7, respectively.

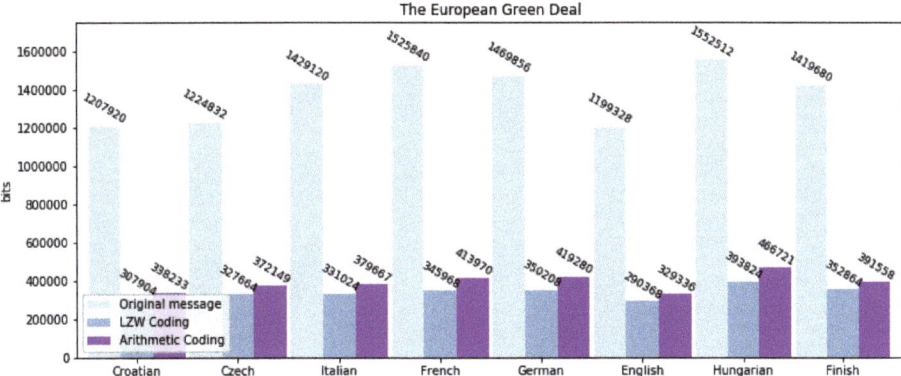

Figure 6. Encoding The European Green Deal.

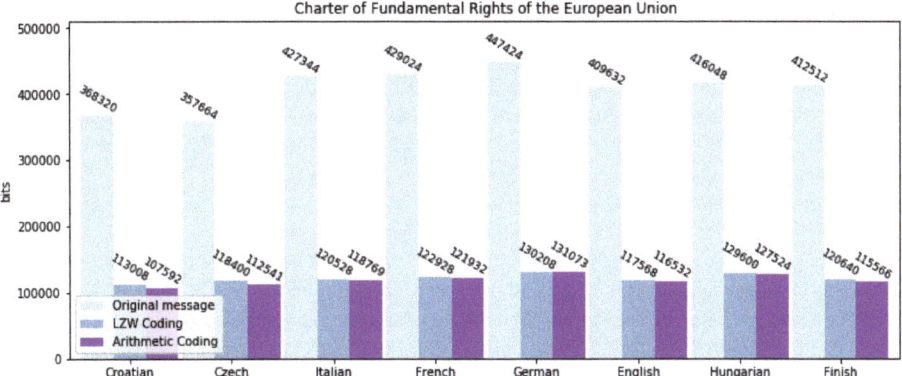

Figure 7. Encoding Charter of Fundamental Rights of the European Union.

3.3. User Manual Compression

We present compression results for Samsung Q6F Smart TV user manual and Candy CMG 2071M Microwave Oven user manual shown in Figures 8 and 9, respectively.

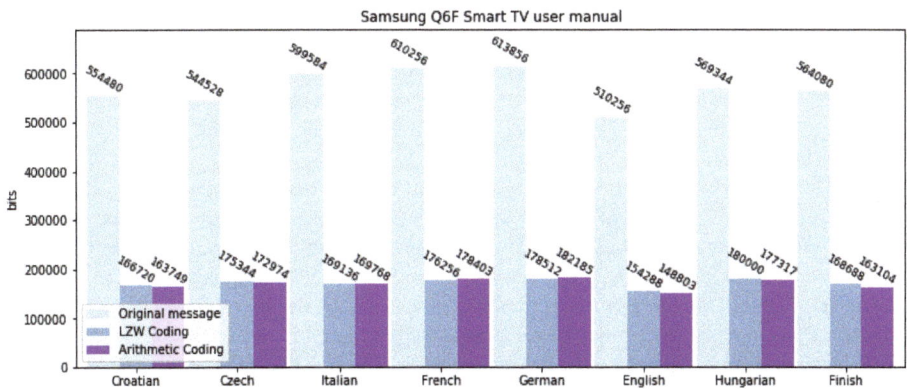

Figure 8. Encoding Samsung Q6F Smart TV user manual.

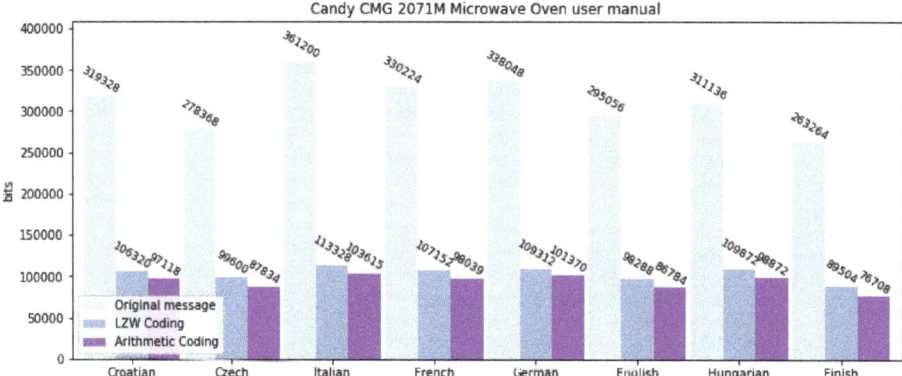

Figure 9. Encoding Candy CMG 2071M Microwave Oven user manual.

4. Discussion

Both compression algorithms (arithmetic and LZW) have proven effective. The compression ratio varies depending on the text language. The Italian, French, and English alphabets consist of 26 letters. The Croatian alphabet consists of 30 letters, 3 of which are composed of two characters from the rest of the alphabet. Therefore, the Croatian alphabet may be considered to consists of 27 different characters. The Finnish alphabet consist of 29 letters. The German alphabet consists of 30 letters. The Czech alphabet consists of 42 letters or 41 different characters. The Hungarian alphabet consists of 44 letters or 35 different characters.

Figures 3–9 present the compression results. In terms of the percentage of text size reduction, the compression results are as follows. Arithmetic compression results for Croatian, Czech, Italian, French, German, English, Hungarian, and Finnish translations of The Little Match Girl are as follows: 72.39%, 70.14%, 73.54%, 72.87%, 72.19%, 73.34%, 70.94%, and 73.83% respectively. The compression results for Croatian, Czech, Italian, French, German, English, and Hungarian versions of The Decameron Tale translations are as follows: 72.69%, 70.28%, 73.29%, 72.83%, 72.4%, 73.08%, and 71.15%. The results for arithmetic compression of The Metamorphosis are 72.78%, 63.87%, 73.01%, 72.97%, 71.87%, 73.33%, and 71.1% for the listed languages. Arithmetic compression results for The European Green Deal translations are as follows: 72%, 69.62%, 73.43%, 72.87%, 71.47%, 72.54%, 69.94%, and 72.42% for the Croatian, Czech, Italian, French, German, English, Hungarian, and Finnish respectively. Finally, compression results for Charter of Fundamental Rights of the European Union are 70.79%, 68.53%, 72.21%, 71.58%, 70.7%, 71.55%, 69.35%, and 71.99%. Arithmetic compression results for Samsung Q6F Smart TV user manual are as follows: 70.47%, 68.23%, 71.69%, 70.77%, 70.32%, 70.84%, 68.86%, and 71.09% respectively. Finally, the compression results for Candy CMG 2071M Microwave Oven user manual translations are as follows: 69.59%, 68.45%, 71.31%, 70.31%, 70.01%, 70.59%, 68.22%, and 70.86% for the Croatian, Czech, Italian, French, German English, Hungarian, and Finnish respectively.

The compression of texts in Italian, French, English and Finnish achieved the best compression ratio. The compression ratio of Croatian and German texts is close to the compression ratio of texts in languages with smaller alphabets. Compressing texts in Czech and Hungarian stands out the most. Czech versions of The Little Match Girl, The Decameron Tale, The Metamorphosis and Charter of Fundamental Rights of the European Union compression is >2% lower than compression of the same texts in different languages with fewer letters in the alphabet. Figure 10 shows arithmetic compression results. Compression ratio change compared to English is shown in Figure 11.

The number of different characters impacts compression performance. More different characters in alphabet increase the number of subintervals in Arithmetic Coding and extend the encoded message accordingly.

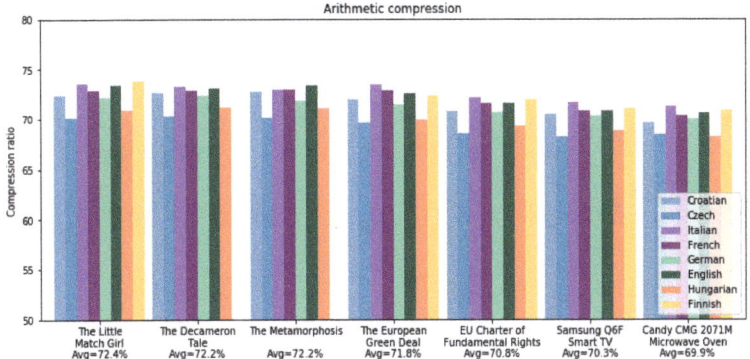

Figure 10. Arithmetic compression results.

The Little Match Girl is 4–6 thousand characters long text, depending on the text language, which makes it the shortest of three prose texts that are shown in this paper. The LZW compression results for compressing this text are 57.11%, 52.96%, 57.85%, 59.43%, 60.21%, 60.62%, 55.67%, and 59.46% for the Croatian, Czech, Italian, French, German, English, Hungarian, and Finnish respectively. These results show that LZW compression is not ideal for shorter texts. The Decameron Tale is approximately twice as long as The Little Match Girl, and the results of compressed Tale are as follows 62.35%, 59.21%, 64.02%, 64.16%, 64.31%, 64.62%, and 61.41% for the Croatian, Czech, Italian, French, German, English, and Hungarian, respectively. The Metamorphosis is up to 130 thousand characters long. Results of LZW compression of The Metamorphosis are 74.22%, 71.46%, 75.03%, 76.63%, 75.76%, 76.83%, and 73.78% for the Croatian, Czech, Italian, French, German English, and Hungarian, respectively. We can conclude that LZW compression is affected more by the text length than the arithmetic coding. The LZW compression results for Croatian, Czech, Italian, French, German, English, Hungarian, and Finnish translations of The European Green Deal are as follows: 74.51%, 73.25%, 76.84%, 77.33%, 76.17%, 75.79%, 74.63%, and 75.14%, respectively. The compression results for Charter of Fundamental Rights of the European Union translations are as follows: 69.32%, 66.9%, 71.8%, 71.35%, 70.9%, 71.3%, 68.85%, and 70.75% for the listed languages. The LZW compression results for Croatian, Czech, Italian, French, German, English, Hungarian, and Finnish translations of Samsung Q6F Smart TV user manual are as follows: 69.93%, 67.8%, 71.8%, 71.12%, 70.92%, 69.76%, 68.38%, and 70.1%, respectively. Finally, the compression results for Candy CMG 2071M Microwave Oven user manual translations are as follows: 66.71%, 64.22%, 68.62%, 67.55%, 67.66%, 66.69%, 64.69%, and 66%, respectively for the for Croatian, Czech, Italian, French, German, English, Hungarian, and Finnish.

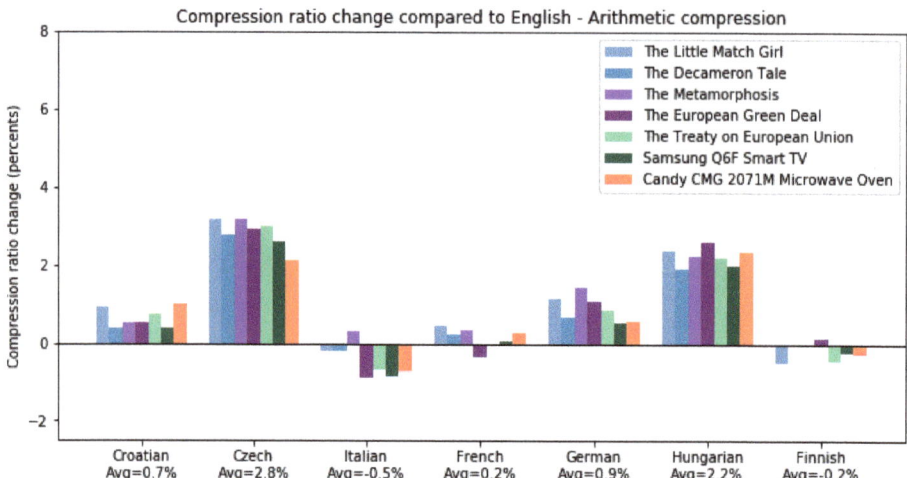

Figure 11. Compression ratio change compared to English—Arithmetic compression (positive percentages signify larger compressed file size when compared to English).

Figure 12 shows LZW compression results. Compression ratio change compared to English is shown in Figure 13.

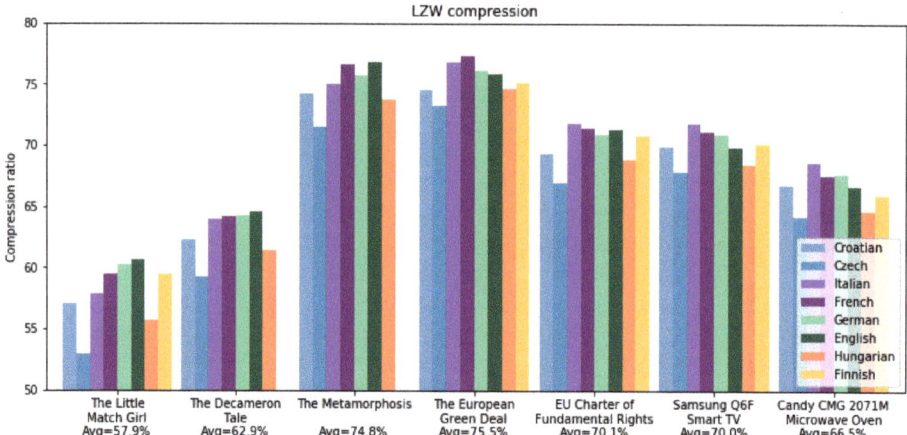

Figure 12. LZW compression results.

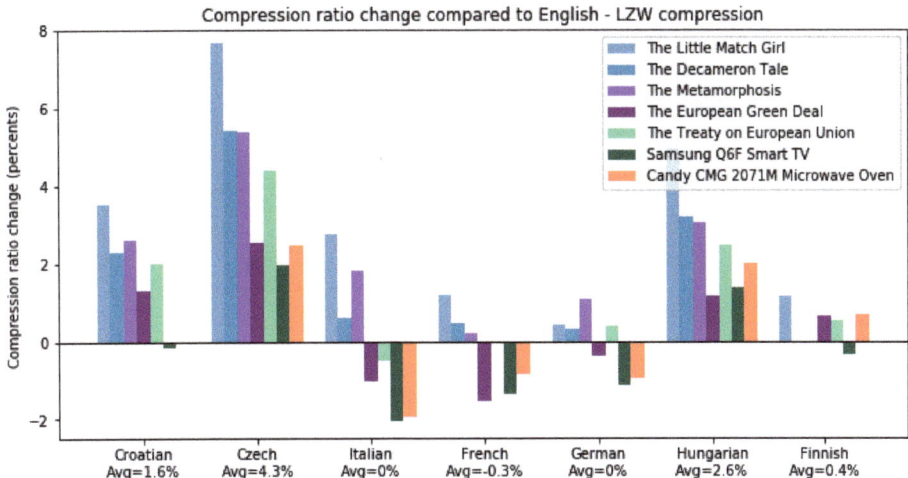

Figure 13. Compression ratio change compared to English—LZW compression (positive percentages signify larger compressed file size when compared to English).

Figure 14 shows the compression rate for different lengths of text. Generally, as text length increases, the compression ratio of the LZW algorithm increases. In our test texts, the exception is the compression ratio of Charter of Fundamental Rights of the European Union which compression achieves better results than compression of, longer text, Smart TV user manual. The reason for this irregularity is the repetition of the word 'Article'. As stated in Section 2, LZW compression is based on encoding character strings that frequently appear in the text. Arithmetic encoding achieves significantly better compression ratio for compressing texts up to 20,000 characters, the LZW algorithm achieves better compression ratio for compressing texts longer than 100,000 characters.

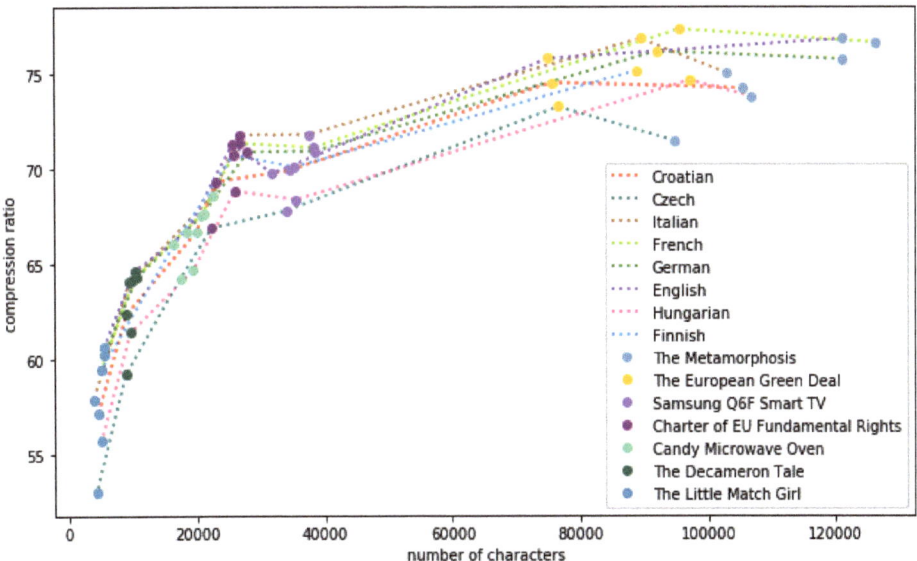

Figure 14. LZW compression results—text length dependence.

In addition to the size of the alphabet and text length, the LZW compression also affects the form of the word. We corroborate this by comparing Croatian and English grammar. Croatian grammar is more complex than English grammar. In Croatian grammar, the form of the word depends on the tense, case, and position in the sentence; English grammar also changes the form of the word but in far fewer cases. The LZW compression is based on encoding repeating strings. Because of these differences in grammar, English texts achieve a better compression ratio than their Croatian equivalents. In Figure 15 there are several values from the end of the LZW dictionary. It is shown that encoded strings in English are longer and contain more complete words.

KEY	VALUE	KEY	VALUE
. Gro	28386	u. Po	27437
owi	28387	ostavš	27438
ing mo	28388	ši sve	27439
ore si	28389	e šu	27440
ilent	28390	utl	27441
and al	28391	ljivij	27442
lmost un	28392	ji i	27443
ncon	28393	i spo	27444
nsc	28394	oraz	27445
ciousl	28395	zumi	27446
ly und	28396	ijevaj	27447
ders	28397	jući se	27448
standing e	28398	pogledi	27449
each other	28399	ima, na	27450
r in t	28400	amata	27451
their g	28401	ali su	27452
glances	28402	u mis	27453

Figure 15. Example from LZW dictionaries in English and Croatian.

5. Conclusions

Data compression is the process of reducing the number of bits needed to represent data. Compressing data both reduces the need for storage hardware and speeds up file transfer.

Choosing the right compression algorithm is not a simple task because the performance of each algorithm depends on the text type, length of data, and other text characteristics. Arithmetic Coding achieves a significant compression ratio regardless of the length of the text, but algorithm performance decreases as text length increases. Time and space complexity are crucial parts of any algorithm, and that makes the algorithm not suitable for universal use.

The LZW Algorithm achieves excellent compression ratio when compressing long text files that contain repetitive strings. The algorithm takes a short time to execute and uses minimal resources.

The main question posed in this paper is—"How does the language of a text affect the compression ratio?" and, as it can be seen from results, the answer is positive—there are some differences in compression ratios between texts in different languages and different types of texts. When choosing a compression algorithm, it is important to determine which algorithm achieves the best compression ratio for each language and/or type of text.

Author Contributions: Conceptualization, M.I. and J.L.; methodology, M.I. and J.L.; software, M.I.; validation, L.S. and M.D.; formal analysis, M.I., J.L., L.S., and M.D.; investigation, L.S. and M.D.; resources, M.I.; data curation, M.I.; writing—Original draft preparation, M.I.; writing—Review and editing, J.L., L.S., and M.D.; visualization, M.I.; supervision, J.L.; project administration, J.L., L.S., and M.D.; funding acquisition, J.L., L.S., and M.D. All authors have read and agreed to the published version of the manuscript.

Funding: This work was fully supported by the Croatian Science Foundation under the project IP-2018-01-3739 and IP-2020-02-4358, Center for Artificial Intelligence and Cybersecurity—University of Rijeka, University of

Rijeka under the projects uniri-tehnic-18-17 and uniri-tehnic-18-15, and European Cooperation in Science and Technology (COST) under the project CA17137.

Conflicts of Interest: The authors declare no conflict of interest.

References

1. Celikel, E.; Dalkilic, M.E. A New Encoding Decoding Scheme for Text Compression with Embedded Security. *Math. Comput. Appl.* **2004**, *9*, 475–484. [CrossRef]
2. Rozenberg, L.; Lotan, S.; Feldman, D. Finding Patterns in Signals Using Lossy Text Compression. *Algorithms* **2019**, *12*, 267. [CrossRef]
3. Shahbahrami, A.; Bahrampour, R.; Rostami, M.; Mobarhan, M. Evaluation of Huffman and Arithmetic Algorithms for Multimedia Compression Standards. *arXiv* **2011**, arXiv:1109.0216.
4. Mbewe, P.; Asare, S.D. Analysis and comparison of adaptive huffman coding and arithmetic coding algorithms. In Proceedings of the 13th International Conference on Natural Computation, Fuzzy Systems and Knowledge Discovery (ICNC-FSKD), Guilin, China, 29–31 July 2017.
5. Robert, L.; Nadarajan, R. Simple lossless preprocessing algorithms for text compression. *IET Softw.* **2009**, *3*, 37–45. [CrossRef]
6. Katugampola, U.N. A New Technique for Text Data Compression. In Proceedings of the 2012 International Symposium on Computer, Consumer and Control, Taichung, Taiwan, 4–6 June 2012; pp. 405–409.
7. Howard, P.G. Lossless and lossy compression of text images by soft pattern matching. In Proceedings of the DCC '96: Proceedings of the Conference on Data Compression, Snowbird, UT, USA, 31 March–3 April 1996; pp. 210–219.
8. Al-Dubaee, S.A.; Ahmad, N. New Strategy of Lossy Text Compression. In Proceedings of the 2010 First International Conference on Integrated Intelligent Computing, Bangalore, India, 5–7 August 2010; pp. 22–26.
9. Quddus, A.; Fahmy, M.M. A new compression technique for binary text images. In Proceedings of the Second IEEE Symposium on Computer and Communications, Alexandria, Egypt, 1–3 July 1997; pp. 194–198.
10. Xu, J.; Zhang, W.; Xie, X.; Yang, Z. SSE Lossless Compression Method for the Text of the Insignificance of the Lines Order. *arXiv* **2017**, arXiv:1709.04035.
11. Sayood, K. *Introduction to Data Compression*, 5th ed.; Elsevier: Amsterdam, The Netherlands, 2018; Chapter 6, pp. 165–185, ISBN 978-0-12-809474-7.
12. Kavitha, P. A Survey on Lossless and Lossy Data Compression Methods. *Int. J. Comp. Sci. Eng. Technol.* **2016**, *7*, 1277–1280.
13. Shanmugasundaram, S.; Lourdusamy, R. A Comparative Study Of Text Compression Algorithms. *Int. J. Wisdom Based Comput.* **2011**, *1*, 68–76.
14. Bhattacharjee, A.K.; Bej, T.; Agarwal, S. Comparison Study of Lossless Data Compression Algorithms for Text Data. *IOSR-JCE J. Comp. Eng.* **2013**, *11*, 15–19. [CrossRef]
15. Abliz, W.; Wu, H.; Maimaiti, M.; Wushouer, J.; Abiderexiti, K.; Yibulayin, T.; Wumaier, A. A Syllable-Based Technique for Uyghur Text Compression. *Information* **2020**, *11*, 172. [CrossRef]
16. Zhang, N.; Tao, T.; Satya, R.V.; Mukherjee, A. A flexible compressed text retrieval system using a modified LZW algorithm. In Proceedings of the Data Compression Conference, Snowbird, UT, USA, 29–31 March 2005; p. 493.
17. Garain, U.; Chakraborty, M.P.; Chanda, B. Lossless Compression of Textual Images: A Study on Indic Script Documents. In Proceedings of the 18th International Conference on Pattern Recognition (ICPR'06), Hong Kong, China, 20–24 August 2006; pp. 806–809.
18. Mohamed, A.S.; El-Sawy, A.H.; Ahmad, S.M. Data compression for Arabic text. In Proceedings of the Fifteenth National Radio Science Conference, Cairo, Egypt, 24–26 February 1998.
19. Kuruvila, M.; Gopinath, D.P. Entropy of Malayalam language and text compression using Huffman coding. In Proceedings of the First International Conference on Computational Systems and Communications (ICCSC), Trivandrum, India, 17–18 December 2014.
20. Morihara, T.; Satoh, N.; Yahagi, H.; Yoshida, S. Japanese text compression using word-based coding. In Proceedings of the DCC '98 Data Compression Conference, Snowbird, UT, USA, 30 March–1 April 1998.

21. Farhad Mokter, M.; Akter, S.; Palash Uddin, M.; Ibn Afjal, M.; Al Mamun, M.; Abu Marjan, M. An Efficient Technique for Representation and Compression of Bengali Text. In Proceedings of the 2018 International Conference on Bangla Speech and Language Processing (ICBSLP), Sylhet, Bangladesh, 21–22 September 2018; pp. 1–6.
22. Kattan, A.; Poli, R. Evolutionary lossless compression with GP-ZIP. In Proceedings of the IEEE World Congress on Computational Intelligence, Hong Kong, China, 1–6 June 2008.
23. Grabowski, S.; Swacha, J. Language-independent word-based text compression with fast decompression. In Proceedings of the VIth International Conference on Perspective Technologies and Methods in MEMS Design, Lviv, Ukraine, 20–23 April 2010; pp. 158–162.
24. Saad Nogueira Nunes, D.; Louza, F.; Gog, S.; Ayala-Rincón, M.; Navarro, G. A Grammar Compression Algorithm Based on Induced Suffix Sorting. In Proceedings of the 2018 Data Compression Conference, Snowbird, UT, USA, 27–30 March 2018; pp. 42–51.
25. Langdon, G. An Introduction to Arithmetic Coding. *IBM J. Res. Dev.* **1984**, *28*, 135–149. [CrossRef]
26. Sarkar, S.J.; Kar, K.; Das, I. Basic arithmetic coding based approach for compressing generation scheduling data array. In Proceedings of the 2017 IEEE Calcutta Conference (CALCON), Kolkata, India, 2–3 December 2017; pp. 21–25.
27. Husodo, A.Y.; Munir, R. Arithmetic coding modification to compress SMS. In Proceedings of the 2011 International Conference on Electrical Engineering and Informatics, Bandung, Indonesia, 17–19 July 2011; pp. 1–6.
28. Vijayvargiya, G.; Silakari, S.; Pandey, R. A Survey: Various Techniques of Image Compression. *arXiv* **2013**, arXiv:1311.6877.
29. Behr, F.; Fossum, V.; Mitzenmacher, M.; Xiao, D. Estimating and comparing entropies across written natural languages using PPM compression. In Proceedings of the Data Compression Conference, DCC, Snowbird, UT, USA, 25–27 March 2003; p. 416.
30. Ezhilarasan, M.; Thambidurai, P.; Praveena, K.; Srinivasan, S.; Sumathi, N. A New Entropy Encoding Technique for Multimedia Data Compression. In Proceedings of the International Conference on Computational Intelligence and Multimedia Applications (ICCIMA 2007) Sivakasi, Tamil Nadu, India, 13–15 December 2007; pp. 157–161.
31. Shannon, C.E. A Mathematical Theory of Communication. *Bell Syst. Tech. J.* **1948**, *27*, 379–423.
32. Dheemanth, H.N. LZW Data Compression. *AJER* **2014**, *3*, 22–26.
33. Hasan, M.R.; Ibrahimy, M.I.; Motakabber, S.M.A.; Ferdaus, M.M.; Khan, M.N.H. Comparative data compression techniques and multicompression results. *IOP Conf. Ser. Mater. Sci. Eng.* **2013**, *53*, 012081.

© 2020 by the authors. Licensee MDPI, Basel, Switzerland. This article is an open access article distributed under the terms and conditions of the Creative Commons Attribution (CC BY) license (http://creativecommons.org/licenses/by/4.0/).

MDPI
St. Alban-Anlage 66
4052 Basel
Switzerland
Tel. +41 61 683 77 34
Fax +41 61 302 89 18
www.mdpi.com

Mathematics Editorial Office
E-mail: mathematics@mdpi.com
www.mdpi.com/journal/mathematics

www.ingramcontent.com/pod-product-compliance
Lightning Source LLC
LaVergne TN
LVHW070619100526
838202LV00012B/681